OFFICIAL REPORT

OF THE

TWENTY-FIFTH INTERNATIONAL

CHRISTIAN ENDEAVOR CONVENTION

HELD ON

THE MILLION-DOLLAR PIER AND IN MANY CHURCHES,

ATLANTIC CITY, N.J., JULY 6-12, 1911.

First Fruits Press
Wilmore, Kentucky
c2015

First Fruits Press
The Academic Open Press of Asbury Theological Seminary
204 N. Lexington Ave., Wilmore, KY 40390
859-858-2236
first.fruits@asburyseminary.edu
asbury.to/firstfruits

THE STORY OF THE OCEANIC CONVENTION

THE OFFICIAL REPORT

OF

THE TWENTY-FIFTH
INTERNATIONAL . .

Christian Endeavor Convention

HELD ON
THE MILLION-DOLLAR PIER AND IN
MANY CHURCHES

ATLANTIC CITY, N. J., JULY 6-12, 1911

Copyrighted, 1911 by the U. S. C. E.

UNITED SOCIETY OF CHRISTIAN ENDEAVOR
BOSTON, MASS.

LINOTYPED AND PRINTED AT
The Arakelyan Press
BOSTON, MASS.

CONTENTS.

Officers of the United Society of Christian Endeavor		5
Trustees		5
The Atlantic City Convention Committee		8
Thank You		9
Chapters.		
I	Salt Breezes	11
II	A Magnificent Opening Session	15
III	The Quiet Hour	30
IV	Reaching Out	34
V	The Greatest Evening	36
VI	Rallying the Juniors	51
VII	Choral Service and Camp-fire	56
VIII	Memorable Sabbath Meetings	61
IX	Denominational Rallies	77
X	International Brotherhood and Good Fellowship	95
XI	The Best in Christian Endeavor	100
XII	Training in Interdenominational and International Fellowship	107
XIII	Williston's Great Meeting	111
XIV	Christian Endeavor in Conference	114
XV	The Field Secretaries	135
XVI	Training for Missions	139
XVII	A Feast of Addresses	142
XVIII	The Closing Session	188
XIX	Resolutions	198
XX	Corporation and Trustees' Meeting	206
XXI	What They Say	209
Index		211

ILLUSTRATIONS.

The Oceanic Convention Committee	Frontispiece	
Young's Million-Dollar Pier and Beach	facing page	9
Rev. Francis E. Clark, D.D., LL.D.	" "	17
William Shaw, General Secretary	" "	25
William Howard Taft, President of the U. S.	" "	33
The Auditorium during President Taft's address	" "	41
At Captain Young's	" "	49
Officers and Trustees of the United Society	" "	57
Group of United Society Officers	" "	65
Texas and Oklahoma Delegation	" "	73
The Temple, and Board-Walk Crowd	" "	81
Convention Speakers	" "	89
California Headquarters. Board-Walk Scene	" "	97
Conference Leaders	" "	105
Minnesota and Iowa Delegates	" "	113
Convention Speakers	" "	121
Canadian Delegation	" "	129
Speakers and Conference Leaders	" "	137
The Maine and New Hampshire Delegation	" "	145
Convention Speakers — The Ladies	" "	153
The Corridor of State Booths	" "	161
Our Foreign Brethren	" "	169
Christian Endeavor's Best — The Field Secretaries — and Florida Booth	" "	177
Convention Speakers	" "	193
Philadelphia Delegation and Wheel-Chair Procession	" "	209

OFFICERS OF THE UNITED SOCIETY OF CHRISTIAN ENDEAVOR.

Office:
TREMONT TEMPLE, BOSTON, MASS., U.S.A.

President:
REV. FRANCIS E. CLARK, D.D., LL.D.

General Secretary:
MR. WILLIAM SHAW.

Treasurer:
MR. H. N. LATHROP

Editorial Secretary:
PROF. AMOS R. WELLS.

Publication Manager:
MR. A. J. SHARTLE.

Interstate Secretary:
MR. KARL LEHMANN.

Superintendent of Builders' Union:
REV. R. P. ANDERSON.

Auditor:
MR. ROBERT H. BEAN.

DENOMINATIONAL TRUSTEES.

REV. THOMAS ASHBURN, D.D., Knoxville, Tenn.
PRESIDENT JOHN WILLIS BAER, LL.D., Pasadena, Cal.
REV. W. C. BITTING, D.D., St. Louis, Mo.
PRESIDENT C. I. BROWN, D.D., Findlay, Ohio.
REV. W. L. BURDICK, D.D., Alfred, N.Y.
REV. DAVID JAMES BURRELL, D.D., New York, N. Y.
REV. J. C. CALDWELL, Nashville, Tenn.
HON. S. B. CAPEN, LL.D., Boston, Mass.
REV. G. C. CARPENTER, Warsaw, Ind.

REV. J. WILBUR CHAPMAN, D.D., New York, N. Y.
REV. FRANCIS E. CLARK, D.D., LL.D., Boston, Mass.
GEORGE W. COLEMAN, M.A., Boston, Mass.
REV. W. J. DARBY, D.D., Evansville, Ind.
REV. FRANK J. DAY, Montreal, Quebec.
REV. H. A. DENTON, Troy, N. Y.
BISHOP SAMUEL FALLOWS, D.D., LL.D., Chicago, Ill.
REV. J. H. GARRISON, D.D., LL.D., St. Louis, Mo.
REV. ALEXANDER GILRAY, D.D., Toronto, Ont.

Rev. Howard B. Grose, D.D., Boston, Mass.
Rev. N. B. Grubb, D.D., Philadelphia, Penn.
Mr. William Phillips Hall, New York, N. Y.
Rev. A. W. Halsey, D.D., New York, N. Y.
Mr. Elmore Harris, Toronto, Ont.
Rev. P. S. Henson, D.D., Dorchester, Mass.
Rev. James L. Hill, D.D., Salem, Mass.
Prof. James Lewis Howe, Ph.D., Lexington, Va.
Rev. C. H. Hubbell, D.D., Adrian, Mich.

Rev. E. Humphries, D.D., Fall River, Mass.
Rev. Albert W. Jefferson, Portland, Me.
Rev. W. T. Johnson, D.D., Richmond, Va.
Rev. Gilby C. Kelly, D.D., Charlottsville, Va.
President Henry Churchill King, D.D., Oberlin, Ohio.
Rev. Ira Landrith, D.D., LL.D., Nashville, Tenn.
Rev. Cleland B. McAfee, D.D., Brooklyn, N. Y.
Rev. W. H. McMillan, D.D., Allegheny City, Penn.
Rev. Samuel MacNaugher, Boston, Mass.

Rev. Rufus W. Miller, D.D., Philadelphia, Penn.
Rev. Allan B. Philputt, D.D., Indianapolis, Ind.
Rev. Robert E. Pretlow, Brooklyn, N. Y.
Rev. M. Rhodes, D.D., St. Louis, Mo.
Rev. P. J. Rice, El Paso, Texas.
Venerable Archdeacon J. B. Richardson, London, Ont.
Rev. W. F. Richardson, D.D., Kansas City, Mo.
Rev. John Balcom Shaw, D.D., Chicago, Ill.
Mr. William Shaw, Boston, Mass.

Rev. H. F. Shupe, D.D., Dayton, Ohio.
Rev. Wilton, Merle Smith, D.D., New York, N. Y.
President George B. Stewart, D.D., Auburn, N. Y.
Bishop U. F. Swengel, D.D., Harrisburg, Penn.
Rev. A. D. Thaeler, Bethlehem, Penn.
Rev. Floyd W. Tomkins, S.T.D., Philadelphia, Penn.
Rev. Hugh K. Walker, D.D., Los Angeles, Cal.
Bishop Alexander Walters, D.D., New York, N. Y.
Hon. John Wanamaker, Philadelphia, Penn.

Rev. E. A. Watkins, M.A., Greenville, Ohio.
Rev. Earle Wilfley, D.D., Washington, D. C.
Dean H. L. Willett, D.D., Chicago, Ill.
Rev. W. F. Wilson, D.D., Toronto, Ont.
Rev. Samuel H. Woodrow, D.D., Washington, D. C.

Honorary Trustees:

Rev. J. M. Lowden, D.D., Portland, Or.
Rev. J. Z. Tyler, D.D., Cleveland, Ohio.

Trustees Representing Denominational Christian Endeavor Unions and Work:

Rev. Willis L. Gelston, Philadelphia, Penn.
Rev. P. A. Heilman, D.D., Baltimore, Md.
Rev. Claude E. Hill, Valparaiso, Ind.
Rev. J. G. Huber, D.D., Dayton, Ohio.
Rev. J. S. Leland, Pittsburg, Penn.

STATE TRUSTEES.

Alabama,	Mr. Walter D. Shepard, Montgomery.
Arkansas,	Mr. Surry Wood, Little Rock.
California,	Mr. A. W. Johnson, San Francisco.
Colorado,	Mr. H. G. Fisher, Denver.
Connecticut,	Mr. F. C. Bidwell, Bloomfield.
Delaware,	Rev. J. Ernest Litsinger, Seaford.
District of Columbia,	Mr. D. C. Davis, Washington.
Florida.	Mr. Alexander Linn, St. Petersburg.
Hawaiian Islands,	Rev. Moses K. Nakuina, Honolulu.
Idaho,	Mr. J. O. Baum, Caldwell.
Illinois,	Mr. C. W. Dyer, Decatur.
Indiana,	Judge Charles J. Orbison, Indianapolis.
Iowa,	Rev. H. E. Van Horn, Des Moines.
Kansas,	Rev. O. L. Smith, Emporia,
Kentucky,	Mr. J. F. Logeman, Jr., Carrollton.
Louisiana,	Mr. Archie Hickman, Lake Charles.
Maine,	Rev. William F. Slade, Portland.
Maryland,	Mr. W. M. Robinson, Baltimore.
Massachusetts,	Miss Emma Ostrom Nichols, East Lexington.
Michigan,	Rev. Harry L. Crane, Alma.
Minnesota,	Mr. J. W. Miller, Minneapolis.
Missouri,	Mr. Cree J. Henderson, Kansas City.
Nebraska,	Mr. Ray G. Fletcher, Lincoln.
New Hampshire,	Mr. Herbert D. Collins, Keene.
New Jersey,	Mr. John T. Sproull, Arlington.
New Mexico,	Rev. J. Wilburn Rose, East Las Vegas.
New York,	Mr. John R. Clements, Binghamton.
North Carolina,	Rev. R. E. Steele, Spencer.
North Dakota,	Mr. George L. Hempstead, Jamestown.
Ohio,	Rev. T. C. Lawrence, Cleveland.
Oklahoma,	Miss Adeline Goddard, Oklahoma City.
Oregon,	Mr. G. Evert Baker, Portland.
Pennsylvania,	Rev. William A. Jones, D.D., Pittsburg.
Rhode Island,	Rev. W. W. Deckard, M.A., Arlington.
South Dakota,	Rev. W. M. Evans, Faulkton.
Tennessee,	Mr. Eugene L. Philpot, Nashville.
Texas,	Mr. Fred M. Roach, McKinney.
Vermont,	Rev. Fraser Metzger, Randolph.
Virginia,	Rev. R. E. Elmore, Roanoke.
Washington,	Rev. E. A. King, North Yakima.
West Virginia,	Rev. Aubrey F. Hess, Buckhannon.
Wisconsin,	Rev. Edgar T. Farrill, Kenosha.
British Columbia, Can.,	Mr. D. J. McPhail, Vancouver.
Manitoba,	Mr. A. R. Walkey, Winnipeg.
Ontario,	Rev. W. A. Mactaggart, B.A., Toronto
Quebec,	Mr. W. R. Leroux, Montreal.
Saskatchewan,	Mr. F. R. Sebolt, Regina.

CONVENTION COMMITTEE

Chairman, MR. JOHN T. SPROULL, President of the New Jersey Christian Endeavor Union, Arlington, N. J.

First Vice-Chairman, REV. GEORGE D. JONES, Atlantic City, N. J.

Second Vice-Chairman, REV. R. G. BANNEN, D.D., Williamsport, Penn.

Third Vice-Chairman, MR. H. A. KINPORTS, New York City.

Secretary, MR. WILLIAM SHAW, 600 Tremont Temple, Boston, Mass.

Treasurer, MR. H. N. LATHROP, 600 Tremont Temple, Boston, Mass.

Press, MR. WALTER D. HOWELL, 600 Tremont Temple, Boston, Mass.

Music, MR. PERCY S. FOSTER, Washington, D. C.

Pulpit-Supply, REV. N. W. CALDWELL, D.D., Atlantic City, N. J.

Evangelistic, REV. B. S. HUDSON, Atlantic City, N. J.

Reception, MR. H. W. MERRILL, Y. M. C. A., Atlantic City, N. J.

Hotels and Registration, MR. ALBERT T. BELL, Atlantic City, N. J.

Halls and Churches, REV. CHARLES D. SINKINSON, D.D., Atlantic City, N. J.

Ushers, MR. CALVIN S. SMITH, Atlantic City, N. J.

Decorations, REV. JOHN J. MACMILLAN, Atlantic City, N. J.

Copyright, 1910, Geo. A. McKeague Co. Used by permission.

Entrance to Young's Million-Dollar Pier.

By permission

SCENE DURING BATHING HOUR.

YOUNG'S MILLION-DOLLAR PIER.
SHOWING THE TWO GREAT AUDITORIUMS AND OPEN-AIR PAVILION.

THANK YOU.

The compilation of a report that will do justice to a great International Convention of Christian Endeavor, like our Oceanic Convention held in the City-by-the-Sea, is no easy task. When you take into consideration the many simultaneous meetings necessary in order to meet the requirements of a programme with more than one hundred meetings scheduled, it becomes an impossibility for one man. It is, therefore, with a keen sense of appreciation that the compiler hereby desires to acknowledge the splendid services of Rev. Ira Landrith, D. D., Mr. John T. Sproull, Prof. Amos R. Wells, Rev. R. P. Anderson, Mr. Arthur W. Kelly, Mr. William Shaw, Mr. H. N. Lathrop, Mr. John R. Clements, the Field Secretaries, and also the many leaders of meetings and conferences, whose co-operation in reporting the several sessions of the Convention made the publication of this Report a certainty.

Trusting that its perusal may be the means of stimulating the young people throughout all the land to do their best for the Master, and set aglow the fire of Christian Endeavor in the heart of the individual, and with a fervent prayer for the divine blessing upon all our young people, this Report of the proceedings of the Twenty-Fifth International Convention of Christian Endeavor is submitted.

A. J. SHARTLE,
Publication-Manager
United Society of Christian Endeavor.

Boston, Mass., July 18, 1911.

CHAPTER I.

SALT BREEZES.

The entire country was a furnace.

States ordinarily cool were as hot as the hottest.

Men were falling in the streets, all over the country, by the hundreds; there were deaths by the score.

It was in this terrific atmosphere that the Endeavorers made their way to Atlantic City.

They carried with them a good cheer and a patient serenity that triumphed over all discomforts, and through regions that were sullen in the fearful heat they bore a continuous song.

Was ever a sea-breath so glorious as the splendid salt breezes that burst upon us from the ocean as we neared Atlantic City?

The wisdom of the United Society in selecting this superb meeting-place was commended by all, and especially when we got out on the Million-Dollar Pier.

There, with the waves on either hand and swinging beneath us, and with the cool winds sweeping through the open windows, our brains were clear to think the high thoughts brought us by our speakers, and our bodies were kept fresh and alert.

Imagine a great, broad, stanch pier extending farr out from the beautiful beach. On the extreme tip is the immense net drawn every day in the presence of an interested company of Endeavorers, full of strange fishes, small and large. Back of it is a wireless telegraph station. The fishnet is a good gospel symbol of the ingathering work of Christian Endeavor, its foodful and instructive character; and the wireless station is a fine modern symbol of the outgoing, unifying work of our society. Two of the very earliest Christian Endeavor Conventions were held at a seashore summer resort, Old Orchard, Me.; but not once, since our gatherings became large, have they made the experiment that was made in going to Atlantic City.

And it was a superb and entire success.

Physical comfort has a large share in spiritual exaltation. It is hard indeed to be enthusiastic, even for the noblest causes, with garments soaked in perspiration and seared lungs panting for breath. It is hard to sing praises at 100° Fahrenheit.

First, therefore, in the long list of Atlantic City congratulations is the weather. While the rest of the country was broiling and baking and frying, we by the ocean were fanned with invigorating breezes. Between sessions we could plunge into the cool billows. The salt tang was in the Convention as well as in the air. The Atlantic swell buoyed up every gathering as it rose and fell beneath the Pier. Christian Endeavor has never enjoyed a more comfortable Convention than this in the middle of one of the hottest periods the country has ever known.

The second notable feature of the Convention, and the one for which, probably, our twenty-fifth assembly will be chiefly remembered, was the presence and participation of the President of the United States. Mr. Taft's predecessors have honored Christian Endeavor, and have shown their regard for our society in many ways; but none of them have been able to do more than send telegrams and letters to our Conventions. But at what must have been considerable personal discomfort and sacrifice President Taft came to Atlantic City, and gave us two addresses that were carefully prepared, full of thought, and of great weight as they spoke with the highest authority on the most important national and international questions of the day. He accomplished this service, also, with the utmost heartiness and cordiality, and evidently enjoyed thoroughly his visit with these thousands of representatives of the best young manhood and young womanhood of the country.

The Speaker of the House of Representatives has an influence in our republic second only to that of the President, a power far exceeding that of most monarchs. The Hon. Champ Clark, who addressed the Convention, is an orator of high rank, and a Christian who for many years has been glad to speak boldly for Christ. He is just the type of man that fits into a Christian Endeavor Convention, as was Mr. Bryan, who honored our last Convention with his presence.

The President, the former Vice-President, and the Speaker of the House! Men of different religious and political faiths, yet uniting in their earnest desire for the religious uplift of their people, and the training of young men and women in all the essentials of Christian citizenship! Never before since the dawn of time has such a trio of eminent statesmen adorned a religious convention. The event is worthy to be emblazoned in letters of diamond as marking the new attitude of men of affairs toward the religious forces of this country. It is a notable tribute to Christian Endeavor, but it is all the more notable that it has this larger and most blessed significance.

Next only to these three conspicuous figures we must name among the reasons for the success of the Convention the other speakers that gave so freely of their best. Equally to be honored in the kingdom of God, equally powerful intellectually, themselves Presidents of the Republic of God — there were scores of them that would add lustre to any platform.

The glorious interdenominational character of Chistian Endeavor makes easily possible an unparalleled programme. Think of the men and women whom we heard at Atlantic City! — Dr. Tomkins, Secretary Grose, Bishop Fallows, Dr. John Balcom Shaw, President Capen, Dr. Wilson, Dr. McAfee, Dr. J. Wilbur Chapman, Dr. Sylvanus Stall, President Horsefield, Secretary Blecher, Mrs. Chapman, Judge Lindsey, Dr. Hill, (*two* Dr. Hills!) President Stewart, Secretary Halsey, Bishop Walters, Dr. Darby, Secretary McGaw, Principal Booker T. Washington, Dr. Tyndall, President Landrith, Secretary Fred B. Smith, Archdeacon Richardson, President William Phillips Hall, Dr. Hascall, Rev. Herbert Anderson, Secretary Gelston, Dr. Caldwell, Dr. Johnson, Bishop Coppin, Dr. Wilfley, Dr. Conwell, Judge Warner, Judge Orbison, Dr. W. H. Roberts, Secretary Wolf, President Lewis, Bishop Swengel — we began easily enough, but we do not know where to stop. The crowded pages of the programme, with their hundreds of names, constitute a "Who's Who" of most eminent leaders in fully thirty denominations. What a privilege to hear their God-given messages, and to mingle with them for seven inspiring days!

The field secretaries added much to the Convention. Other union officers we have had with us in large numbers in the past, with their consecrated hearts and brains — God bless them! But this was the first Convention after the rise of a strong body of paid workers who are giving their whole time to Christian Endeavor. It is a brilliant set of young men and young women, and their work made a foundation on which the great programme stood secure.

Many of the delegates took advantage of the unsurpassed opportunity for surf-bathing, and the generous spaces left in the programme for recreation were well used. Those that did not "get into the drink" found endless pleasure in visiting the long lines of pretty State reception-booths, wandering among the attractions and curiosities of the Pier, or simply sitting quietly and watching the lively panorama of sky and ocean, surf and shore. It was a genuinely recreative Convention.

That was one reason, though only one, for the abounding enthusiasm that reigned. The writer has attended all the International Conventions since, and including, New York, 1892, and in none of them have the Endeavorers shown a spirit so exuberant, a zeal and a zest so superb. The new generation of Endeavorers is in no way behind their predecessors in this happy essential for the best Christian service.

One cause of this enthusiasm was undoubtedly the splendid success of the Increase Campaign that has filled the two years since the St. Paul Convention with strenuous and purposeful activity. It is hard to realize what it means to add more than a million new members to any organization in two years. Ten thousand new societies! Why, few organizations have so many constituent bodies, all told. There are only a few States in the United States that possess a million inhabitants. That Christian Endeavor has done this great work, and done it with comparative ease, is an evidence of the on-moving power of our society that rejoiced us all at Atlantic City, and that sends us with conquering vigor into the Betterment Campaign that will fill the next two years.

We have not yet mentioned one of the most important and blessed triumphs of the Convention, the singing. It was pre-eminently a Convention of song. No attempt was made to introduce new songs, but the standard hymns and the well-known gospel songs were used exclusively. It was a happy thought to bring together the Christian Endeavor choruses of Philadelphia, Washington, Reading, and Harrisburg, and their leaders, Messrs. Lincoln, Foster, Wieand, and Palmer, brought us all heavily into their debt.

Especially did Percy S. Foster distinguish himself with an abounding inventiveness, a ready adaptability, and an infectious good cheer that added even to the many laurels he has won as director of Convention singing in the past. Mr. Lincoln also, another veteran Christian Endeavor chorus-leader, accomplished wonders. The Convention was much helped also by the solo singing of Mr. W. C. Weeden and the various lady singers, while the unique double voice of Mr. Enos Bacon, "the Yorkshire Nightingale," provided an attraction in all the sessions that was absolutely novel, and as beautiful as it was novel.

But when all this is said, with a whole-hearted tribute to the magnificent singing of the vast audiences, so ready, responsive, and full-volumed, all will agree that the one musical feature that excels the others was the presence of that chief hymn-writer of the world's history, the beloved Fanny Crosby. This aged poet, in spite of her lifelong blindness, is the very personification of good cheer. She has not only written more hymns than any other writer that has ever lived, but more hymns of the first rank, that are sure to live in the heart of the church. The sight of Fanny Crosby at the age of ninety-one, and the privilege of listening to her strong and beautiful words, was alone worth the longest journey to Atlantic City.

And now our faces are turned to Los Angeles. From the Atlantic to the Pacific. From one ocean to another even greater. May it be a second Oceanic Convention full of Californian sunshine and beauty, fragrance, and fruitfulness. And may the two Efficiency years between be the best that Christian Endeavor has ever known.

CHAPTER II.

A MAGNIFICIENT OPENING SESSION.

Thursday Evening, July 6.

"There is only one man in all the world," said Secretary Shaw, "who can properly open this twenty-fifth Christian Endeavor Convention, and that is Dr. Clark."

As our leader came forward he was greeted with a magnificent demonstration of loyalty and personal affection.

It was a glorious assembly that filled every corner of the great Auditorium Endeavor with a sea of more than six thousand young faces, the most inspiring audience that a speaker could ever meet.

At Dr. Clark's request the opening sentence of the Convention was the opening sentence of our pledge, "Trusting in the Lord Jesus Christ for strength, I promise Him that I will strive to do whatever He would like to have me do."

All were standing as the solemn promise rolled out, and as they stood they joined in the Bible prayer, "Establish thou the work of our hands upon us; yea, the work of our hands establish thou it."

Prof. Percy S. Foster is an ever-welcome leader of our Convention singing. His white suit, his cheery face, his ready enthusiasm, his unfailing freshness and ingenuity, and above all his deep consecration, are known the length and breadth of our land.

He caught the Convention at once, and bound them with the magic of song. Professor Foster has a most happy way of weaving together songs, a stanza here, a stanza there, forming a chain of inspiring thought; and this faculty was well used in his opening song service.

Another prime favorite of Endeavorers is Dr. Floyd W. Tomkins. No one could better conduct the opening devotional services. After a sweet, simple, and profound opening prayer, he gave us three key-words for the Convention.

First he bade us remember our origin, saying over softly to ourselves, "I came from God." Then as he led us we sang softly, "Nearer, my God, to Thee."

Second, we were to remember what God has done for us, saying over softly, "Christ died for me," and then singing, "My Jesus, I love Thee."

Finally, we are to serve this dear Saviour; and the thousands of earnest young voices spoke it with sincerity, "I will serve Him," raising their hands as they said it, and completing the consecration with the song, "I will go where you want me to go, dear Lord."

In introducing New Jersey's leading Endeavorer, that noble bank president, Mr. John T. Sproull, Dr. Clark spoke of the good fortune of Christian Endeavor in the devoted service of many men of affairs.

President Sproull's address was hearty, spirited, thoughtful, and eloquent. He introduced the following letter from New Jersey's popular governor, Hon. Woodrow Wilson:

"It is with the most genuine regret that I find myself unable to be present at the International Convention of Christian Endeavor to be held in Atlantic City, July 6.

"May I not, as the chief executive of the State, convey, through you, my warm and cordial greetings to the great Convention; and may I not express, through you, my feeling of the great importance of the work carried on by the Society of Christian Endeavor? Its influence has been world-wide and profound, and every man who values the deeper influence of Christianity must subscribe himself a friend and admirer of that great organization.

"Cordially and sincerely yours,
"WOODROW WILSON."

President Sproull gave to Dr. Clark a unique and beautiful gavel.

Permit me, said President Sproull, in behalf of the Endeavorers of New Jersey to present to you this gavel.

New Jersey has twenty-one counties, significant of majority, and the head of the gavel is composed of twenty-one different pieces of wood, a piece from each county, thoroughly cemented together for service and banded by the most precious of metals, gold, and the handle, which makes the head effective for service, is a piece of wood from the Life-Saving Station at Atlantic City.

This we feel is a mosaic of our great organization of Christian Endeavor now in its full majority of strength, composed of young people of all lands, of all ages, cemented in interdenominational fellowship for service in the hands of the Great Master of Assemblies and which service is actuated and controlled and made effective by the one dominant underlying principle of Christian Endeavor, life saving and developing, and banded together by the richest and most precious of all motives, the love of Christ which constraineth us.

In presenting this to you for service at this Convention, it is with the prayer that it will open a Convention that shall not only be signalized by its great speakers and grand addresses, splendid music and large attendance, but by the mighty outpouring of the Spirit of God that shall bring to every one present a new vision of Jesus Christ and the blessedness of service for him.

It is now my very great pleasure and privilege in behalf of the Endeavorers of the State of New Jersey and of the religious and busi-

REV. FRANCIS E. CLARK, D.D., LL.D.
PRESIDENT WORLD'S CHRISTIAN ENDEAVOR UNION, PRESIDENT UNITED SOCIETY OF CHRISTIAN ENDEAVOR.

ness interests of Atlantic City to extend a most cordial and hearty welcome to you, the officers and Board of Trustees of the United Society and to all Endeavorers gathered for this Twenty-fifth International Convention.

While New Jersey is small in its area, it gives place to none in the largeness of its hospitality. New Jersey has many things which in the past have added to her fame and renown and of which she may be justly proud, but we feel that her highest honor will be this Convention just opening, in view of its world-wide and eternity-lasting effect, and for this we welcome you.

We welcome you in behalf of the pastors and churches of this City, who realize that the presence in their midst of this magnificent body of Christian young people will be an inspiration and uplift to all their religious life and activities.

We welcome you in behalf of the business and hotel interests of this city, whose assistance and co-operation have so materially aided in our plans and who to-night, we believe, are glad of the presence of those who unitedly stand for that righteousness that exalteth a city.

We welcome you because of the fellowship of Christian Endeavor, as international as it is interdenominational; because of the principles for which the organization stands of personal consecration and loyalty to Jesus Christ and for efficient service to the church.

Dr. Grose, vice-president of the United Society, made a bright response to this address of welcome.

He enlivened the occasion by wittily commenting upon the sú*pier*ior provisions for our comfort here, as ap*pier* to those that *pier* about the Pier."

Referring to Captain Young's lovely home built out on the Pier, he remarked that the Captain seemed to be the only citizen perfectly happy with fifteen feet of water in his cellar; and further that when the Captain invited his friends he doubtless urged them to "just *drop in* at any time."

Dr. Grose spoke of the three great words of Christian Endeavor: *Conscience, Comity,* and *Efficiency.*

"Christian Endeavor" means Conscience Energized, Comity Expressed, and Co-operative Efficiency. These are meaningful phrases, and they will bear study.

It was a genuine surprise when at this point Field Secretary Lehmann stepped forward, and, in thought of the thirty years of Christian Endeavor and Dr. Clark's coming sixtieth birthday, presented to him a gold watch-chain bearing a diamond-studded Christian Endeavor monogram. The links of this chain are square-cut, and upon each face is engraved the name of a State or a Canadian Province; for all States and Provinces had a share in the gift.

After Dr. Clark's words of hearty gratitude, he introduced Dr. Grose as presiding officer for the remainder of the session, and Dr. Grose proceeded to introduce Dr. Clark, for his presidential address. The vice-president's characterization of Dr. Clark was so fine and just that we must include it in this account.

Dr. Grose said of him:

"Thirty years ago there came to a young pastor in Portland, Maine, a great ideal, a great idea, and a great name to represent them. The ideal has since been enshrined in the hearts of millions who have embodied the idea in development of personality and in beneficent activities in all parts of the world, until to-day under the name of Christian Endeavor a mighty army of young people belt the globe with unselfish service for Christ and the church. The man to whom ideal, idea, and name were given as a sacred trust; who has for all these years represented them worthily in his own character, work, and influence; who has been welcomed in every land and by races of every color and condition; who through such varied experiences as come to few has kept the faith in simplicity and his own manhood in sincerity, immune against the allurements of deserved praise — the leader whom we all love, I now have the privilege to present to you — the Founder and Master Builder of Christian Endeavor — Francis E. Clark."

Dr. Clark's address sounded a call for the Efficiency or Betterment Campaign of the next two years, and its plans were accepted by the approving plaudits of the Endeavorers.

EFFICIENCY.

Motto: "In the name of our God we will set up our banners."

The past two years have been years of wonderful enlargement of our Christian Endeavor circle. The Secretary's report will tell of the thousands of new societies and the hundreds of thousands of new members added since last we met in International Convention. For these let us thank God, the Giver of all, who has made possible the seemingly impossible task proposed two years ago.

The great advance of recent days, which proves that the divine favor rests upon the Christian Endeavor movement, should only be an incentive to make our societies better in every way, that we may be worthy of His continued blessing. As the motto of our Increase Campaign at the last Convention was "Enlargement," I propose that this year it should be "Efficiency."

Our enlargement is given us only that we may increase our efficiency. Every new society, every new member that joins the Christian Endeavor ranks, is a challenge to us to make each one more effective in the service of Christ. We miss our God-given opportunity when we do not transform our Enlargement into Efficiency.

Let us not think for a moment that our Increase Campaign is at an end. It should never cease, for increase should mean, and usually does mean, efficiency; since enlargement means effort, and effort, wisely directed, means effectiveness. The two words should be inseparable, but I desire this year to put the emphasis on the word *"Efficiency,"* as two years ago the stress was put upon the word "Enlargement."

Let me suggest a few lines of achievement which I think are within the bounds of our accomplishment during the twenty-four months to come. They are, you will see, all along the lines of the providential development of Christian Endeavor. I would only ask you to enter the doors God opens to us.

The Promotion of World-Wide Peace.

First. We have become in the broadest sense, more than ever during these two years past, an *international* organization. In every land beneath the sun the name "Christian Endeavor" is known, and its principles are acknowledged. Almost without knowing it, certainly without much human guidance, we have become a world-wide brotherhood that embraces every race and region.

What, then, is more natural or more important than that we should stand in every land for the fellowship of the nations and the peace of the world? What organization has a better chance or a more imperative call to unite the future leaders of the religious world in a pact that can never be broken by the hideous god of war?

This is peculiarly the year to press the peace idea. President Taft has uttered his ringing note that has aroused the echoes in every land. Sir Edward Grey and the leaders of both great English parties have seconded his brave words. Endeavorers in many lands have already expressed their gratitude that some statesmen dare to refer *every* question of national import to arbitration. British Endeavorers are peculiarly enthusiastic over the possibilities of a compact which shall unite English-speaking peoples in an indissoluble treaty. Let this Convention go on record with equal urgency, and let these two years to come mark a great advance the world over in promoting the fellowship of mankind so far as Christian Endeavor can promote it.

Most of my time for the next two years will be spent among the Endeavorers of Europe. I will try to do my little best there to promote this pact of peace. Will you do your best at home?

The Fellowship of the Churches.

Second. Our duty to promote the fellowship of the churches as well as of the nations must never be forgotten or minimized. It is our God-given privilege and duty to continue, as in the past, to be, perhaps, the chief agency in bringing the young people of all Protestant denominations together on a non-sectarian basis of love and service to God and man.

These two years past have seen new denominations join our ranks, have seen, indeed, greater advances along these lines than any other years, and should only spur us on to do our best to make the fellowship complete.

The Endeavorer as a Citizen.

Third. But our society has not only relations to every nation and denomination, but its relations to State, county, and city are equally important. An Endeavorer must never forget that he is a citizen, and he is not a good Endeavorer unless he is a good citizen. Our State and local unions are every year growing in value and influence, and should receive the wisest and most energetic guidance.

Perhaps the most important contribution of the last two years to Christian Endeavor history has been the splendid work of the Field Secretaries in fully half of our States. Their need, their value, their indispensable importance, where the right man is found, has come to be recognized everywhere.

Field Secretaries.

Let one of the watchwords for the coming biennium be, "A Field Secretary for every State and Province in America!" His services may not be needed in every State for the entire twelve months, but active field work for at least a portion of the year may well be the ambition of every commonwealth and Province.

But unions for world, nation, State, city, or county are but expressions of our fellowship, and furnish us opportunities for united service. The most important work of the individual Endeavorer is done in his own society, under the direction of his own church and pastor. To make this efficient, let me propose one or two plans which every society can enter upon before we meet again in International Convention.

A Campaign of Education.

a. Mission study-classes are already well known in our societies. Why should we not have a Christian Endeavor study-class in every society? Text-books are cheap; the little time necessary is not wanting; the advantages would be enormous. Remember that half a million new Endeavorers join our ranks each year. We must catch them young and train them unceasingly.

Because you older Endeavorers of ten or twenty years ago knew what the pledge meant, and why we adopted it, how to conduct a prayer meeting and carry on a committee efficiently, is no proof that the boys and girls who joined week before last understand these things.

We cannot afford to omit the education of Endeavorers in Endeavor principles any more than we can afford to shut up our high schools or close the doors of the little red schoolhouse in the country.

Christian Endeavor Experts.

In every society should be some, at least, who have thoroughly studied our principles; and I propose not only that in every society a Christian Endeavor study-class be instituted, but that pastor and president confer the degree C. E. E., "Christian Endeavor Expert," on every proficient student.

Rating for Efficiency.

b. I suggest for our local societies that some system of rating be adopted, that the faithful may be distinguished from the faithless and the conscientious from the careless. If our highest universities find the marking system necessary to promote scholarship, why should not this training-school of the church take a leaf out of their book of experience?

Let attendance, participation, and reverence in the meetings count. Let faithful and efficient service on the committees and worthy monthly committee reports also count for points. Let proportionate and systematic giving to missions and the support of denominational enterprises be recognized in the rating. Let the winning of new members of course always be considered worthy of recognition, and faithfulness to other services of the church than the Christian Endeavor meeting never be forgotten. Full details concerning this plan of Rating for Efficiency will be given in THE CHRISTIAN ENDEAVOR WORLD and in other Christian Endeavor papers and publications.

The contests between two or more societies, or two sides of the same society, when carried on in a spirit of friendly emulation, when efficiency is not sacrificed to numbers, and when all is done in the spirit of our motto, "For Christ and the Church," are often most helpful.

A New Bond of Unity.

c. One more suggestion I would make, that we everywhere begin and close each meeting with a simple service perhaps like that which we use in this Convention, that will emphasize our unity and yet will not be so elaborate as to stiffen into mere routine formalism.

We might at least begin each meeting with the first clause of our pledge, which is our confession, not of doctrinal but of practical unity and service, and close by singing a verse of that universal hymn of Christian brotherhood,

> "Blest be the tie that binds
> Our hearts in Christian love."

A Summary of Suggestions.

Shall these, then, be our ambitions and our efforts for the biennium which is before us?
1. *As an International organization, the promotion of world-wide Peace.*
2. *As an Interdenominational organization, a still wider Fellowship of all young Christians.*
3. *As State organizations, Field Secretaries who will promote our principles and our fellowship in every section.*
4. *As a Local organization,—*
   (a) *A Campaign of Education in every society.*
   (b) *A Campaign of Efficiency, promoted.*

The Real Source of Our Strength.

Never for a moment would I forget, or have you forget, the Source of our strength. Ours is a religious society, and it prospers only as such a society. Hundreds of young people's societies have been born, have been loudly trumpeted abroad, have dwindled and died, within the last thirty years. They have never gripped the hearts of the young people for long, or commended themselves to the church at large, because the religious idea involved in the pledge, the prayer meeting, the consecration meeting, and the committees was left out or minimized. They have been young people's societies, sometimes young people's societies of Endeavor, but not young people's societies of *Christian* Endeavor; and so they have had no long life or wide acceptance.

While I believe in the utmost flexibility of Christian Endeavor, and its ability to adapt itself to all conditions, and to incorporate within itself everything that young people need for their religious training, let us never lose sight of our cardinal principles.

Let me repeat it. Ours is a religious society. We stand for training the youth along four great lines: Outspoken Acknowledgment of Christ, Constant Service for Christ, Loyalty to Christ's Church, Fellowship with Christ's People. Whatever features we introduce or omit, let us not forget or minimize these features, which really spell Christian Endeavor, which for thirty years have made it increasingly successful, and which have caused it to find a home in every land beneath the sun.

Two Dangers to Be Guarded Against.

There are two dangers to be guarded against. First, a narrow exclusiveness which would make the society merely a prayer meeting, with a very narrow round of duties for a few of the spiritually gifted; and, on the other hand, an unintelligent inclusiveness which, for the sake of numbers or prestige, adopts every latest young people's fad, thus belittling or perhaps crowding out the very things which Christian Endeavor was established to maintain, until at last, as one has graphically expressed it, "the guest has eaten up the host."

Against both of these dangers we have one great safeguard. It is found in our pledge, which is both inclusive and exclusive, including whatever Christ the Master would like to have us do, yet limiting our society and defining it as promoting in any way and all ways the distinctively religious life of young people.

O fellow Endeavorers! In all our plans for enlargement and efficiency remember that there is but one Source of real strength and growth. Plans, methods, new ideas, are important; but one thing is *all*-important. There is One who is all and in all. In all our meetings, in all our committees, in all our unions, never leave Him out of your plans. Keep close to His heart and to the heart of His church. Glory in the cross of Christ, and be willing to take up your own cross and follow Him. Then we will go on to greater enlargement than ever, and to nobler efficiency. In the name of our God we will set up our banners.

Five able speakers said Amen to the statesmanlike proposals, and Dr. Grose confined them to two minutes each — "men who usually take," as he said, "forty minutes each."

But they proved their rapid-fire quality, every one of them — Dr. W. F. Wilson of Canada, Bishop Fallows, Dr. Cleland McAfee, Dr. John Balcom Shaw, and President Capen of the American Board.

Dr. Capen declared that nearly all of the foreign missionaries commissioned by the American Board for years have proved, on examination, to have received their early training in the Christian Endeavor Society.

Dr. McAfee asserted that it is time that the Christian Endeavor movement should become a world-wide peace movement; and the many references throughout the evening to the present proposal for international arbitration were gloriously applauded.

One of the surprises of the evening was the singing by Mr. Enos Bacon of England, "the Yorkshire Nightingale," the man with the double voice, a genuine bass and a clear, powerful soprano — not a falsetto, but a fine soprano.

He sang two solos of his own composing, passing so marvellously from soprano to bass and back to soprano that he seemed to be at least two soloists singing a duet. The Endeavorers were thoroughly delighted, and their applause was tremendous.

"It's an awful drop," said Treasurer Lathrop, "from poetry to prose, from a Yorkshire Nightingale to a Yankee treasurer." But he held his crowd for the really remarkable facts of the report.

FACTS AND FACTORS.

There are some things that need to be said pretty often, even to tried and true Endeavorers who read THE CHRISTIAN ENDEAVOR WORLD and keep posted on the United Society's literature. I refer to the wonderful financial facts and the particular factors that make up the record of twenty-five years' operations of the Publishing Department, that dynamo which has furnished the "sinews of war" at home and abroad ever since the United Society was organized.

The busy world knows in a general way that Christian Endeavor is the name of a great young people's movement, but comparatively few know the tremendous fact that not one of its members has ever been taxed one cent for its support. Nor the other tremendous fact that, aside from paying all its running expenses for twenty-five years, the Publishing Department has enabled the United Society to contribute nearly a quarter of a million dollars to world-wide work for young people.

To accomplish this has meant rigid economy in business administration, it has meant little salaries and no salaries to its officers. President Clark draws no salary, but makes his living by editorial and other literary work; the treasurer draws no salary, but keeps the wolf from the door by other business activities; and General Secretary Shaw works overtime. Nobody is complaining, because the cause is worthy of every ounce of time and strength; and we give God all the praise that He has provided us with other sources of income.

We only want Christian Endeavor understood and the world to know how we exist, why we exist, and to be convinced that we are entitled to a building in which to continue our existence. Any movement with nearly four million members ought to command the attention of thoughtful men and women everywhere, even if that movement does not continually advertise itself; but when such a movement is universally recognized as a great religious training-school for young people, the marvel is that consecrated men and women have not a score of years ago provided a Christian Endeavor Headquarters Building for this Society.

Spend just a moment with me on one year's statistics.

In 1910 the Publishing Department received $60,021. The printing and binding, salaries, rent and office expenses cost $46,413; $10,147 was contributed to the Missionary Department; and we have a balance on hand June 1, 1911, of $3,452.

Our *total assets* are now as follows:

Publishing Department, Net Inventory, and Accounts receivable, ...	$28,066.66
*Real Estate cor. Huntington and Longwood Aves., Boston, at cost	31,625.52
Cash on hand and invested for International Christian Endeavor Building	41,284.83
This makes a grand total of	$100,977.01

That isn't Dr. Clark's money, it isn't Secretary Shaw's money, it isn't my money; it is *your money*. We recognize it as a consecrated trust fund. It belongs to every member of a Christian Endeavor society from the rising sun round the world to the point of its rising again. There is no "setting sun" for Christian Endeavor.

To our assets must be added good pledges for the Building Fund amounting to $70,973.10; and, to return to my text, the *fact* is we need just *$25,000* more than is now pledged to complete that building. Will you be a contributing factor?

Here came in a telegram from the Missouri, Kansas, and Oklahoma delegations — Endeavorers in distress, on the way, greatly delayed; but they wanted us to know that they would arrive before long.

The following most inspiring and significant message of brotherhood was then read:

"Five thousand Endeavorers in the Far East send greetings to the thousands gathered in Convention at Atlantic City. Japan joins hands with America in pledging her utmost efforts toward preserving peace between the nations, fostering the moral and religious culture of children and young people,

* It's worth at least $5,000 more now.

strengthening the ethical safeguards of society at large, and making regnant in all hearts and lives the teachings of Jesus Christ, Lord and Saviour of mankind.

"For the Japan Christian Endeavor Union.
TOKIYUKI OSADA, *President*.
TATSUJIRO SAWAYA, *Secretary*.
JAMES H. PETTEE, *Treasurer*.

"Kyoto, Japan."

We heard also a message of hearty greeting from the European Christian Endeavor Union, sent by its president, the beloved Rev. John Pollock, of Belfast, Ireland

The Washington chorus filled the platform, and at this point sang Kipling's "Recessional" (Reginald de Koven's music). It was splendidly sung, the solo part being charmingly taken by a Christian Endeavorer, Miss Agnes Green Preston.

No one but Secretary Shaw could have held that vast throng at that late hour, after so long a programme, especially for a secretary's annual report; but he succeeded in his difficult task.

Calling out Secretary Poling of Ohio and Secretary Gates of Illinois, he bade them "hold his manuscript."

This was a series of sheets on which, in letters read across the auditorium, were printed the salient facts of the superb Increase Campaign of the last two years.

Secretary Shaw had the audience read these facts in a mighty chorus, and often as the new page was turned, with its announcement of a gain in two years of more than ten thousand new societies and more than one million new members, or its tribute to the large contribution made by the Allen Leagues of the A. M. E. churches or the Varick Leagues of the A. M. E. Zion, the burst of applauding joy for a time quite drowned the reading.

TWO YEARS OF GROWTH.

Two years ago, at the St. Paul Convention, President Clark challenged our Christian Endeavor host with the proposition that we start a two years' Increase Campaign for ten thousand new societies and one million new members.

The first impression was that the task was impossible, but after a gasp of surprise the very magnitude of it appealed to the imagination of the young people, and with a cheer, from the North and the South, from the East and the West, they threw themselves into the campaign with the daring and enthusiasm of youth, led by our splendid corps of Field Secretaries and union officers.

We are here to-night to announce that

We Have Arrived,

that the task is completed, and more.

Since July, 1909, there have been reported to the United Society by national, State, provincial, and denominational unions 10,345 new societies of Christian Endeavor, and in these and in the societies already

WILLIAM SHAW.
General Secretary United Society of Christian Endeavor.

organized 1,002,500 new members, and the remarkable thing about these reports is that over 7,000 are young people's societies.

The honor roll of the States that secured their full apportionment or more is as follows: California, District of Columbia, Idaho, Illinois, Indiana, Kansas, Nebraska, Texas, Virginia.

Worthy of especial mention is the splendid record made by the Allen and Varick Leagues of Christian Endeavor, a token of the new day of opportunity and leadership that is coming to the young people in the colored churches of our land.

The list of States organizing one hundred or more new societies during the campaign includes California, Illinois, Indiana, Kansas, Massachusetts, Michigan, Minnesota, Missouri, Nebraska, New Jersey, New York, Ohio, Pennsylvania, and Texas.

Every State, Territory, and Province is represented in the Increase Campaign.

These figures do not, of course, represent a net gain, as it must be remembered that Christian Endeavor, unlike every other organization in the church, is steadily graduating its members out of the society into the wider work of the church, and has to fill their places with new material, and that Junior and Intermediate societies fluctuate according to the demands of the churches.

The total world-wide enrolment of societies is now 79,077 with a membership of 3,953,850, the largest in the history of the movement. Of these societies 57,589 are in the United States and Canada, and 21,488 in the world field, with practically every country represented. Notable among the foreign countries showing marked gains in Christian Endeavor is China, with a total of 781 societies, an increase of 381 over the last report, or nearly one hundred per cent, and India with 1,337 societies.

Intermediate and Junior Work.

Two of the most hopeful and successful divisions of our Christian Endeavor army are enrolled under these headings. They stand for men and women in the making. Their dreams and visions of to-day will become the realities of to-morrow.

If the church has real work to do in the world, it must arouse itself to the need of training its future members for that work. The hour a week in the Sunday school is not sufficient in time, nor the teaching method alone an adequate plan for the proper equipment of these workers. The secret, social, and athletic organizations, whose name is Legion, are not sufficient. These young people need the definite religious training that Christian Endeavor supplies, and this training should begin in the Junior society, and continue through the Intermediate and Young People's societies into the Senior grade of active church service.

Other Activities.

That the Increase Campaign has not absorbed all the time and energy of the Endeavorers is shown by the splendid progress reported along many lines of effort. First in order and importance should be mentioned

The International Headquarters Building.

For thirty years Christian Endeavor has demonstrated its usefulness to the churches and the wider work of the Kingdom. Reports show that the large proportion of efficient workers in the churches and the trained leaders in other organizations "found themselves," and received their call to service, while engaged in the definite work that Christian Endeavor provides for each member.

Among all the varied organizations for young people, Christian Endeavor stands supreme as the most practical and efficient training-school for normal church workers.

During all these years of demonstration Christian Endeavor has not only given literally millions of dollars through the missionary and benevolent channels of its own churches, but it has paid its own bills. For more than twenty years the United Society has carried on its work from the profits of its publication department, without receiving contributions from either societies or churches.

Of the $200,000 needed for the International Headquarters Building, $155,021.15 has been secured in cash and pledges. Building banks have been distributed which should yield $20,000 more, leaving a balance of $25,000 that should be raised at this Convention, so that Christian Endeavor can start on its fourth decade with the memory of a glorious past and the assurance of a suitable equipment for a still greater future.

Manifold Activities.

Christian Endeavor does not live unto itself. The whole spirit of the movement is for others, and its object is happily expressed in the theme of this great Convention, "Training for Service." Its centre is the local church, but its circumference is the kingdom of God.

The Moving-Picture Fight.

When the country was threatened with moving-picture reproductions of the brutal Johnson-Jeffries prize-fight in every city and town, demoralizing our youth and provoking race antagonism, Christian Endeavor stepped into the ring, and in one round knocked out the whole business, which was expected to yield its promoters millions of dollars in profits.

Governors of States and local authorities joined in the campaign that practically suppressed the pictures in all parts of this country, while the authorities in South Africa, Australia, India, and England joined in suppressing the pictures there. It was a magnificent demonstration of moral earnestness and of the efficiency of our world-wide movement.

Sunday Labor.

Thousands of mail clerks and carriers in the Post-Office Department have been robbed of their Sunday rest-day because of the selfishness or indifference of the people. The Christian-citizenship department of the Chicago Christian Endeavor Union began an investigation, with the result that they found that the clerks and carriers were losing their weekly rest-day to accommodate about half of one per cent of the patrons of the post-office. They appealed to the pastors, churches, and other organizations. They carried the matter up to the Postmaster-General, who was most cordial and sympathetic in his attitude. The result was an order to limit the Sunday work to the absolutely necessary minimum, and the restoration of the rest-day to an army of toilers.

This movement started in Chicago, has spread to other cities and towns, and promises to become general throughout the country.

Fresh-Air Camps.

The needs of the children in our large cities have not been forgotten by our wide-awake Endeavorers, and the Brooklyn, Baltimore, New Jersey, and other unions have purchased seashore homes, where hundreds of children are entertained during the hot summer months.

Friendly relations are established with the families from which the children come, and they are made to realize by personal experience that these Endeavorers are indeed followers of Him "who went about doing good."

Hospitals and Missions.

The beautiful ministry to the sick in hospitals, carried on by the California and Chicago Endeavorers and many others, meets the need of a field too often neglected. The little group of earnest Endeavorers in Hungary have bought, and maintain, Bethsaida Hospital, a model institution in Budapest. The comfort and hope of the gospel has brought to many a discouraged one strength to bear the physical pain and weariness; and the hand that has smoothed their pillows, and the voice that has cheered their hearts, has been like unto that of the Son of man.

City missions, and summer tent meetings and outdoor services, find in the Christian Endeavor societies their most constant and helpful workers, while in the country the visits to the almshouses and homes for the unfortunate are greatly appreciated.

Our Immigrant Brother.

With a million or more immigrants pouring into this country every year, the question of our attitude toward them becomes a vital one. Naturally suspicious of strangers, alienated from the church, and against the government, as are most of those who are now coming to our shores, the problem is a difficult one. Only the spirit of Christ is able to solve it. But that spirit must be incarnate in men and women who can see in each one of these people our brother man.

Many societies are gaining approach to the immigrants by holding evening classes in the winter months to teach them English. Five nationalities are being reached in this way by the Christian Endeavor society of the South Congregational Church of New Britain, Conn.

Societies are also being organized among the German, French, Italian, Finnish, Bohemian, Armenian, Chinese, Japanese, and other nationalities in this country. It is hoped to bring the members of these societies, through the fellowship of our Christian Endeavor unions, into touch with the best elements in our civilization, and so to transform them into good citizens and earnest Christians.

Extent and Variety.

The movement we represent is so great in extent and so varied in expression that its importance is often overlooked or underestimated.

"Only a society of young people," is the way some people look at it. But consider for a moment that these societies of young people furnish the leaders and the field for thousands of mission-study classes that make use of the text-books issued by the Young People's Missionary Movement;

That in these societies are organized the personal workers' classes to train the members for personal evangelism;

That unions of these societies have fought hard battles for Christian citizenship and have won notable victories for temperance, Sabbath-observance, and other moral reforms;

That they have stood in the front rank of those that believe in international brotherhood, and in the peaceful arbitration of all questions between nations;

That since last we met in Convention, more than 5,000,000 prayer meetings have been held, with an estimated attendance of more than 200,000,000 young people;

That more than 1,000,000 missionary meetings have been held, with an attendance of 50,000,000;

That 5,000,000 temperance meetings have been held, with an attendance of 20,000,000;

That more than 500,000 socials have been held, where genuine good times have been substituted for questionable amusements;

That more than 100 State and more than 10,000 district, county, and local-union conventions have been held;

That millions of bouquets of flowers have brightened the pulpits of our churches, and have then carried the spirit of the Christ in their fragrant blossoms as they have been taken to the sick and shut-ins of the congregation;

That tens of thousands of young people have been learning how to win others to Christ by their service on the lookout committees;

That tens of thousands of music, calling, relief, information, good-literature, and other committees have been training young people for faithful service in the name of Christ through His church for the upbuilding of His kingdom.

Tenth Legion, Quiet Hour, etc.

But having referred thus briefly to a few of the many lines of successful service conducted by our Christian Endeavorers, what shall I more say? for time will not permit any emphasis of the Tenth Legion, which is training 27,320 young men and women in the principles of Christian stewardship; of the Comrades of the Quiet Hour, numbering 57,410, who know what it means to practise the presence of God; of the societies among the soldiers in camp and barracks; of the work with the Indians on the plains; of the Floating societies that minister to the men of the sea; of the Prison societies that have brought freedom from sin to the men behind the bars; and of all the multiplied forms of Christlike service that our Endeavorers are engaged in.

Profoundly grateful for the privileges and opportunities of the past, may we not enthusiastically face the future, and join our beloved president and trusted leader, Dr. Clark, in the "1913 Efficiency Campaign" which he has just outlined, and make Christian Endeavor increasingly effective in training the youth of our churches for the service of the Kingdom?

As our general secretary finished his inspiring record of work accomplished, the Endeavorers sung with feeling and force the Convention hymn by Mr. Wells, "Praise God for Thirty Golden Years."

A CONVENTION HYMN.

In Remembrance of the First Thirty Years of Christian Endeavor.
By Amos R. Wells.

Praise God for thirty golden years,
For faith and hope that conquer fears,
For our united, world-wide host,
Praise Father, Son, and Holy Ghost!

Praise God for purpose true and strong,
For loyal hearts, for joy and song,
And for the strength of Jesus Christ,
That all our need has aye sufficed.

> Praise God for voices leal and bold,
> For glad endeavors manifold,
> For churches drawn to one accord,
> For answered prayers praise the Lord!
>
> Praise God for all the coming time
> Of peace and growth and joy sublime;
> Yet still for Thee we praise the most,
> Dear Father, Son, and Holy Ghost!

Thus closed what was undoubtedly in every way the finest opening session of all our magnificent series of Christian Endeavor Conventions.

CHAPTER III.

THE QUIET HOUR.

Getting in touch with God in the quiet hours of the early morning is always a feature very much enjoyed at our great conventions. Atlantic City proved no exception, because, following the beautiful example of Jesus Himself, who delighted to gather the multitudes by the seaside to teach them, so Christian Endeavorers assembled each morning where the mighty sea rolls in all its majesty to listen anew to the story of Him who loved the dweller by the sea.

The Quiet Hour services on the pier, conducted by Dr. Chapman, Dr. Kelly, Secretary Gelston, and Rev. Huber Ferguson, proved to be a great stimulus and blessing when each morning more than one thousand voices raised songs of thanksgiving, and their hearts went out to God in prayer, while the waves underneath their feet rolled an accompaniment, and the breezes carried the joyful sound upward to the throne of God. Here it was that tender impressions were made, and the budding life blossomed out into rich, fragrant power.

The Quiet Hours of our conventions always come like calms in the storm, lulling and restful alike to both speakers and hearers. It is in these moments of restful devotion that the quiet waters deep down in many a soul are stirred. The mountain-top climaxes of the great meeting are thrilling experiences, and the desire to do something great for God almost sweeps one off his feet, but it is the little lulls that come in the early morning hour of devotions, when the Spirit of God breathes softly o'er the meeting, and the eyes grow wet, the heart warms to the power of God, and the will determines to bear witness for Him, that bring the greatest results.

Dr. Chapman.

At the time for the opening of the first of the Quiet Hours all the chairs provided for the service were filled, and a continuous stream of later comers was pouring in, each bringing his own chair from another hall. The gathering-place was the Pavilion, open on all sides, and with the flooring giving glimpses of the waters beneath, whose plashing mingled with the hymns feelingly sung under Mr. Foster's leading.

The Shepherd Psalm furnished the theme, and Dr. J. Wilbur Chapman gave fresh emphasis to the familiar words, making the thought centre about the phrase, "I shall not want." All joined in repeating the psalm before he spoke, and after he had dwelt upon it all united once more in reciting very softly the words, giving special stress to the first personal pronoun throughout the whole, recalling the strengthening truths that had been presented, and which were echoed in the brief prayers that closed the session.

Saturday morning the Quiet-Hour session was transferred from the Pavilion to Auditorium Williston, and the thousands that flocked to this gathering at half past six would have made a good audience for one of the main meetings. Yet the atmosphere of the meeting was such that in the inspiration of numbers there was no loss of tender impressiveness and sense of personal communion with God. Much of the singing was done very softly, and the solo, "Moment by Moment," by Miss Flora Rondabush, added to the effect of the service.

Dr. Chapman asked all to repeat John 3:16, which was afterward given by the men alone; and then he spoke on "He first findeth his own brother." At the start he stated his wish to lead up to a definite act of consecration on the part of Christians present. As reasons for personal work he gave these: The majority come to Christ as the result of personal work; such work leads to a kind of endless chain of results; we are our brothers' keepers; there is no thrill like that of winning a soul. To do such work, the worker must get right with God, get right with his fellows, surrender fully, and follow the Spirit's leading.

After a series of brief prayers from different sections of the room, two or three sometimes seeking to take part at once, Dr. Chapman clinched his address by asking as many as would to write for themselves a dedication to the work of soul-winning with God's help, using letters, the spoken word, and prayer to bring others to Christ. In response to the invitation practically the whole company, it seemed, rose to their feet as an expression of such consecration. What an endless chain of results that act may mean no one can foresee.

Mr. Gelston.

In opening the Quiet-Hour service on Monday morning Rev. Willis L. Gelston, honored Presbyterian superintendent of young people's work, told how in his own church at one time when he felt especial need of such a step he asked that each one in the congregation try to make the preacher's words in prayer his own. The effect was most marked. He asked the company in Auditorium Williston to do the same with prayer and address and every part of the service. Thus the feeling of participation was kept although the leader was the only speaker.

After picturing the situation when Christ washed the feet of His disciples, Mr. Gelston introduced the subject of service, asking each to put to himself the question, "How much am I worth?" not in property, but in service helping to pay the debt due to the world. Nothing is needed in this country to-day more than volunteers to enter the army of those truly great through service. Our friends need service, and the habit is gained only by training. We ought to form the habit of serving in the church. If a dozen persons in our societies would serve half an hour a day as they would serve in business, the efficiency of almost any society could be multiplied. We ought to serve our country, making sacrifices of personal advantage if needed, and recognizing that we are saved to serve.

Dr. Kelly.

One of the long-time trustees is Dr. Gilby C. Kelly, of the Methodist Episcopal Church, South. We were especially glad that he conducted the Quiet-Hour service on Tuesday morning.

Williston Auditorium was well filled with shining morning faces. Secretary Chain of the Pennsylvania Union conducted a helpful praise service.

"Service," said Dr. Kelly, "is the great word of the church of our day. Indeed, it is the great word of serious-minded people the world over. Service is only the impersonal word of our Lord and Master. In the record of Christ's life the word is written in great capitals."

The morning's theme was "Christ Our Hope in Time of Storm," and the Scripture was the storm rescue on the Sea of Galilee. "Let us not think," said the speaker, "that we can go out to sea in any unworthy craft, and Jesus will deliver us. Let us not think, either, that Jesus will ward off all danger even from His obedient children. Jesus does not make men effeminate. He does not take the heroism out of life. He teaches us to conquer the sea, and not be afraid of it. If a man serves, he must suffer. The only kind of servant that is worth while is the suffering servant."

The morning's lessons were summed up by the quiet singing of three great old hymns, "Rock of Ages," "Jesus, Lover of my soul" and "How firm a foundation."

President Ferguson.

The final Quiet-Hour service, led by Rev. Huber Ferguson, the Ohio president, centred around Christ's commission to

WILLIAM HOWARD TAFT.
President of the United States.

Peter, "Feed my sheep," following the three questions, "Lovest thou me?" The thought emphasized was "Christ's command: does He mean me?"

Remember that Jesus Christ wants you a great deal more than you want Him. But He makes some demands. He wishes to be first in the heart of the man whom He will reinstate in His service. Rev. F. B. Meyer tells how when he was a young minister he saw that Charles Studd had a power that he had not himself, and he asked Studd about it. The answer was, "I have nothing that you cannot have; but have you yielded your life wholly to God?" Mr. Meyer knew that there was one thing that he not given up. He surrendered on that one point, and his whole life depended upon that one night. There is just one thing that Jesus asks, whether we love Him first.

All were asked to bow their heads and to answer audibly, "Does Jesus desire my service?" "Do I love Jesus Christ?" Then the question was put for each to answer in his heart, "Lovest thou me more than these? Shall I place Jesus Christ first in my life?"

With heads still bowed all sung softly, "My Jesus, I love Thee," prayer was offered, and the company left the room quietly, dwelling on the closing thought.

CHAPTER IV.

REACHING OUT.

Auditorium Williston.

A very practical programme filled Auditorium Williston on Friday afternoon with a fine company of Endeavorers that meant business.

Dr. James L. Hill was the resourceful presiding officer, and the singing was led by the splendid Philadelphia Christian Endeavor chorus conducted by that skilful leader of song, known for years in our conventions, Mr. H. C. Lincoln.

Our Presbyterian trustee, Dr. A. W. Halsey, brought into the meeting the spirit of prayer, obtaining from the audience volunteer prayers for the six great subjects of the afternoon.

It is a splendid work for the sick that the Chicago Endeavorers are doing through and with the hospital board of the city union. A member of that board, Rev. E. L. Reiner, told about it so earnestly and forcefully that hundreds must have been inspired to attempt a similar work for other "retreats of suffering." Last year the Chicago Endeavorers gave to their hospital friends 60,220 bouquets, 13,335 papers and magazines, 6,940 tracts, 1,500 garments, and more than a thousand Testaments — this in addition to the regular Sunday-evening services and Friday-evening concerts. What a world of comfort and uplift these figures mean!

For years Judge Edgar M. Warner, prison superintendent of the Connecticut Union, has borne upon his heart the sad case of our prisoners, the men and women that live in "the homes of the forgotten." Judge Warner urged the Endeavorers to send good books and papers to the prisons, to write heartening letters to the prisoners, to get work for discharged prisoners, to work for the observance of "Prison Sunday" — the fourth Sunday of October, and to offer constant prayer for the prisoners. Judge Warner distributed a prayer cycle for the last-named purpose.

At this point we paused while our honored trustee from the A. M. E. Zion Church, Bishop Alexander Walters, led us in a most inspiring service of intercession for the six causes under consideration during the session.

Chaplain Steele is in the habit of urging that the sailors need Christian work more than any other class of men on earth, because their calling keeps them away from church services and influences. Christian Endeavor alone can bring the church of Christ to them. Its simple organization can be maintained by Christian sailors on board ship, and Endeavorers on shore can keep up the zeal of their brothers afloat by means of correspondence. Mr. Alfred S. Cox, chairman of Philadelphia's admirable Christian Endeavor Floating department, told us of the splendid possibilities of this service for the Master.

If any one of the audience thought that Christian Endeavor had no special work to do for the lepers, this thought vanished long before Mr. John Jackson ended his stirring address. He told of the wretched myriads of lepers in Asia and elsewhere, and of the heroic character of the four thousand Christian lepers cared for by his own mission society for lepers.

Dr. W. J. Darby, assistant secretary of the Presbyterian Board of Education, is chairman of a committee of the trustees which for a year has been actively at work promoting Christian Endeavor among the colored churches. The splendid way in which our colored brothers have rallied to the Endeavor banner is shown by the fact that the A. M. E. churches have organized one-fifth of the ten thousand new societies, and the A. M. E. Zion churches bring the proportion up to more than one-fourth. Dr. Darby's discussion of the negro question was exceedingly frank, very courageous, and so fair and sane as to win the hearty approval of the distinguished colored leaders in his audience.

The field secretary of the National Reform Association, Rev. James S. McGaw, had a theme close to his heart in "Christian Endeavor and Civic Problems." With an eloquence both fiery and thoughtful, in an address that bristled with startling facts, Secretary McGaw pictured the contest between the Christian and secular democracy that is waging to-day. He pleaded for the Bible in our public schools; for the right observance of the Sabbath; for the placing of chaplains on our ships, in prisons, and in the army; for the abolition of the divorce evil, polygamy, and the liquor traffic; for the supremacy of Christ in our national life.

"He leadeth me" the Endeavorers sung as they marched from the room, and surely the words were most appropriate. As the hymn was carried out along the Pier and into the streets, so may it be carried out into the lives of all the singers!

CHAPTER V.

THE GREATEST EVENING.

Auditoriums Endeavor and Williston, Friday Evening, July 7.

Presidents of the United States have sent messages of greeting to our Christian Endeavor Conventions. President McKinley delivered a magnificent address before the Cleveland Convention, but it was when he was governor of Ohio. Mr. Taft is the first president to honor our assembly with his presence and his spoken words.

Everybody was looking forward eagerly to his coming. It was the chief subject of conversation among the Endeavorers and through the city also; for not since Grant's administration has a president visited Atlantic City.

The Pier was crowded to the limit, and hundreds were unable to obtain admission to either auditorium. Within the halls all were ready with their flags, to wave them as the chief magistrate of the nation appeared.

And then he came in so quietly, and so far ahead of time, that the Endeavorers were taken completely by surprise. They were putting in the time with their State yells, ending each with a vigorous spelling of "T-A-F-T, Taft!" And the President was as happy as any jolly schoolboy at catching them in their fun.

Mr. Taft was also much interested in the singing, which Professor Foster engineered. When we came to "Like a mighty army," all the men were bidden to rise and sing the stanza. As about three thousand men arose, Mr. Foster cried, "Who said there wouldn't be enough men in heaven to sing bass in the choir?" "That's great!" exclaimed the President as the men's voices rolled out a splendid volume of sound.

"Bringing in the sheaves" was sung — at least the chorus — here on the left a line, yonder on the right the next line, this gallery and that gallery and far in the rear and the fine Indianapolis chorus in front, as the leader pointed to each. "And when I point nowhere, the preachers are to sing," said Mr. Foster; nor were the hundreds of preachers once caught napping. Later in the evening we heard the President, talking to one of the members of his own party, praise in high terms the singing of the Endeavorers.

Dr. John Balcom Shaw conducted the devotional exercises in a unique way, repeating from memory a noble selection of Scripture passages descriptive of our Saviour: "God so loved the world," etc.; "I am the bread of life"; "I am the resurrection and the life"; "Ye believe in God; believe also in me"; "Come unto me, all ye that labor" — a score of passages thus exalting Christ. He followed this with a most inspiring prayer for God's blessing upon our nation and its beloved chief magistrate.

Dr. Clark sought not to present Mr. Taft to the audience, but to present the Endeavorers to the President, and outlined the wide reach of our societies and the scope of their work. "For many years," he told the President, "it was said that nothing could get over our tariff walls into Canada but the birds and Christian Endeavor, and we have always practically illustrated the doctrine of reciprocity."

There was tremendous applause when Dr. Clark referred to Mr. Taft's proposal of an unrestricted treaty of arbitration between this country and Great Britain, the first time since the dawn of history that the responsible ruler of a nation has dared to make such a proposal.

"I would rather," said Dr. Clark, "go down in history as William the Peacemaker than as William the Conqueror."

Of course we all rose to greet the President as he came forward to speak, and of course we gave him the heartiest applause that ever a Christian Endeavor audience can give. I say "of course"; but there was nothing perfunctory about it; the greeting was a glad welcome to one whom every one recognized as a cheery friend, as well as the most powerful of all earth's rulers.

President Taft read his address, but he spoke with great earnestness, with evident feeling, and with the force that these alone can give. His voice is strong, as befits his massive body, and he must have been heard easily by all of the immense throng. They listened with quick appreciation of every point, and constantly adopted the sentiments of the speaker with their delighted applause. We give the address entire:

Mr. Chairman, Members of the Christian Endeavor Society, Ladies and Gentlemen:

As I stand upon this platform, I am conscious of being in the presence of a religious force for progress and good in the world that had its genesis nearly thirty years ago, and now is making its influence felt completely around the world and through the expression and activity of four million living souls.

This Convention commemorates the organization of a movement based upon the principle that the time to influence men and women in their lives is in that formative period between youth and manhood, and that the making of the character of men and women is best achieved by trainng and practice rather than by instruction and preaching. It does not discountenance either instruction to the infants in the Sunday-school or preaching to the adults in the church; but it furnishes a link between the two that in its actual influence has resulted in marvellous development, and shows itself in the conscious and enthusiastic demonstration of biennial meetings like this, in the history of its progress that is recounted at these conventions by representatives from all quarters of the globe. By insistence upon open confession of religious faith, and the bringing forth of works needful for the expression of that faith, and in the fellowship which follows a common confession and work, the Christian Endeavor Society has made its mark in the religious history of the world.

But I did not come here to discuss before an audience that knows them very much better than I the principles upon which your society is founded and the methods by which these principles have been embodied in the present glorious and useful development. I may take one sentence to express my profound and sincere admiration for Dr. Clark and his estimable wife, the founders of this society, who have lived long enough to see it grow from one small organization in Portland, Me., to a world-power for good; and as the chief magistrate of this country to recognize the debt it owes for their work, and especially in the development of individual Christian character among the members of the evangelical Protestant churches of this country. Such a movement can not but have the most beneficial effect upon the citizenship of a nation like this, and I should be lacking in appreciation of these currents of popular reform and individual uplifting if I did not seize such an opportunity to pay a just tribute to those who have deserved so well of the republic; for, while this country has no state church, and encourages the utmost freedom of religious belief and practice, it is a fundamental error to suppose that those who are responsible in any degree for the public welfare may not in every proper way encourage all instrumentalities for the betterment of the individual man, all normal and religious movements for his higher spiritual welfare, without regard to the denominational jurisdiction in which such movements take their course or exercise their influence. They necessarily tend to a leaven of the whole community and to the righteousness that exalteth a nation.

But, as I say, I did not come here to tell you about your own organization. I came to talk on a subject and cause in which I have, in common with all the civilized people of the world, an intense interest; and that is the avoidance of war by providing such instrumentalities for the settlement of international controversies as to make war remote because unnecessary.

I observe that in your last Convention, the Twenty-fourth International Convention, one of your resolutions was as follows:

> "*Resolved,* That as followers of the Prince of peace we ally ourselves with every effort that is being made for the suppression of war. The immense and ever-increasing tax which war and preparations for war levy on peaceful industries, and the frightful horrors of war itself, demand that every lover of God and humanity should unite for its suppression."

In the last twenty-five years we have made great progress toward an international condition in which war is less likely than heretofore. It is true that in that time we have had several great wars — the war between China and Japan and the war between Russia and Japan, the war between the United States and Spain, the war between England and the Boers, and perhaps some others. Nevertheless, as between the great countries of Europe which have armed themselves to the teeth since the

German-French war of 1870, peace has been maintained; and under the inspiration of a common desire for peace treaties have been made with reference to arbitration at The Hague and for the establishment of a court at The Hague for the settlement of international disputes, and have pointed to the ideal of the utmost use in the promotion of the cause of peace. We have ameliorated in many ways the ancient cruelties of war by Red Cross agreements, by the immunity of private property on land from destruction. Now we are agreeing upon what is called the Declaration of London, which, if confirmed, as it seems likely to be, will take away from war on the sea those principles of lawful piracy that have always characterized in a naval war the dealing with the private property of the citizens of enemies.

Just to-day four great powers — England, Russia, Japan, and the United States — signed a treaty by which we agree in effect to banish the shooting of seals at sea, in order to preserve the valuable herds on the land, and to allow them to propagate in such a way as to maintain the fur-seal industry and secure for human use the valuable furs that such seals furnish. It is the beginning, I hope, of the adoption of useful game laws for the open ocean, which has heretofore been subject to the wanton and irresponsible use of men of every nation. It is the settlement by treaty of a controversy that has troubled these four nations for several generations, and it ought to be the cause of great congratulation.

By negotiation and mediation and the formation of arbitration agreements wars in the last decade have been stopped in Central and South America in a most gratifying number of instances. Not all wars have been stopped in those countries lacking stability and power to enforce law and order; but that there is a marked improvement throughout Latin America in this regard, and especially in Central America, no one who has consulted the statistics of revolutions can fail to recognize. The heroism and exhibition of the noblest qualities of the heart and soul and mind of men that war makes possible, every student of history and of human nature must admit; but that this is accompanied with the horrible cost and sacrifice of human suffering and lives, and that an associated exhibition of the lowest moral qualities in man, of ambition, lust for power, of cruelty, ghoulish rapacity, and corruption, is equally true; and in very few cases, if any, can the historian say that the good of war was worth the awful sacrifice. And hence it is that we should all welcome, as far as we can, the effort to dispense with the necessity of war altogether. Even if that effort may not be entirely successful, every movement which tends to discourage war, and to furnish a means of avoiding it, ought to receive, and does receive, the earnest support of an organization that has the purposes and principles that actuate the Society of the Christian Endeavor.

I am glad to say that to-day we have reached such a point in the negotiations for a treaty of universal arbitration with one of the great European powers that we can confidently predict the signing of a satisfactory treaty. The arbitration treaty heretofore with Great Britain and other countries has excepted from the causes which may be arbitrated those which involved the vital interests of either party or its honor. The treaty which we are now closing with Great Britain eliminates these exceptions, and provides that all questions of international concern of a justifiable character shall be submitted to the arbitration of an impartial tribunal, and that, whenever differences arise, before they are submitted to arbitration at all, they shall be taken up by a commission composed of two or more representatives from each government, that shall investigate the controversy and recommend a solution, without arbitration if possible, and then shall decide whether the issue is capable of arbitration, and, if so, the arbitration shall take place. In this way the treaty in one sense, instead of making arbitration necessary, interposes mediation of a year between the happening of the differences and the bringing of the matter to arbitration, with the growing possibility, as the ruffled feelings of the nation may be smoothed out by time, that the differences may be adjusted by mediation instead of judicial action, but holding judicial action as the ultimate resort to prevent war.

I am exceedingly hopeful that other countries besides Great Britain will accept the form of the treaty or one like it, and that we may have half a dozen treaties with the European countries looking toward arbitration of international differences. This will not abolish war, but will provide a most effective and forcible instrument for avoiding it in many cases. Of course war between Great Britain and the United States, between France and the United States, and between Germany and the United States, is quite remote; but the adoption by these great countries of arbitration and mediation as a means of meeting all controversies must have the most healthy moral effect upon the world at large, and must assist all the friends of peace in their effort to make it permanent. To this audience, and this great society with its world-wide influence, I do not hesitate to appeal to give the tremendous weight of its support to such a cause.

On the conclusion of the address Mr. Ernest R. Ball sung with excellent effect a new song, "Let Us Have Peace," which he had written, and dedicated, by the President's permission, to Mr. Taft. The accompaniment, by Mr. George Graff, Jr., was played by Mr. Foster.

While this was sung a group of international Christian Endeavor representatives formed themselves behind President Taft — leaders in our work from England and Japan, Germany and India, China and Canada, Bohemia and Ruthenia. It was a striking tableau of world-wide peace, and the lesson was still further driven home as we first read in concert and then sung the International Hymn.

"Good-by," then said the President heartily to the audience, and the memorable visit was over.

It would seem certain that an anti-climax would follow, but the next speaker was Judge Ben B. Lindsey, of Denver.

Dr. Clark went with the President to Auditorium Williston, and Dr. John Balcom Shaw, left in charge, introduced the famous reformer as "a man who stands with a halo around him, everywhere known as a friend of downtrodden manhood."

"Everywhere known"? Even the President of the United States might well have been proud of the welcome given to this dauntless fighter against corruption, this tender friend of the boys, this judge who is a statesman and this statesman who is a Christian!

Judge Ben B. Lindsey's address, which is given entire, stirred the great audience to a heightened sense of duty. His subject was "The Christian Citizen in Politics." He said:

I should be false to my feelings if I did not express to this magnificent assemblage my appreciation of your generous reception and of this great honor that has been conferred upon me by the Christian Endeavorers. It is rather your regard for the great cause of Christian uplift in

PRESIDENT TAFT ADDRESSING THE ATLANTIC CITY CHRISTIAN ENDEAVOR CONVENTION.
From a photograph taken by *The Philadelphia Press*, used by courtesy of that paper

which it has been my privilege, with others, to take a small part. Then there is the added honor to appear on this platform with the chief magistrate of the nation with his great message for universal peace.

Without intending to minimize the importance of that message and our approval of the efforts of our President to bring about so Christian a result, this occasion may also remind us that there are other wars to be settled. There are the battles of peace, as truly calling for arbitrament as the battles of war. It is another kind of war actually going on in this country of ours, in which men are dying, women perishing, and children starving. The toll of suffering, mingling with the tears and the fears of the helpless in the conflict, is as real as any ever exacted by the tyranny of war. The weapons of the new warfare are different, but they are employed with as deadly effect as those of the old warfare. It is this conflict that is already upon us, in which we are already engaged, with all of its poverty, its misery, injustice, and suffering unnecessarily imposed upon unnumbered thousands of our brothers, that also cries out for our interest and attention; that also demands even now the application of Christian conduct and Christian courage.

Under a new guise, less direct, less understood, but nevertheless affecting as many people, there is a new slavery as truly as there was an old slavery, as truly an irrepressible conflict that must be settled right. It is going on. It is here. It must be bravely met and rightly settled. It must be fought out by courageous and intelligent people with those tools of a new democracy rather than the brutalities of old arbiters. It is a struggle that rightly calls for the interest and activity of Christian men and women, for their activity in politics; for these great issues can be settled only through what men call "politics." It is the duty of the citizen to devote sufficient of his time to a study and understanding of the issues and the leaders. He owes it to himself and his country to exercise judgment to choose wisely, to act justly, patriotically, if it consists only in the deposit of his ballot on election-day.

One of the most dangerous citizens in a republic is that cynic-minded individual that affects an indifference to politics. He is deserving of contempt when he makes a pretence of being above the performance of such duties. There can be no worse enemy to the republic, because none could more surely accomplish its destruction.

It is difficult to conceive even how one's first duty to his family could interfere with so simple and yet so necessary a devotion to the state. Every Christian that follows the injunction, "Be ye doers of the word, and not hearers only," must not only understand, but act up to his responsibility. For the disciple said, "He that looketh into the perfect law, the law of liberty, and so continueth, being not a hearer that forgetteth, but a doer that worketh, this man shall be blessed in his doing."

The citizen that makes no effort to understand the politics of his time is more than likely to become the dupe or servitor of the very worst enemies of his country. He must know enough to exercise his will and judgment so as to distinguish between the real and the false champions of public rights — how to avoid not only the mere demagogue, but his more dangerous rival, the modern plutagogue; that is, the apologist for rich criminals and those unnecessary and unjust conditions that make for poverty and crime.

It may not be for us to set a standard by which a Christian should measure his duty in politics. But have we not a right, if not indeed a duty, to search the teaching and the example of Christ for that test? I wish, therefore, to direct your attention to some things He said and some things He did as furnishing a guide. In the sixth chapter of Matthew we find Him discussing our necessities, difficulties, and duties on this earth. In that marvellous sermon is the command, "Seek ye first His kingdom and His righteousness." Was He not talking about the kingdom on this earth, righteousness here and now? The things that Christ discussed most, about which He was concerned most,. were not those things in the next world, but in this world.

This is the first great teaching of the life of Jesus. He would have us make the first great motive of our lives the coming of the kingdom of God on this earth. The Christian owes it to himself to find out what Christ meant by this kingdom on earth. I do not believe there can be any question as to what He meant. He meant a new social order. He meant that the old social order should be destroyed; that there should be builded upon its ruins a new social order pervaded by the spirit of the Golden Rule; an order that would so completely deliver man from temptation, from evil, that he could in truth and in fact live the Golden Rule, so that he could in truth and in fact treat his neighbor as he would wish to be treated if he and his neighbor could change places. He meant an order that would make the world a better place to live in; a world in which love, peace, and good will would be possible; a world where cooperation and mutual service would as naturally emanate from the hearts of men as would strife, envy, violence, and hate under the old order; a new order that would naturally promote fellowship with God, a participation in the divine life He would have us live.

The only excuse for that cynic who would have us believe that the social teachings of Jesus were visionary or impractical is that we are not yet doing as we should do the *first* thing that Christ taught us we must do in order that "all these things shall be added unto you." We are not seeking *first* the kingdom of God on this earth. It is only just as we approach that kingdom on earth that men as a whole can live the Christ life. We have through past ages too much sought the kingdom in some abstract unknown world. We were more concerned as to how to die to enter the kingdom hereafter than how to live to enter the kingdom here.

The kingdom of God will not come on this earth unless we seek, unless we work, unless we struggle. Only men can change conditions under which they live. God is not going to do it for us except in so far as He has abundantly equipped men with the power to work out their own salvation. We have the tools, but the old house will not come down and the new rise in its place unless we work and struggle. The temple is not torn down in a day or rebuilt in a day; neither is it expected that the old order shall be changed in a day, a decade, or perhaps a century. But the old order changeth, and it must continue to change till the kingdom comes on earth. He realized that conditions were primarily responsible for unrighteousness, injustice, misery, hate, poverty, and crime. He said (Matt. 18:7), "Woe unto the world because of occasions of stumbling! for it must needs be that the occasions come; but woe to that man through whom the occasion cometh!"

He denounced the men of His time who were responsible for the occasions, the conditions. He never denounced in any such fashion those who were the result of the conditions, who were in a measure the victims of their environment. "The kings of the Gentiles," that "have lordship over them," and "that have authority over them," were chastised for their hypocrisy in permitting themselves to be "called benefactors."

If any reformer of modern times should denounce the scribes and Pharisees of this age as Christ denounced the same men in His age, he would scarce escape the charge of being a scold or a muck-raker. For the indignation of Jesus at certain eminently respectable and reactionary men of His time knew scarcely any bounds. To them He constantly repeated, "Woe unto you!" He called them "hypocrites," "fools," and "blind guides," "like unto whited sepulchres," "outwardly appearing beautiful, but inwardly being full of dead men's bones," "outwardly appearing righteous unto men," but inwardly "full of hypocrisy and iniquity." "Ye serpents, ye offspring of vipers, how shall ye escape the judgment of hell?"

He told us very simply why He abused them (Matt. 23:13), because "ye shut the kingdom of heaven against men; for ye enter not in yourselves, neither suffer ye them that are entering in to enter," because "ye tithe the mint and anise and cumin," but leave "undone the weightier matters of the law, justice and mercy and faith"; it was these that needed most to be done, even if those other duties were not to have been left undone; but to do them and leave the weightier things undone made of them hypocrites, who "devour widows' houses, and for a pretence make long prayers"; "because ye load men with burdens grievous to be borne, and ye yourselves touch not the burdens with one of your fingers."

Those in Jerusalem who were enjoined to "bear ye one another's burdens" were just as much opposed to such "dangerous doctrine" then as the greed of big business is opposed to it now. And they treat His prophets very much now as they did then. The form changes, but the substance endures. He said, "I send unto you prophets, and wise men, and scribes; some of them shall ye kill and crucify; and some of them shall ye scourge in your synagogues, and persecute from city to city; that upon you may come all the righteous blood shed on the earth."

And the first great cause of all of this bitter invective was that "ye shut the kingdom of heaven against men"; and He meant that kingdom on this earth, and not in the next world.

It was the Pharisees and big-business crooks of His time who said He preached "dangerous doctrine." It was through their influence that He was denied the right to preach in the churches. Yet we are told that these men whom Jesus condemned were, as a rule, strict observers of that round of ethics or moralities involved in purely personal conduct. They observed the conventionalities of the better classes; they approved and contributed to the conventional charities; as society leaders they no doubt patronized the charity ball; they threw crumbs to the beggars and offered incense in the temple; they were no doubt good to their families, refrained from beating their wives, and with orthodox regularity on the Sabbath day attended the church in which they were pillars.

These classes had nothing against Jesus because He healed the sick, consoled the poor, and preached the personal virtues. Every one would have spoken well of Him, had He placed such a limitation on His work and His mission. They were against Him because He preached "dangerous doctrine," "knocked the town," "hurt business," and refused to "let us alone"; because of His hostility to the Pharisees, the eminently respectable men of His time, who wanted Him to "smile and push." They were against Him, not only because He abused them, but because He was willing even to be violent against them, as He had shown in the temple market-place.

They knew well enough that Jesus had not attacked them because they were rich, but because they insisted on the maintenance of a social order that made them rich at the sacrifice of right and justice to others. Jesus must have known that it was not the poor who could change conditions. They had neither political power nor influence. It was the rich and powerful that ruled and controlled. They could change conditions.

It is very much the same to-day. It is the rich and powerful that rule by controlling political parties, churches, business, courts, and public officers, and who insist upon the maintenance of an order that robs, enslaves, and kills its tens of thousands that they and the few they represent may, at the expense of the many, pile up more wealth, more power,

You can name on the fingers of one hand in nearly every large city in America the men that are most likely responsible for the larger injustice and crime of that city. Many of these men, as well as their most effective agents, are as often the pillars of the church now as they were in the time of Jesus, and would just as surely turn on Him now as they turned on Him then. They are just as truly "like unto whited sepulchres" now as then, just as truly make pretence and "outwardly appear righteous unto men" while inwardly "full of hypocrisy and iniquity"; for they just as truly now as then "load men with burdens grievous to be borne," and themselves "touch not the burdens with one of their fingers."

During His very brief time among men His larger mission necessarily was not so much Himself to change those conditions, but so to preach and act that those that would truly follow Him must necessarily perform that service. That is to say, they must battle against those conditions that make impossible the kingdom on earth and for those that will make it possible.

To bring that kingdom on earth we must necessarily concern ourselves with two great sources of strength, of power. These are the hearts of men and the conditions under which men live. And it is impossible to deal with the one and neglect the other. Neither the church nor any other institution claiming to represent Christ on earth can get the best out of men and for men so long as they are blind to the conditions under which men live. Our work for the child is twofold — that which concerns his heart and mind; and that environment, conditions, under which there may be the best development of heart and mind. In working for children we learn from them how we must work for men, for men are only children grown up. Both are more or less the creatures of environment.

We cannot entirely solve our moral questions along industrial or economic lines, but it would be equally unwise to assume that we could bring about moral reform, changes in the hearts of men, without regard to industrial or economic problems. It would be a foolish teacher whose stolen pocketbook had been left on her desk, offering a constant temptation to children that come from different kinds of homes, if she expected to end the scandal in the school that resulted from its theft by continuing to leave the pocketbook lying around loose. We can do much to furnish the answer to the supplication of our prayers, "Lead us not into temptation, but deliver us from evil." The scandal in the school is the scandal in the city. We leave our public rights, privileges, and franchises, that as truly belong to the people as the teacher's pocketbook belonged to the teacher, lying around loose to tempt little boys grown up.

There will as truly follow the scandal in the city as there followed the scandal in the school; for as truly as the teacher tempted the children, we tempt the little boys grown up, who understand the value of a franchise for the city railroad company, the gas company, or the water company, and the unearned millions in trafficking in the watered stocks of public-service corporations.

So long as we permit the conditions, we shall reap the scandals. We cannot excuse the boys for their weakness in yielding to temptation.

But what about the teacher? We cannot excuse the men that steal privileges, franchises.

But what about those that permit the "occasions," that as truly provoke the shame of the cities as they provoke the scandal in the school? Punishment, jails, and prisons are necessary; but they will not reach the cause. We must change the conditions, the occasions. That is what Christ meant.

If the water supply of your city is tainted, corrupted, we know it is a condition from which we may expect typhoid fever.

If, then, you have typhoid fever in your city, it is because of the conditions rather than the men that are attacked by the germ of disease. Like conditions in any city will produce like results.

We have discovered the cause of many diseases, and we know it is more important to fight the cause of disease than the result of disease. What is true of disease is true of poverty and crime. If you point out the cause of typhoid fever, because the men that own the stocks and bonds of the water company may assail you is no reason why you should not, if necessary, submit to their persecutions rather than be deterred in your fight against the cause. Neither should we be intimidated by the Pharisees in our fight against the cause of poverty and crime or against those "through whom the occasion cometh."

It is generally conceded that Christ was not a theologian, that He was not a churchman, that He was not a socialist or a social reformer; but we cannot escape the conviction that He was much concerned about the social order. His activity there is as positive as it was indifferent to those activities and conflicts growing out of the mere matter of dogma or creed. He was not concerned about building an ecclestiastical machine that might add as much strength as a political machine to the social order that Christ opposed.

His message was chiefly for those that have a passion for social justice, and since that involves activity in politics, if the Christian would seek first the kingdom of God and His righteousness on earth, he must take some part in the politics of his time.

One of the disappointing things to the Christian is to find that the church, generally speaking as an institution, is not only often in politics, but it is too often in politics on the wrong side; that is to say, because of a negative attitude, it does the very thing that the Pharisees of our time want it to do.

Silence or inaction for a righteous cause may be as effective against it as open hostility. He who is not with us is against us. As Christians in politics we need the church on our side. The result has been that many Christian Endeavorers and others in the church are struggling heroically to save the church from becoming an institution that merely gives respectability and strength to an established order that forbids the coming of the kingdom on earth to-day as it did in the time of Christ.

It is a sad thing, but a true thing, that one of the tasks of the Christian in politics struggling against the conditions that Christ opposed has been, in a measure, to help save some of the preachers to Christianity and some of the churches to religion. It is no small part of the task of many Christian preachers in the church or out of the church. The church cannot save others if it cannot save itself. Without a vision of social justice and a more militant determination to fight for a reign of righteousness and the coming of the kingdom on earth, the church may become an institution of those Pharisees who "shut the kingdom of heaven against men."

But one of the most hopeful signs of the times is that to be found in the interest shown by many Christian ministers and organizations like the Christian Endeavorers in the great social, political, economic, and industrial problems of our time. They are beginning to take a more active and courageous part in these struggles. It is a part of true Christianity that they should do so.

No one would suggest that the Christian church or Christian minister should become mixed in that questionable kind of politics that too often marks the cause of strife between political parties as such. It is generally a mere fight for office and a scramble for privilege, and the good influence of the minister or church would often be jeoparded by any such activity.

But that is altogether different from the real, vital political struggle now going on in this country. It is not between parties or between men. It is that injustice tolerated by many men that support the churches now, as in the time of Christ; it may be found in the death-dealing slums of the cities; the overworked employees of employers, many of whom claim to be Christians; the girls and women whom they are selling into shame; the profits and the wealth derived from the labor of others that is being turned into the stocks and bonds that the owners never earned; the privileges in city, State, and nation which they gained through the enslavement and corruption of men; the active opposition of the modern Pharisees to those that are honestly trying to follow Christ by fighting the causes of poverty and crime.

If Christ were on earth to-day, He would not be much interested in those charities and palliatives that are promoted mostly by the institutions that often share in the graft that comes from the greed and injustice of the present order. He would go straight at the causes that are making for social injustice, poverty, and the degradation that keep the rich and the poor separated from each other. He would expose the whole miserable system. He would have a contempt for those that preach the platitude while they continue to profit by the injustice that they make no real effort to destroy.

He would do that even if He only showed His displeasure and His indignation, even as He did it in the temple, which had become a sort of combination of a certain type of modern church and a stock exchange. For there those that came to worship had to exchange their foreign coin for the Hebrew coin. The priests had exclusive privileges. Their privilege grew into a trust. They were simply piling up wealth through the unjust profits from extra charges that privilege and monopoly enabled them to levy. The graft was shared by the priests and the politicians. It was in Christ's day, as nearly as the conditions of His time permitted, precisely what we have in our day in those lobbyists that make the temple of justice a place for bartering and trading and the levying of unjust burdens on the people, the stealing of franchises and the trafficking in the needs and necessities of the people.

Christ faced the situation with an act that spoke louder than any word, an act that marked the beginning of persecution and final crucifixion then as it would mark precisely the same results now. He gathered up rushes from the temple floor, wove them into a lash, and, advancing on the big-business crooks of His time with all the fury of His indignation, drove them from the temple, for

> "He knew to curse as well as bless,
> To pity and be pitiless,
> To make and mar,
> The fierceness that from gentleness
> Is never far."

If, then, we are true Christians in politics, true soldiers of humanity, we have no right to content ourselves with anything short of attacking ignorance, the causes of poverty, and the real forces of evil that are exploiting our brothers, destroying our government, and making necessary human misery and crime.

Politically, this country is no longer divided by two great parties. That, indeed, is only a part of the sham that obscures greater issues, issues that are desperately struggling for expression and recognition *within* the parties, not *between* the parties. The alignment is rather between progressives and reactionaries, those who are moving forward towards the Kingdom and those who are standing still or moving backward; those who are not content with the existing order, as against those who are content with the existing order; those who believe there is a cure for poverty and those who do not; those who believe that men can solve the problem of the unemployed and those who believe that God only knows what the solution is; those who believe that the science of production is so completely mastered by men as to furnish humanity with every necessity in food, housing, clothing, and the reasonable enjoyment of life; those who believe that men through the powers with which God has endowed them are wise enough, brave enough, and unselfish enough to work out a system of production and distribution that shall serve best all men rather than a few men; who believe this can be done without being hostile to those rights and rewards that belong more to one citizen than another citizen; without being hostile to those rules of justice, reason, and common sense that properly permit one man to profit more than another man from a greater service to be rendered society; who believe that excessive ownership is a burden, sacrificing the happiness of the excessive owner as truly as it destroys that of the victim who is, under the sanction of unjust law, robbed or enslaved. As against them are arrayed the Pharisees, the scribes, the princes of privilege, and those that would maintain the injustice of the present order.

The first battles in this struggle are being fought, but they are for reforms of an institutional rather than an economic kind. They are merely a means to an end, the working tools of a new democracy; how perfect a means, how effective a tool, must depend upon the wisdom, the intelligence, and the sincerity of the people as a whole, and especially of those that are chosen as leaders of the people. If we are to build well with these tools coming into our possession through the progressive movements of the past decade, we must bring to bear in our work all the spirit and purpose of the Master; religion must be most of all a passion for social justice; and it must necessarily follow that religion must be possessed by a passion for democracy, a democracy that is the embodiment of the highest ideals of the teachings of Christ; the kingdom of God on earth, which alone can usher in all those other things which "shall be added" unto us, the universal brotherhood of men under the universal fatherhood of God, with whom "is no respect of persons," the deliverance from evil, a life on this earth that may embody that love expressed in "the great commandment," which was not only the first, but the second, "like unto it," and the embodiment of them all, "Thou shalt love thy neighbor as thyself."

The great audience that gathered in Auditorium Williston was musically irrepressible. Under the magic touch of Mr. H. C. Lincoln and his Philadelphia Christian Endeavor chorus it thrilled the very heart with enthusiastic song.

The devotional service, presided over by Rev. Cleland B. McAfee, D.D., one of our trustees, was deeply reverential and touching.

With his well-known graceful tact Rev. Howard B. Grose, D.D., led the meeting. But stop! The audience is on its feet. Flags wave, handkerchiefs flutter like snowflakes, and from thousands of voices peals the national song, "My country, 'tis of thee." It is the President!

In presenting President Taft Dr. Grose paid him this eloquent tribute: "It is fortunate for us when we can unite respect for high office with respect and regard for its occupant. Such is the happy lot of our country to-day. In the chosen ruler of this free people we behold the world's foremost promoter of international arbitration and universal peace, the steadfast champion of the rights of all as against the privilege of the few, the enforcer of law without fear or favor, the man of serious purpose, blessed with a saving sense of humor."

President Taft came from addressing the Endeavorers in

the other auditorium. He wore his famous genial smile that captivates all hearts.

"There are some things," he began after the volume of applause that greeted him subsided, "about your association that are embarrassing, and one of them is its size, which demands that a speaker deliver his address twice. I am glad to stand here in the presence of a force that upholds the nation in righteousness, and to know that this organization works for international peace."

In the other auditorium the President read his speech. Now he discarded the manuscript and spoke out of his heart. With vigorous gestures he drove his points home, and gave his hearers a glimpse of the force that has carried him so far and so high. There is nothing lethargic about Mr. Taft. He has vision, and the power to realize much of it.

The apparent slow progress of international peace — for that was his theme — he explained by the fact that the conscience of a nation is less than the conscience of an individual. Yet progress is being made. He pointed out the various treaties that are in force, making for more humane conditions; one was signed on the very day of his speech, in which half a score of nations agree to cease killing female seals, thus preventing the extinction of the species. This, he said, may be the beginning of ocean game laws. The respect for law, for which Mr. Taft is well known, came to view in a ringing sentence: "It is our hope that soon there will be no spot on earth where man can be outside the jurisdiction of law!"

The President recalled the fact that the St. Paul Convention passed a resolution in favor of world-wide peace, and he expressed his confidence that the support of Endeavorers for this cause would not be appealed for in vain.

"I wanted to hear you, Mr. Washington," said the President, as he bade Principal Booker T. Washington good-by. And the great negro educator was worth hearing. He caught the audience at the start, and held it with sober fact and witty sally until the end.

First of all came a grateful tribute to Christian Endeavor for the recognition that the movement has given for twenty-five years to the black citizens of the United States. To-day there are, he said, more than 3,000 negro Christian Endeavor organizations.

One can hardly realize that this big, brainy negro was once a slave. "I have been a slave in my life," he cried, "but I have forgotten all that, and I love you all. The spirit of Jesus Christ in this organization is able to break down all racial hatred and strife."

His theme was "The Uplift of a Race."

THE PRESIDENT ENTERTAINED AT CAPTAIN YOUNG'S.

In order from the left: Mr. Sproul; Mr. Shaw; Rev. Robert Arthur Elwood; Senator Briggs of New Jersey; Captain Young; President Taft; Mrs. Young; Dr. Clark; Mr. Wells; Mr. Hilles, the President's secretary; Mr. Lathrop; Major Butt.—Standing, the Misses Young.

AT CAPTAIN YOUNG'S

After the President's two addresses he was taken to the Italian villa of Captain Young, on the pier. The officers of the United Society and his own party, including Senator Briggs of New Jersey, Secretary Hilles, Major Archibald Butt, Rev. Robert Arthur Elwood, messenger, and secret service men, accompanied him.

We were most graciously entertained by Captain Young and his wife and daughters, who refreshed the party with pleasant viands, and interested us mightily with the sight of their unique home.

Captain Young's career is typically American. He has risen from the smallest beginnings to great wealth by the exercise of thrift and ready enterprise, and his life history is still at its vigorous prime.

CHRISTIAN ENDEAVOR SOCIETY 49

The colored race in America is grateful for the privilege of being represented at the Twenty-fifth International Convention of the Christian Endeavor Society. From the very first this organization has manifested its interest and its liberality toward my race in no uncertain way. The International Christian Endeavor Society is so broad in its scope and in its methods and work that it cuts through racial and color lines, and aims to lift up and encourage all people regardless of race, color, or nationality. My race in America owes much to this organization. It has been the means of inspiring, encouraging, and saving a large number of young people who otherwise would have led useless lives.

It is always a help to a race, as it is to an individual, to fall into line with a great organization, a world-movement such as this organization represents.

The American negro has not been slow in responding to the helpful influences exerted in his behalf through the church, through the Sunday-school, through the Christian Endeavor Society and foreign-missionary organizations and institutions. To indicate what I mean more definitely, let me make a little comparison.

Since the negro has during the past forty years been the subject of so much missionary effort, I wish to call attention to some of the ways in which he is helping himself, is making progress. I find that a good way to judge of the progress of one people is to compare it with that of another. An interesting comparison is that between the negro and the Russian peasant.

Fifty years ago fourteen million Russian serfs were given their freedom. By means of loans from the government they were able to secure small tracts of land. After fifty years of freedom their property accumulations amount to $500,000,000. Forty-eight years ago to four million negroes was given their freedom. Without any government aid these four million negroes have been able to accumulate $600,000,000 worth of property. That is, in fifty years the Russian peasants have accumulated about $36 worth of property per capita, or an average of about $200 a family. In forty-seven years the American negroes have accumulated $150 per capita, or about $900 a family.

The progress of the Russian peasant along religious lines is scarcely to be compared with that of the negro because of the great difference in the religious conditions under which each lives. The religious progress of the negro has kept pace with his economic and educational progress. Every colored religious denomination maintains one or more institutions for the better training of its ministers. For moral and religious instruction the negroes through their churches are maintaining 35,000 Sunday-schools, in which there are 1,750,000 pupils, who are taught by 210,000 teachers. For their moral and religious instruction the people of my race have 35,200 ordained ministers. They have 35,160 churches. They have accumulated church property to the value of more than $56,650,000.

The negro has done and is doing much more for his own education than the Russian peasant. Ever since emancipation the negroes out of their poverty have contributed liberally for education. The negroes of this country are each year paying in direct property and poll-taxes something like a million dollars for their education. Almost one-half the running expenses of negro educational institutions are paid for by the cash and work of the students. It is estimated that in nine years the students in seventy-four negro institutions have paid in cash and work for the running expenses of these institutions more than $5,000,000. Negro churches in the past forty years have contributed more than $16,000,000 to education.

The churches of my race have been very liberal in their contributions for missionary work. They are giving each year more than

$100,000 for missionary work. They are supporting 280 missionaries, and are giving aid to hundreds of needy churches. At the same time they have not been neglectful of their brethren in Africa. They are contributing annually about $50,000 for the African work.

The liberal way in which the negroes are giving money to build churches, to support mission work, to the Young Men's Christian Association work, and to their education is very encouraging. All these efforts indicate the capacity of the colored people for good citizenship. The recent work of the colored people of Philadelphia, of Chicago, and of Atlanta in raising money for the colored Young Men's Christian Associations has given the entire country a better appreciation of the capacity of the colored people to respond to appeals for those things that go to help make better citizenship.

These efforts have also caused the colored man and the white man to work side by side for a common end, and as a result they have been brought into closer touch with each other, and have come to understand each other better. In Atlanta, Ga., the colored people in ten days raised $57,000 for the Young Men's Christian Association work. The greatest result in Atlanta, however, was not the raising of this money by the colored people, but the moral effect that it had upon the white people, not only of Atlanta, but of the South in general; for it was discovered that the negro responds much more readily to those things that assume his good citizenship than he does to those that assume his instincts towards criminality. It emphasized the fact that the negro has race-consciousness and that he has civic pride, that he will work as enthusiastically as the white man when assigned a task that assumes his good citizenship and his manhood and all the possibilities that inhere therein. We have here an improved method of dealing with the race-problem everywhere, and that is, in whatever effort is made for his improvement, to give the negro an opportunity to assist in this effort.

Booker T. Washington is proud of his people — a new race, he called them, a race with a future before it, and not *behind*. One day he met an old negro woman on the road, and asked, "Susie, where are you going?"

"Mr. Washington, I done been where I's goin'."

So some races have been where they are going, and have turned back. The negro is going forward.

The Indian refused the white man's customs, his religion, his clothes, his houses; but the negro says, "We'll take everything that we can get from you, and weave it into our life."

Making the point that the negro is not content with an inferior article, but wishes the best, Mr. Washington created merriment by saying, "You don't find a negro eating stale food if there is fresh meat around." The negro wears good clothes. The negro woman may fall behind the fashion, but not more than a week.

One day, in a pretty little negro settlement he asked his guide, "What is the name of this place?" Usually ignominious names like Bug Hollow or Little Africa are appended to such places, but in this case the reply was, "This is Columbia Heights!"

CHAPTER VI.

RALLYING THE JUNIORS.

Auditorium Endeavor, Saturday, July 8.

If ever a fairer sight has been seen on earth than the procession of Juniors on the Board Walk at Atlantic City, we certainly do not know where it was.

It was half a mile of lovely, bright, innocent faces. Young America swung stoutly along with his banners, proud to step to band music. The girls' bright dresses made long lines of white and pink and blue, with touches of more vivid colors where groups were costumed in foreign garb. A moving picture of the procession was taken; would that we could show it here!

Inside, Auditorium Endeavor was crammed with an expectant multitude. The Juniors marched down the broad central aisle to their seats on the platform and the floor.

Then came a period of Junior "yells"—for the Juniors know how to cheer quite as well as their elders. Hurrah! what vim they put into it! There was life there, buoyant and irrepressible; and what joy that it was being captured for the Master!

Dr. Clark's arrival gave another occasion for enthusiasm, and he was greeted with the tumultuous waving of hundreds of Christian Endeavor flags.

More Junior vigor when "Onward, Christian soldiers" was sung, and Mr. Foster had the great audience rise and wave flags, handkerchiefs, and programmes in time with the chorus.

Dr. Clark presided over the Junior rally, and said he was just as glad to do that as to preside over the meeting at which the President spoke, because there might be a future president among the Juniors, or at any rate there were Christian workers of the future, and they are even more important.

Rev. R. P. Anderson, associate editor of THE CHRISTIAN ENDEAVOR WORLD, led an uplifting opening exercise. He had the Juniors and the older folks recite the Twenty-third Psalm in alternate verses. Then the Juniors, standing, raised their right hands as they repeated the first sentence of the Christian Endeavor pledge. Finally the audience rose with the Juniors while Mr. Anderson offered a fervent prayer for all those young lives.

A very delightful feature was unexpectedly introduced, a voice-and-violin solo by Dr. Clark's youngest son, Sydney Clark, who has come up from the Junior society into a vigorous and most promising young Christian manhood. He is a skilful violinist and played on the beautiful instrument his own accompaniment to his song, "I was wandering and weary," a tender and moving song with a touching appeal for the Christian decision.

A most remarkable rendering of the cantata, "The Healing of Naaman," was next given by the Juniors of the First Presbyterian Church of Swarthmore, Penn. The superintendent of this society is Mrs. Grace Livingston Hill-Lutz, the story-writer whose fame is so wide-spread among Endeavorers.

The cantata is long and elaborate. It was committed perfectly to memory, and was given with spirit and charm by the young singers. The costumes were effective, and the entire entertainment would have done credit to musicians twice the age of the Juniors. The great audience, children and adults, were held in the deepest interest to the end, and watched spell-bound the panorama of brilliantly arrayed kings, — Syrian and Hebrew,— glittering soldiers, ladies of the court, little Hebrew maids, and white-bearded Elisha. There was the greatest enthusiam as Dr. Clark introduced Mrs. Lutz, the superintendent of these talented Juniors, Mr. Lutz, who wrote the music for some of the solos, and Miss Hill, who played the music on the piano.

There was a wonderful contrast, to those of us that remember it, between this vast Junior rally and the first one, held in 1892, at the New York Convention, in Dr. Deems's church. The principal speaker at that little first rally was Dr. C. H. Tyndall. He gave a remarkable balloon-talk, and since then has become famous all over the land for his object-talks.

At this rally Dr. Tyndall gave the children a wonderful object-lesson on "The Windows of the Soul." He had a big, five-foot box in the shape of a heart, painted red. It had a door on the one side and a window on the other. Dr. Tyndall said:

> Did you ever see a soul? We cannot see it, feel it, or hear it; yet we know it is a real thing. It is the I in us. It is that which lives, loves, wills to do things, and lives beyond the grave. While we cannot see it, we have things that represent it, and I will show you one of them. It is a heart. It represents the soul, the I in us; for it is the part of us which lives, loves, and does. It is the centre of us as our physical heart is the centre of the body.
> You see this heart has a door. All hearts have doors, though we often find it difficult to get into the door of some hearts.
> This door has a small bolt on the outside. It is like a latch that we can lift to enter. So the heart of every boy and girl, man and woman, has an outside bolt, which we can draw if we know how. Sometimes a little kindness draws this outside bolt, some candy, or it may be a whip,

or a threatened punishment. We think the kind way into one's heart is generally the best way.

If you will look through this window, you will notice that this door has also an inside bolt. That bolt in us is the *will*. Even small boys and girls have wills. When I was preparing this talk, I heard an Italian mother going along the street with her small child. She had him by the hand, and he had to go; but he was resisting with all his might, and was screaming with anger at the top of his voice. He had a will. Every one that is good for anything has a will.

Sometimes that small will bolt is very difficult to have drawn. One from the outside cannot draw it. Only the one that lives within can draw it.

When I began my ministry, a wonderful revival occurred in the village, and many young people were converted. One evening all the young converts and I had a meeting in the lecture-room, and at the close I asked whether there were any present who wished to become Christians, and one little boy on the front seat said he did. I explained that it was to have Christ come to live in our hearts, and asked him whether he would let Christ come into his heart; and he said, "No, I will not." I thought he misunderstood, and so asked him again whether he wished to become a Christian, and he replied that he did; but, when I asked him whether he would become one, he said again that he would not. And so for some time I tried to explain the way to him; but each time he said he wanted to be a Christian, but would not be one. Then it dawned upon me that even little boys have wills, and that no one can force his way past one of them. Each one must draw that bolt for himself.

You notice, also, that this heart has a curtain. Curtains let in the light, and shut it out. The curtain can be drawn aside, or can exclude the light. You have such a curtain. You can let in some light, or a great deal; or you can see but a few things, refusing to see what you do not wish to see. We can all let whatever light into our soul we wish. This curtain is in front of a window. We remove it, and you see a window behind it.

This is a strange window. It is iron. Often when you visit factories, you see a notice, "No Admittance. Apply at the Office." Once in a great while one reads, "Keep Out." That is what this window says. Those that have such windows shut people out. They do not wish to be friendly or to make friends.

On the inside of this window you notice another thing. It says, "Keep All." Those having this iron window before their souls shut out their real friends, and then shut into themselves all that is good. They are selfish souls. They would keep for themselves all their toys and good times when children, and when grown to be men and women they keep their money and all that they think is of value.

I think Judas had this kind of a window before his soul. He would not let the truth into him, and he held on to all he had. The Bible says he was a thief. Many others still shut out the good, and shut into themselves what they have, until there is nothing but a dungeon within them.

We are glad to leave this, and look at another window. This is the blue one. If you look through a blue window, all things look blue. That is, they are of a dark, sombre color. The cheeriness is all gone. Some have this blue window always before their souls. They see nothing that cheers and helps them. They look on the dark side of things; they have the blues. All the evils that depress, and lead to doubt and misery, come through this blue window. Anger, hatred, a grudge, worry, all depress and injure, and should not be let into our hearts.

Then, if one lets such light get into him, it is the very kind of light that will go out of him. He will depress and irritate and anger and tempt and annoy and worry all that come near him. You cannot let blue light into your soul, and have pure white light come out of it. To take such light into us is to scatter frowns and not smiles. We sometimes sing, "Scatter the sunshine"; and we can do it only by letting the cheery light into us.

Last August I saw a small boy selling pansies in a railway station at Burlington, Vt., who I am sure must have let the pure light into him; for he was pleasant and smiling to every one.

He came up to us, and said: "Have one? Only a nickel this morning." And so pleasant a smile!

I said, "No, thank you"; and he smiled, and went to others in the same pleasant way and with the same smile. I said to Mrs. Tyndall that the boy's smile was worth five cents, and so I went into the station, and found him, and bought a bunch of flowers.

The train came, and we all hurried into it, and some people left a camera behind them; and he hastened in with it, and gave it to them; and, when they offered him money, he refused with a smile; and the man said, "Here, give all these ladies flowers." So he sold a quarter's worth. I called the gentleman's attention to that smile, and he followed the boy into the car; and soon all his flowers were gone.

Here is the red window. This is at the other extreme. It represents those that want to see everything in a bright and glowing color. It represents the pleasures of life. Some boys and girls and young people seem to live only to have a good time. That good time is play. That is the way the grown men and women of Israel did in the wilderness when Moses was on the mountain with God. "They sat down to eat and to drink, and rose up to play." They were called idolaters. They must have their games. With the boys it is the ball game and other sports, and these are all right in their place in good proportion. But all play and no study makes Jack a dull boy.

The next is the yellow window. It is the color of gold. It signifies that those who have that window before their souls see everything through money. Their first thought is of money. If one has plenty of money, he is satisfactory to such people. They work for gold; they live for gold; they suffer for gold; they marry for gold; they sacrifice the feelings of others for gold; they sell their character for gold; they die for gold; they forfeit heaven for gold.

Those that let little other than the light of gold into their souls show out gold wherever they go. If they have it, they love to display it, to prate about it, to boast over it, and to teach their children to regard it as the best good.

All the windows we have thus far seen are faulty, but here is one that has all the beauties of all the others with none of their faults. It is a beautiful copy of Guido Reni's celebrated "Christ Crowned with Thorns." It signifies that those that have this window before their souls see everything in life through Christ crucified.

It means seeing Him in our play; and to have sport into which He cannot come is a curse, not a blessing. It is to see Him in our studies, in the tests. It is to see Him in all our work, and in our calling in life, to ask Him to help us in them, and then to be truthful and not to cheat, and in our trials to lead and help us.

It is to see Him as our salvation, our peace, our safety from the temptations of life, and our eternal blessedness.

We may travel around the world, and see all the wonders that are to be seen. We may look through the telescope, and see the suns and all the glories of the heavens.

Then, when we have seen Him and let His light into our souls, His light will shine out of us. People will love Him better because of what we are and do. All true Christian Endeavorers let Him in, that they may show Him out to others.

Auditorium Endeavor.

On the conclusion of this heart-talk Mr. Bacon's double-voiced song immensely interested the Juniors, and all the rest of us.

The last exercise of this shining session was a series of songs by the different Junior societies of Atlantic City and County. One after the other these beautiful bands of young people marched upon the platform and sang their well-prepared songs. One society was dressed as Indians, another as Japanese; others wore red Christian Endeavor monograms on white clothes; all had distinctive features. The singing of the colored Juniors was fine, but all the societies did nobly. As the Juniors rose and sang "America" with the waving of flags, Dr. Clark conducted to the front "the little superintendent," Mrs. Alexander Brownlee, who so splendidly leads the Atlantic County Juniors.

Dr. Clark surprised some of his audience when he declared that probably in the world there are more Methodist Endeavorers than Endeavorers of any other denomination; but Methodism in many lands takes the lead in Christian Endeavor.

CHAPTER VII.
CHORAL SERVICE AND CAMP-FIRE.

Long before the opening hour on Saturday evening the big auditorium was crammed with an audience that evidently had come determined to enjoy itself. Gallery, floor, and every inch of standing-room were soon crowded. Then the fun began.

First, a yell! This was the spark to the fire. Every delegation wanted to get in its yell—and did it, too. Half a dozen delegations, each led by a stentorian voice, were on their feet at one time,—all yelling,—gloriously, hilariously, enthusiastically, having what the leader, Prof. Percy Foster, of Washington, called a "bully" time.

Indiana delegates, who had put in a strong plea for the 1913 Convention, created a furore by their cry: "One, two, three, four; whom are we for? whom are we for? Indiana is for *California*."

Then the sunshiny Californians responded with a resounding ninefold "Rah-rah-rah! Come to golden California!"

What an ovation! Led by Dr. and Mrs. Clark, the best-loved Christian song-writer of this or any century, Miss Fanny Crosby, came to the platform. The entire audience rose to welcome her, and it was with reverence that the great throng that had so often sung the songs that have gone forth from her fertile mind and devotional spirit gazed upon her face. Touching, too! Frail and worn with the burden of more than ninety years, she is young at heart as the youngest, interested, alive, alert, eager, consecrated, a saint that serves through song.

A moment later she went back to speak at the big meeting in the other hall.

But the song service has begun, Professor Foster leading. He himself is an Endeavorer, and understands an Endeavor crowd like a book. If necessary, he could find a way to bring music from stones; but this alert, bright-eyed audience needs no spurring.

It is a choral service. The choir is a combination of Washington, Harrisburg, and Philadelphia choirs. It sings with spirit, verve, and understanding. The old-time hymns are always favorites, but Kipling's "Recessional" is rendered in excellent taste and with deep feeling.

But the choir has no monopoly. The audience is another and bigger choir. This is a people's meeting.

OFFICERS AND TRUSTEES OF THE UNITED SOCIETY.

Of course there are delightfully witty sallies by the leader, and solos by "the Yorkshire Nightingale," and by Mr. W. C. Weeden, who has consecrated his splendid voice to the Master's service.

But now Fanny Crosby is again on the platform, and Mr. Foster starts one of her favorites, "Blessed assurance, Jesus is mine," the chorus of which is sung by sections of the audience. A pretty effect is made by the far-away, echo-like sound of the lines sung by the back gallery.

Mr. Enos Bacon, "the Yorkshire Nightingale," sang Miss Crosby's hymn, "Safe in the arms of Jesus." It was touching to see the aged author's eager expression as she drank in the sweet words. Did she feel the need of the "rest that remaineth to the people of God?"

Mr. Bacon rarely escapes with one hymn. He chose for his second another of Fanny Crosby's, which he had sung at five years of age at an entertainment—"Pass me not, O gentle Saviour."

Miss Crosby was surprised at Mr. Bacon's two voices. "I never heard anything like that before," she said, as she grasped him by the hand. "Your singing broke my heart all to pieces."

"I am proud to meet you, Miss Crosby. I would rather meet you than meet the King."

"O, thank you. We can pray for each other although we are far apart. Come and see me."

Dr. Clark is now ready formally to introduce Miss Crosby. "I would consider it a privilege," he began, "could I see and greet Isaac Watts, or Charles Wesley, or Toplady, or Montgomery, but we enjoy the privilege to-night of seeing one that has written more hymns than all these song-writers put together. She was 91 years old on March 24, but she is still young. She might even belong to a Junior society; you can never grow too old to belong."

At his invitation Miss Crosby stepped forward and received one of the heartiest and sincerest ovations ever given any one, whether King or Kaiser, Then Dr. Clark ranged beside her her friends, Mr. Wells, Mr. Foster, and Mr. John R. Clements, three Christian Endeavor hymn-writers, and Dr. Elijah W. Stoddard, 91 years old April 23, whom Miss Crosby jocularly calls her twin brother. These stood beside Miss Crosby while she spoke as follows:

"Friends of this large and noble assembly:

"My heart is filled to overflowing, and I cannot find language with which to express my emotions.

"Dr. Clark has done more for the souls of humanity than any other man. He has worked day by day in this land and in foreign countries. Dr. Wilbur Chapman told me that when he reached the Fiji Islands he found there a Christian association waiting for him. Who has done this? Who? I repeat. Dr. Clark has done it.

"He gave me a Christian Endeavor badge to-night, and while my heart beats it will throb with joy because of it, and I shall remember the giver, and will pray that great blessing may rest upon him."

In spite of her 91 years Miss Crosby is a vigorous speaker, and could be heard all over the hall. Turning to Mr. John R. Clements, she paid him a gracious tribute; then to the venerable Dr. Stoddard, who has preached for seventy years.

"This meeting has done me good." she continued. "I am obliged to this society for asking me to come. God bless the Juniors also. Why, I am only 19, not 91. I could not keep still if I tried. I have a niece, and when she wants quiet for thought she says, 'Now, chatterer, I want you to keep still, *if you can*'; and I have to mind her."

Miss Crosby's home is in Bridgeport, Conn. The delegation from Connecticut sat in a body in the hall. Unannounced they rose and sang "Safe in the arms of Jesus." It was a happy thought that made Bridgeport Endeavorers present Miss Crosby with a beautiful bouquet of white carnations.

More singing, and such singing! The wizard of song on the platform made the audience do anything he wished. The women hummed alone. The men whistled alone. The women hummed and the men whistled together while Mr. Bacon sang the words with his soprano voice. The effect was indeed striking, like the tone of some strange, vibrant instrument.

Two moving-picture pieces—urging pure milk and a sane Fourth—closed the most enthusiastic and successful choral service ever held in Christian Endeavor history. It turned every heart to praise.

One may not sing on the famous Board Walk, but in other less sacred streets groups of young people, going homeward, acting under the inspiration received, awoke the city and the echoes of the night. Later, however, special permission was granted by the authorities for Endeavorers to hold open-air meetings on the Board Walk.

THE CAMP-FIRE.

Christian Endeavor camp-fires under the lead of Secretary Shaw are full of enthusiasm, but on Saturday evening in the other auditorium, Williston, it broke out in applause and song before the leader was on the platform. The audience caught sight of the loved Christian singer, Fanny Crosby, coming into the hall, and she was promptly welcomed with the strains of "Saved by Grace."

Introduced by Dr. Clark, the sightless singer was received by the audience standing and waving their handkerchiefs. Here is what she said:

"If 'Fanny Crosby has sung herself into the hearts of the people' [referring to Dr. Clark's introduction] what has our beloved Dr. Clark done? I will tell you what he has done. He has done a work that is winning for him day by day stars for his crown, stars that will shine through the countless ages of eternity. Ah, friends, let us follow his example of the meek and lowly One, walk in his footsteps as he has walked in the footsteps of Him who said, 'Come unto me, all ye that labor and are heavy laden, and I will give you rest.'

"Friends, I have prayed for this moment. I have prayed that the Lord would permit me to clasp the hand of this noble servant of His, and my prayer is answered; and I will tell you more than that. I have already caught an inspiration from this meeting that will fill my heart with ecstasy, that will bring forth hymns that I have never written yet. [Applause.] O, my work is not done. I feel it in my heart that the good Lord is going to spare me to see one hundred and three years; and, if He does, I will go where He wants me to go; I will say what He wants me to say; and, praise His name, I will be what He wants me to be.

"Friends,

"Some day the silver cord will break,
   And I no more as now shall sing;
But O, the joy when I shall wake
   Within the palace of the King!
And I shall see Him face to face,
And tell the story, Saved by Grace.

"Some day; till then I'll watch and wait,
   My lamp all trimmed and burning bright,
That, when my Saviour opes the gate,
   My soul to Him shall speed its flight;
And I shall see Him face to face,
And tell the story, Saved by Grace.

"And there are others whom I shall see. I shall see Mr. Wells, the managing editor of THE CHRISTIAN ENDEAVOR WORLD; I shall see John R. Clements; I shall see Brother Stoddard. Ah, what a meeting when we stand before the throne of God and hear the welcome plaudits, 'Well done, good and faithful servants; enter ye into the joy of your Lord.'

"O, as I came in here to-night, I heard the ocean waves, and they seemed to tell me the old, old story of their creation; and then, as the evening star arose, it sparkled on their bosom; and then they told the story of this Convention, how they have watched over it; how there was an eye that never slept and an ear that was bent low to catch our humblest prayer, and that the blessed Lord would never leave nor forsake us, glory to His name.

"If I had not to speak once more, I would talk to you longer; but I can see my niece looking out at me from one corner of her eye; and I have got to stop." [Applause.]

Following Mr. Shaw's suggestion, the delighted audience expressed their appreciation by saying together, "Thank you; God bless Fanny Crosby"; and their wish for God's blessing was further voiced in a prayer by Rev. W. H. S. Hascall, missionary to Burma. As the hymn-writer left the hall on her way to the other auditorium, the Philadelphia chorus, led by Mr. H. H. Lincoln, sung her "All the way my Saviour leads me," one stanza being effectively rendered antiphonally by the chorus and the audience.

At this point Mr. John Jackson, secretary of the Mission to Lepers in India and the East, presented vividly to eye and ear, by means of a stereopticon lecture, the conditions of life among the lepers and the relief and blessing that missionary effort is bringing to this most afflicted class and to their children.

"The Yorkshire Nightingale" came from Auditorium Endeavor, saying that he had just had the treat of his life in shaking hands with Fanny Crosby and receiving her words of appreciation after he had sung two of her hymns. He then gave his hearers a treat by singing "The Nightingale's Trill," a song written for Adelina Patti.

Those in charge of the immigration exhibit at the Convention gave a realistic demonstration of the kind of examination through which a newcomer to the United States must pass in order to gain admission. Several persons dressed in the costumes of different foreign countries were made to swing their arms and walk up and down; one impersonating a medical inspector listened to the action of their lungs; another scrutinized them for symptoms of trachoma, that dreaded disease of the eyes; and another inquisitor propounded some twenty questions to a candidate that answered them with a good imitation of Irish wit that kept the audience smiling when it did not smile out loud.

A practical bearing of this exercise was brought out by Mr. Shaw when he pressed upon Endeavor societies generally the example of that society in New Britain, Conn., that is doing its best to help the men and women of five nationalities that have lately become their neighbors, and are in need of neighborliness that is Christian.

The stereopticon again came into use, and the evening closed with a remarkably fine display of views and moving pictures illustrating the charms of southern California. This was provided by the California delegation to the Convention. The plan had been to show it as an argument in favor of "Los Angeles, 1913." Compliance with some police regulations involved a delay, and the treat was enjoyed quite as much after Los Angeles had won its prize, and was simply giving a foretaste of what might be the delights of those that go to the land of sunshine two years hence. Even the pictured orange groves and ostrich farms and alligator farms, the fairy-like avenues, the profusion of flowers used as snowballs or confetti, and the exquisitely beautiful flowers that were made to grow on the screen aroused the enthusiasm of those that feasted their eyes on the sight and longed to behold the reality.

CHAPTER VIII.

MEMORABLE SABBATH MEETINGS.

In many Churches and Auditoriums Endeavor and Williston.

Sunday broke warm and glorious over Atlantic City; and, when the hour of morning worship arrived, hosts of Endeavorers wended their way to the city churches.

In one church it was announced that several hundred had been turned away. In spite of the heat those present crowded together in already crowded pews to make room for a few more; and, when other space was exhausted, the young people manned the steps of the pulpit.

The pulpits were largely occupied by trustees and Convention speakers.

The Episcopal congregations listened to the Canadian Episcopal trustee, Archdeacon J. B. Richardson and the president of the British National Union, Rev. J. F. Horsefield. Strong speakers were assigned to the churches of our colored brethren, who will not soon forget the impression made.

A meeting for men and another for women were arranged for the afternoon, the former to be addressed by Mr. Fred B. Smith and the other by Mrs. Woodallen Chapman. Both were successful, as the following brief account will show.

MEN'S MEETING.

Auditorium Endeavor.

Mr. Fred B. Smith, who was scheduled to speak to men only on "A Fatal Mistake," is a virile personality, whose stirring, straightforward talks always create an appetite for more. He is at the helm of one of the greatest movements of modern times, the Men and Religion movement, and his influence is felt in every city of the land. On Sunday afternoon, therefore, a great audience of men gathered on the Million-Dollar Pier to listen to his message.

Seats had been reserved for the Elks, who had a convention in the city, and many of them took advantage of this courtesy. Especially notable was a large delegation of the dignitaries of the order, the ruler and members of his executive committee, wearing their official badges, who were led to the front by Mr. Shaw.

What a company of men! Fine, stalwart, clear-eyed, keen-faced, eager! What wonder that Mr. Smith, accustomed to seeing audiences of men, should have got that vision of the tremendous power of Christ locked up in such hearts?

Bishop Fallows led the devotional exercises, directing the thought upon the need of watchfulness against the many demons of intemperance, of greed, and of unholy lust.

The leader of the meeting was Mr. William Phillips Hall, the business men's evangelist, who read the story of Cain and Abel.

Mr. Smith began by paying a warm tribute to Christian Endeavor. "As a secretary of the Y. M. C. A., in which position I have served for twenty-five years, it gives me pleasure to testify to the world-power of Christian Endeavor. It has been my joy to circle the globe two and a half times, and in travels far and near I have never been away from the benign influence of the Christian Endeavor movement; and I want here to state that in my judgment the Christian Endeavor organization has in the providence of God fulfilled a function that no other has ever attempted, and it has a large place to fill in the future."

Mr. Smith stopped long enough to make the meeting "a unanimous shirt-waist-meeting." Off came his own coat — and the coats of many others were immediately peeled off.

The sermon was a running commentary on the story of Cain and Abel, and it bristled with fine, searching thoughts.

What is the mark of Cain? A scar? No; sin! Sin always leaves its mark, and I believe that God lets the vicious look of a murderer shine out for evermore from this man's face.

No man can dodge his responsibility. Cain tried it, and is execrated. Many names in the Bible are given to our children, but no one is called by the name of Cain. Why? Not merely because he was a murderer, but because he tried to dodge his responsibility.

Every man is responsible for his brother. Before to-morrow morning every one of us will have influenced somebody for good or ill, for time and eternity. Down in Newport, Ky., I was told of a fine young man who, if he could be won for Christ, would swing a great crowd of young men to righteousness. I met him and asked, "Are you a Christian?" "No." "They tell me that you would influence others if you surrendered to Christ." He said, "I don't believe that theory, and I wouldn't give much for the chap that could be influenced by me. I allow no man to influence me."

Mr. Smith showed him that he wore shoes with toothpick points because they were the style; his hair was parted in the middle because his friends parted theirs in the same way; his coat was in the latest fashion. Habit is branded upon us.

The barber paints his pole red, white and blue because he knows that men are influenced by it. The Indian dummy, made of putty and wheels, that never moved a foot unless somebody pushed it, attracts men to the tobacco-dealer's store. We are what we are because of others, and others are what they are because of what we are. We are responsible. God has made us so.

With tremendous power and a wealth of telling illustrations he drove home the terrible truth. He forced fathers to see their responsibility for their sons. One said to him, "Save my son from drink." Next day this father was seen drinking in a saloon. How could he expect the salavtion of his son while he set the pace that leads to hell?

This led Mr. Smith to a fierce denunciation of the saloon. "If I had the power, I would put up in front of every saloon in the country a sign with letters six-foot high: 'This is the reception-hall to hell. Come in and get a ticket!'"

Then a fervid statement of the truth that men that start an evil going can never shed tears enough to go back and stop it.

I have no use for the Christ-rejecting man who repents on his deathbed. I saw an army officer, standing on a club table, drinking champagne, and heard him boasting of the girls he had ruined. He died at sixty, and when I heard the preacher say that the man had repented at the last moment I thought I should have to go out for air. I have no use for a religion that throws a cloak over a wretch like that. That officer may have repented, but he left hell behind him.

There are other "keepers." The man who votes for saloons on election-day is more of a saloon-keeper that the man who wears the white apron behind the bar. The stylish sneak outside who buys the drinks and treats is the barkeeper.

As to gambling, if I could, I would sweep out the stylish gambling, the gambling for silver spoons and booby prizes, and then I'd starve out professional gambling for gain.

Any man who by hint or look turns a girl from virtue, he is the keeper of the house of disrepute, of that girl's soul.

Get that word "keeper"; that is a good word. I stood not long ago in London before a great audience of orphan boys, six hundred of them. A business man is behind that whole institution. As I stood there, I was strongly swept by powerful emotion, and I could scarcely say anything; for I remembered that this business man was practically the guardian of that group of boys, nearly all of them picked up as waifs in the street. I said, "Sir, you are a good keeper of these boys." He is the keeper, the guardian, the restrainer, the protector of life.

I was leaving Lexington, Ky., some years ago in a fierce blizzard. Near the cars stood an old black man who had a blanket wrapped around his head until you could hardly see his face. He had in his hand a red lantern and a white lantern. "It is a pretty cold night," I said. "Yes, I's 'fraid some folks will freeze to-night." "You'd better go home." "Boss, I can't go home; for, if I do, I am afraid a lot of folks are going to get killed in this yard to-night." Am I my brother's keeper? This is another way we use that word "keeper."

There is the keeper of the saloon. "O," but you say, "you need not talk about him." If you mean the man who puts on a white apron and gets behind the bar to sell the stuff, perhaps not; but I have for the last time in my life stood on the platform to beat over the head with a cudgel the man that stands behind the bar to sell the stuff. The man that will go up on election-day to vote to have it done is far more the keeper of the saloon. If you say to my boy, "Come, and have a drink with me; one drink never hurt any man," and my boy goes on the road to ruin. you are the saloon-keeper to that boy, and God will some day make you pay the price for that murder.

Are there men in this audience who were in either of the Dakotas on the twelfth of January, 1898? One — two — three. You will remember that morning. The sun rose clear, and the air was as balmy as April. My brother and I went from the ranch to see some cattle. During the forenoon we saw in the distance a low, black cloud lying on the horizon. It rose like a hurricane, and in fifteen minutes you could not see your hand in front of your face. For twenty-four hours that storm raged, and we had to stuff the keyholes tight, for enough snow could blow through a keyhole to drift a room.

In a schoolhouse there was a little girl, eighteen years of age, who weighed about one hundred pounds. She had sixteen scholars ranging from fourteen years down to the youngest, my own niece, of eight. She saw she must keep them there in order to be safe. In the fury of the storm, a window gave way. She got up to put a cloak in the place, but another gave away. She saw the building would not stand. She took a rope, and tied it around the waists of all, opened the door, and out she went; and for a mile and a quarter against a blizzard that little, frail one-hundred-pound, eighteen-year-old girl fought her way until she fell with a thud against the hut of a bachelor. I have heard him tell the story. When he bathed her brow, and she opened her eyes, she said, "Are the children all right?" He said, "Yes; they are all safe." She swooned again, and an hour later, the first time she opened her eyes again, she asked, "Are they all safe?" He said he had to take every one of them past her bedside until she had baptized each of them with a kiss. There are big men in this room that have not such moral courage as the physical courage of that little girl. A keeper!

At the close he asked the Christians to rise, and a great multitude responded. Many asked for prayer; many wrote their addresses on cards distributed for his purpose, so that a special message might be sent to them through the mail; and many indicated that they wished definitely to follow Christ. A crowd of this latter class thronged around the speaker at the front of the platform. May they be true to their pledge made that Sunday afternoon, and may this great meeting be "written in heaven"!

THE WOMEN'S MEETING.

Auditorium Williston.

There were no vacant seats in Auditorium Williston on Sunday afternoon, and for the first time in the history of Christian Endeavor an overflow women's meeting was necessary, which was held in the Pavilion. The great assembly of women, with their cool, white dresses and earnest Christian faces, made an inspiring sight.

Mr. Lincoln, Philadelphia's beloved chorus-leader, conducted a sprightly song service. After singing one stanza of a hymn, he asked the Sunday-school teachers of the audience

to sing the next stanza; there was no appreciable lessening of the volume of sound. The next stanza was sung by those who at home were members of quartette or chorus choirs, and again the volume was about the same. "And now," said Mr. Lincoln, "let the fourth verse be sung by those that do *not* go to Sunday-school." Only four or five voices responded to this challenge. "I've just been thinking," said Mr. Lincoln, "how lonely it must be at home with all the workers off at this Convention!"

Miss Emma O. Nichols, president of the Massachusetts Union, read for the opening devotional exercises the love chapter in First Corinthians, following it with a fervent prayer. Next came a charming solo, "The Lord is my Shepherd," by Miss Flora Rondabush.

In introducing Mrs. Woodallen Chapman, Mrs. Clark spoke of the work of her mother, Mrs. Wood-Allen. Mrs. Chapman's address took up for its theme "The Beauty of Holiness." "The beauty of wholeness" was her interpretation of the phrase. If we have in our home a beautiful vase with a piece chipped out, though we may cherish it because of some association, we always must apologize for it. Thus also no life can have the beauty of holiness unless it is wholly given up to God.

"Purity" is another word very close to holiness in its meaning. "There is nothing outside of ourselves," said Mrs. Chapman, "that we really need to fear. We are likely to think that purity is a matter of conduct, but Christ taught us that purity is a matter of the heart."

Mrs. Chapman discussed fully the question so often asked regarding the liberties that young men frequently take with young women, and young women do not always know why it is wrong to permit them. These liberties, however, are the initial point of danger, a playing with fire; and one can never know when they will flash into a flame of passion that will ruin two lives. Moreover, girls and women should keep themselves pure, not only for the sake of preserving their womanhood, but also for the sake of young men, who are exposed to many fierce temptations. And, finally, if we take any part of our lives for our own selfish gratification, we are not worshipping God in the beauty of holiness.

After a solo sweetly sung by Miss Ethel Foster, a good Christian Endeavorer, Mrs. Clark, with a word about the splendid Burmese Endeavorers, introduced Miss N. MaDwe Yaba, of Burma. She wore her beautiful Burmese dress, stood on a chair, and with perfect self-possession, with a clear, strong voice, made a never-to-be-forgotten plea for interest in missions.

This young Endeavor girl has wit and grace and force, and held her audience enthralled; yet, when some years ago she began in Burma her Christian Endeavor work, after hunting up the shortest verse she could find, she was quite unable to muster courage to say a word. So the officers of that society, "to help her out," as she said, got together and appointed her to lead a meeting. Thereupon she hunted up a pencil and paper as soon as she could, and resigned from that society! But since then Christian Endeavor and missions have made her the effective speaker that she is.

Miss Yaba told us what Buddhism does for Burma — how it keeps down womanhood especially, whose only salvation must come through their husbands or their sons, and who cannot engage in any religious work. They have no home life, and no word for home. American women sometimes say: "Why disturb the heathen in their religion? It is good enough for them." But no religion that is not good enough for American women is good enough for Burmese women.

Miss Yaba closed by singing a charming song, the words by her father, the music by herself:

> "A voice that I hear across the sea
> Sings the sweetest songs of the East to me;
> Sings of a land where bright suns glow,
> And beautiful blossoms of Burma blow."

A Chinese society sent an elegant banner to represent it at the Convention, and Mrs. Clark asked "Caroline Cobweb," the daughter of Managing Editor Wells, to hold it up, and read the verse from Hebrews imprinted upon it.

Germany came next, in the person of Mrs. Frederick Blecher, noble wife of the splendid secretary of the German Union. She gave a most inspiring message, telling us a lot about Christian Endeavor work in her great country. Mr. Blecher has three field secretaries with six clerks. Germany has 420 Young People's societies with about 11,000 members, and 75 Junior societies with about 1,500 members. Out of these societies have gone 726 special Christian workers. There are 12 German State unions. German Endeavorers contribute most of the support of fifteen missionaries in the Caroline Islands, a German possession, and have bought their first mission ship, the Peace. Last year more than three million tracts were distributed by German Endeavorers. They also establish Christian Endeavor libraries full of the best of reading, look after the welfare of factory girls, and in Saxony they carry on a Christian school for housework.

England was well represented by Mrs. Horsefield, wife of the president of the British Christian Endeavor Union. In a strong address she urged more of the *prayer* life, to meet the many perplexities of a woman's life; more of *purpose*, that we may live before our home folks the lives that they expect of us; and more of *practice*, that we may illustrate every day and hour the will and character of Jesus Christ.

China again came to the front in the person of Mrs. George Hubbard, who with her husband founded the first Christian Endeavor society in China. She made a class of the thousands of women before her, and taught them the story of Abraham's offering of Isaac just as she teaches it to her Bible women in China.

The work of Christian missions was shown in a lovely way by Miss Grace Joy, a Chinese girl with a fine face, who told how she was adopted into a Christian home, and how her great desire is to go to China and tell her sisters less fortunate than herself about the great love of Jesus. Then very sweetly she sang in Chinese, "I want to tell the story."

The last speaker of this brilliant and moving session was Miss Margaret Koch, of Maine. Miss Koch, the active field secretary of the Maine Union, is one of twelve children, and six of her brothers are ministers of the gospel. She should herself be counted as the seventh, for she knows well how to preach the truth of God.

Her theme was "The Queen's Part in the Kingdom's Work," and her Spirit-filled address was a plea for prayer in the Christian life. She showed how necessary it is to pray if one would be happy and make others happy, and how impossible it is without the conscious communion with God to do God's work in this world. With these strong words closed what was certainly the best women's meeting ever held in a Christian Endeavor Convention.

THE EVENING MEETING.

It was with deep regret that the Endeavorers learned that Commander Eva Booth had been so prostrated by the intense heat that it was impossible for her to come to address the Convention on Sunday evening in Auditorium Endeavor.

The leader of the devotional exercises was Dr. W. F. Wilson of Canada, a man much in demand throughout the Convention. He spoke vigorously about Dr. Clark's motto for the coming two years, "In the name of our God we will set up our banners."

Notwithstanding Miss Booth's absence there was no lack of material for a strong meeting. Dr. Samuel B. Capen, that stanch friend and trustee of Christian Endeavor, and the president of the American Board, brought four messages from the Bible especially for men. He said:

I want to speak to-night as a layman to laymen on the great missionary message that the Bible has for us. If any one wonders why I limit this message to men only, the reply is a simple one, Because we need it the most. We men have to acknowledge with shame that the women in our churches have been far more interested than we in world-evangelization; they are better organized, and have been willing to make far more sacrifices than we.

First. The fundamental message of the gospel is contained in the words, "Go ye, therefore, and make disciples of all the nations." Let us remember that the one that spoke these words was not a priest, or even a Levite, but a carpenter's son; and those to whom the message was spoken were largely fishermen. These laymen sprang to their task, and before the close of the first century they had been everywhere all over the known world. They had the true conception of the Christian church; it was not primarily for worship; it certainly was not a religious club; it was to tell others of the Christ. Then came the church controversies and divisions, and here we are to-day, nineteen centuries since Christ died, and a thousand million human beings have not yet heard of Christ; they have never seen a Bible or spelling-book, and they could not read them if they had.

Second. The reason for this command is based on the fact that only in this message of salvation through Christ is there any hope for the world. We must never forget that this is a lost world to be saved, and not an ignorant one to be educated. All the religions of the non-Christian world are utterly inadequate; if any of them were sufficient, would the awful sacrifice on the cross have been made? We are ready to accept any truth that may be found in any religion; but they are all, with the exception of Mohammedanism, going into bankruptcy, and tottering to their fall. The Swamis come over from India, and fool silly women; but they represent a religion that is rotten through and through. If I should dare to describe it, I should be liable to be arrested for obscenity. In one of the cities of India where Hinduism has full sway, there are five thousand temples that, in the name of religion, live to ruin men and women for gain.

We want to press the work at home as never before, for its needs were never greater than at this hour. But in doing this we must be equally in earnest for work abroad. We must never forget that practically all the people in this nation live within the sound of the gospel bell, and breathe a Christian atmosphere. In the United States there is one ordained minister to every 550 persons; in the non-Christian world there is but one missionary to about 125,000 persons; in the United States there is one physician to every 577 persons; in the non-Christian world there is one medical missionary to every 2,500,000 persons. If there was the same ratio in this country as there is abroad, there would be in the whole United States but about 35 physicians and surgeons; there would be but 2 for all New England.

Third. There is another Bible message that bears upon our subject; namely, "To whomsoever much is given, of him shall much be required." God has given to our nation great resources, both of money and of men, and we are responsible to Him for a proper use of them. This opportunity has greatly increased in recent years; the battle of Manila Bay and the destruction of Cervera's fleet have made the United States a world power as never before. The Golden Rule as inaugurated by John Hay, and which has been followed all through the administrations of Mr. Roosevelt and Mr. Taft, has given to the American missionary a standing in the world such as he did not possess before. With our friends across the border in Canada, the American missionaries can go everywhere, and are universally accepted.

This very time when we are most able to help is the hour when because of rapid changes in the East we are having opportunities for service as never before. The conclusion of the experts gathered from all the world at the Missionary Conference at Edinburgh a year ago was this: "The next ten years will in all probability constitute a turning-point in human history, and may be of more critical importance in determining the spiritual evolution of mankind than many centuries of ordinary experience. If those years are wasted, havoc may be wrought that centuries are not able to repair. On the other hand, if they are rightly used, they may be among the most glorious in Christian history." The victory of Japan over Russia has stirred all Asia from Constantinople to Tokyo; there is a feeling of unrest and a desire for something better. We can get a hearing for the gospel message now as has never been possible in all the past.

Fourth. Another Bible message we need especially to heed is, "Whosoever would become great among you shall be your minister, . . . even as the Son of man came not to be ministered unto, but to minister, and to give His life a ransom for many." The chief glory of the Christian nations is not in the strength of their armies and navies, but in the service they can render to the world. Was it not Gladstone who said that the place of America was to be the chief servant among the nations?

A part of this work of ministering should be to correct the evil that is going everywhere through our selfish and commercial interests. We have become a great manufacturing nation; our looms and factories produce more than we can use; we can manufacture in six or eight months all that our nation can use in a year; we must have broader markets. There is a great industrial struggle going on internationally; these commercial interests are often perfectly selfish and cruel. President Taft has done distinguished service twice, in speaking before the Laymen's Missionary Movement, in calling attention to the sad fact that many that go to the East for business purposes fail utterly to represent worthily a Christian nation. When the worst of the East and the worst of the West meet in the great "port-cities," it is literally a hell on earth. The Christian men of this country are in honor bound to give the antidote to this evil by sending more speedily the gospel message.

This is a great age to live in. There has been a great rising of men through the Laymen's Missionary Movement, and it is interesting to know that it is in some respects a part of the fruit of Christian Endeavor; the one that first suggested the organization of this movement had been an active Christian Endeavorer.

We have been making history rapidly within the past few years; there has been almost a revolution in the thought of the world as well as in the church with regard to the great missionary enterprise; the diplomacy of the world, the press, the philanthropists, the business interests, are all arrayed on this side.

The final message to which I would call your attention is this brief word: "Follow me." If we accept Christ's "Come," we are bound to follow that command to "go." That message is binding on us all; we must either accept it personally or give to the extent of our ability that others may deliver the message to those that have it not. An old sailor said to a young apprentice, "Aboard a man-o'-war, my lad, there's only two things: one's duty; t'other's mutiny." Which is it to be for you and me? May we make such an answer to-night as we shall be glad to remember when we meet Jesus Christ face to face in the other world.

The other address was by Mr. Fred B. Smith. He is not only a men's evangelist, but has a message that appeals to all classes and to both sexes.

He made an impassioned plea for evangelism in the church and in young people's societies, defining it as the divine art of winning men and women to know Jesus Christ as the Son of God. It is its evangelism that marks Christianity as absolutely unique and supreme among religions. In this lies the final solution of every problem of the church.

If history ever records a nation without religion, that country will be our own. A young college man whose faith in the supernatural was shaken by a single year in a university was unmoved by all arguments that could be urged; but a single evangelistic service set him right. If we are going to keep God a reality, evangelism must be emphasized.

Bigger than all world-problems, bigger than the cause of universal peace and the solution of industrial questions, is the need of the world of a personal acceptance of Christ. This need is at the root of modern unrest and modern social entanglements. It is a daring thing to say, but the truth none the less, that all the problems of Christianity have been solved under the spell of the evangelistic spirit.

The world has not changed in its need for Christ, and, though the old-fashioned downright methods of winning souls have been abandoned and tabooed, they will have to be revived before progress can be made toward the Christianizing of the universe. The real issue of Christianity is directly concerned with winning men and women definitely to acknowledge Christ as their Saviour and their Lord. Every organization in the church, the Young Men's Christian Association, the missionary societies, and the young people's associations are losing sight of this. They must go back to former ways to become effectual, and by any and all methods make the personal appeal, which alone can stir the heart and rouse the conscience.

The time is coming when the church will have to make scientific provision for evangelism. It is a deplorable thing that the very name of it has fallen into disrepute and become associated with charlatanism and graft. At present any broken-down corn-doctor can start out as a free-lance evangelist. Without credentials or the sanction of the church the most sacred trust of Christanity is placed in the hands of those who discredit it, and who are in no way capable of upholding it.

To-day we are told that there is no need of constant emphasis on personal confession, but inspiring great ideas of service will answer. Said a leader in the study of social conditions, "You might as well tie roses to dead bushes and call them flowers as to talk about service until you get men related to Christ as Saviour and Lord."

In the time of the great panic in October, 1897, when business men were to be seen rushing through Wall Street, their clothes half torn from them in their frenzy, Mr. Smith saw coming toward him a friend, a president of a bank, a leading man in the financial world. Fearing to meet him, Mr. Smith tried to step out of sight. But the man's eye caught him, and on coming up he said not one word about the panic, but, "Smith, this morning before I came down-town, Thomas, my chauffeur, gave his heart to Christ in my library, and is going to join the church next Sunday." Evangelism is not cheap work that appeals only to small men, but is worthy of the greatest and noblest.

THE EVENING MEETING.
Auditorium Williston.

President Landrith of Belmont College — the big-hearted, big-bodied Southerner — knows well how to wake up a meeting and keep it wide-awake. He is a stanch Bible-lover and Bible-defender, and made an ideal presiding officer for the Bible meeting of the Convention on Sunday evening.

After a most helpful Bible-reading and prayer by Dr. Elijah Humphries, Primitive Methodist trustee, we had a beautiful solo by Mr. W. C. Weeden. This son of the famous W. S. Weeden was for thirteen years on the stage, and was led to Christ by the first speaker of the evening, Mr. William Phillips Hall.

Mr. Hall is a successful business man, the president of the American Tract Society and the Bible League, and a Methodist Episcopal trustee of the United Society; but his noblest title, after all, is "the business men's evangelist." Considering these many and varied activities, no more suitable theme could be given to him than "The Evangelistic Message of the Bible."

It has been my chief delight, said Mr. Hall, for many years to deliver the evangelistic message of the Bible for the salvation of men, for, like the great apostle to the Gentiles, "I am not ashamed of the gospel of Christ; for it is the power of God unto salvation to every one that believeth; to the Jew first, and also to the Greek."

In John's Gospel, in the third chapter, and beginning at the fifth verse, we read that solemn declaration of our Lord Jesus Christ to Nicodemus: "Verily, verily, I say unto thee, Except a man be born again (from above), he cannot see the kingdom of God." "Verily, verily, I say unto thee, Except a man be born of water and of the Spirit, he cannot enter into the kingdom of God." Not that God has elected cruelly and arbitrarily to shut any man out of the Kingdom simply because that man has morally failed to come up to divine requirements, but because in the very nature of things it is spiritually impossible for a man that is "dead in trespass and sins" to be spiritually alive unto God until he has been born again (from above) of the Spirit of God, and because until he is so born he cannot exist in the kingdom of God.

And then, to distinguish the naturally born from the spiritually born man, our Lord observed: "That which is born of the flesh is flesh; and that which is born of the Spirit is spirit. Marvel not that I said unto thee [the eminent member of the Jewish Sanhedrin, the doctor of the law, moralist of moralists], Ye must be born again."

And now, if we carefully note the words that follow, we may learn how the man is born again (of the Spirit), "The wind bloweth where it listeth, and thou hearest the sound thereof, but canst not tell whence it cometh, and whither it goeth; so is every one that is born of the Spirit." Or so doth the Spirit effect the new birth in the heart of the one that meets the divine conditions required therefor.

And now as to how the individual may be born again of the Spirit of God. "And as Moses lifted up the serpent in the wilderness, even so must the Son of man be lifted up: that whosoever believeth in him [in the same way in which the Israelites believed in the brazen serpent unto salvation from the deadly poison of the fiery serpent's sting] should not perish, but have eternal life. For God so loved the world that he gave his only begotten Son, that whosoever believeth in him should not perish, but have everlasting life." In all of this teaching we shall do well to note that eternal life, being born again, and salvation are synonymous terms.

"For God sent not his Son into the world to condemn the world: but that the world through him might be saved" (born again).

"He that believeth on the Son hath everlasting life" (has been born again). We have very briefly and Scripturally considered the content of the evangelistic message of the Bible. Let us now with equal brevity consider how this message was delivered and interpreted in its delivery by the Apostle Paul. Paul and Silas from the depths of the inner prison of Philippi are urgently entreated by the distracted jailer in the midst of the awful earthquake that seemed to betoken the end of all earthly things, in the words, "Sirs, what must I do to be saved? And they said, Believe on the Lord Jesus Christ, and thou shalt be saved, and thy house. And they spake unto him the word of the Lord, and to all that were in his house. And he took them the same hour of the night, and washed their stripes; and was baptized, he and all his, straightway. And when he had brought them to his house, he set meat before them, and rejoiced, believing in God with all of his house." Acts 16: 30-34.

Let us note, first, the fact that the apostles told the jailer that he would be saved (born again) by believing on the Lord Jesus Christ; and, second, that, having believed on the Lord Jesus Christ, it is further stated that the jailer "believed in God." It therefore appears that believing on the Lord Jesus Christ is believing in God, who is incarnate in the Lord Jesus Christ.

It will be seen in the thirty-second verse that Paul and Silas "spake unto him," the jailer, "the word of the Lord." If we will turn to Romans 10: 8-14, we shall learn the content of that "word of the Lord" that Paul preached to the Philippian jailer. "But what saith it? The word is nigh thee, in thy mouth, and in thy heart; that is, the word of faith, which we preach, because if thou shalt confess with thy mouth Jesus as Lord, and shalt believe in thine heart that God raised him from the dead, thou shalt be saved." Now may we not pause a moment to inquire what Paul meant when he spoke of confessing Jesus as Lord? The word "Lord," here quoted, in the Greek is *Kurios*, and the word *Kurios* in the Septuagint, Paul's Old Testament, is the equivalent or substitute word for Jehovah.

There is but one conclusion to be drawn from this fact, and that is the further fact that the apostle clearly and positively taught the jailer that he must confess the Lord Jesus Christ as Jehovah or God incarnate, and believe in his heart that God raised him from the dead, in order to his salvation.

This interpretation is confirmed beyond the shadow of a doubt by the words quoted by Paul from Joel 2: 32, in the thirteenth verse of this tenth chapter: "For whosoever shall call upon the name of the Lord shall be saved." The Lord Jesus and the Lord of the quotation are one and the same. And the Lord of Joel 2: 32 is Jehovah.

THE "WAYDOWN" TEXAS GROUP.

THE OKLAHOMA "WE DO" DELEGATION.

If the Christian church through her ministry had always emphasized the deity of our Lord Jesus Christ as Paul did in his preaching of the evangelistic message of the Bible, do you think that there would have been any question raised in the church concerning the deity of our Lord? And if the church had interpreted the evangelistic message of the Bible as requiring a heart-belief in the fact of the resurrection of our Lord Jesus Christ from the dead, do you think that there would ever have been any question as to that glorious fact?

While it is blessedly true that a simple looking to our Lord Jesus Christ in faith for that purpose effects the salvation of the soul, has not the time come to re-emphasize the apostolic interpretation of the evangelistic message of the Bible by holding up our crucified and raised Lord Jesus Christ as not only "the Lamb of God, which taketh away the sin of the world," but also as our "Lord and our God"?

And now in conclusion just a few words of personal testimony to the present-time saving power of the evangelistic message of the Bible. One year ago last February I was praying one evening in my study for God's blessing upon a men's meeting I was to conduct under the auspices of the Young Men's Christian Association of Baltimore, Md., at Ford's Opera House in that city, upon the twentieth day of that month.

It had been arranged some time before that the late Rev. F. H. Jacobs, whom so many Christian Endeavorers knew and loved so well, should sing at that meeting. But while in prayer for God's blessing upon Brother Jacobs I was impressed with the thought that for some reason or other he was not to sing at that meeting, but that another, who so far as I then knew was singing upon the comic-opera stage, was to sing at that meeting. This was a most extraordinary situation, but I immediately said, "Lord, if that be Thy will, may Thy will be done."

The next morning upon calling Mr. Jacobs upon the telephone I learned that he had made a mistake in the memorandum of the date for Baltimore, and had made another appointment in the city of Brooklyn, from which he could not honorably retire. Immediately after, through a chain of circumstances of the most extraordinary character, I was placed in touch with relatives of the man whose name had come to me in my prayer of the night before. Through those relatives I was placed in touch with the man, who I then learned for the first time had shortly before retired from the stage, and who consented then and there to accompany me to the city of Baltimore the same day. Although, as may be imagined, he was far from God, the following day in Baltimore he resurrendered to God, whose service he had forsaken some thirteen years before, and had a most blessed assurance of his acceptance with his Lord.

As he stepped out on the stage of Ford's Opera House that Lord's Day afternoon, he recalled the fact that just one year before, to the very day, he had sung a leading part in a popular comic opera on that very stage. His first song that day was "The Ninety and Nine," and so wonderfully did God bless his singing and the word that was spoken that a splendid company of men surrendered to Christ.

Since that day he has been engaged with one of the leading evangelists of the country in a great soul-saving campaign, in which thousands confessed their faith in the Son of God. His whole life has been transformed; and now W. C. Weeden, for it is of him that I have been speaking, finds his chief delight in using his splendid voice in winning men to God. From a leading part on the comic-opera stage to the service of Christ is a far cry, but by the grace of God and the power of the evangelistic message of the Bible the change had been made.

After this it was with new zest that the audience followed Mr. Weeden's enthusiastic lead in singing "Will there be any stars?" The fine Harrisburg chorus was on the platform, and next they sang for us, in a delightful way, "Holy Bible, book divine."

This substantial evening's programme closed with two addresses by veteran missionaries, each of them a quarter of a century on the field.

The first of these, Rev. W. H. S. Hascall, of Burma, declared vigorously, "So long as the authorities of any country chain the Bible, so long do they chain the people." "The Bible," he went on to say, "is never a foreign book; it strikes the life of the people every time, whether they live in America or in the jungles of India or in the forests of Africa or in the heart of China."

Mr. Hascall told of an old man in Burma to whom a missionary had given, not a Bible, but only some small tracts. The influence of those tracts — he never had a Bible — was so great that his neighbors testified that it transformed his life. The speaker, out of his long experience, gave many other examples of the changes wrought by the Bible among the people of Burma.

Rev. Herbert Anderson, of Calcutta, is one of the missionaries whom Mr. Shaw called missionary statesmen, men of insight, vision, and faith. Mr. Anderson was twice president of the Christian Endeavor union of India, Burma, and Ceylon. He has been identified with Christian Endeavor in India in every important undertaking. Among other positions he has held he was president of the World's Convention at Agra, and thus was the host of the Endeavor party that made that famous tour around the world.

Mr. Anderson began by expressing the gratitude of India's Endeavorers for all that has been done by Americans for the great Indian Empire during past years. This kindly "thank you" came from 40,000 Endeavorers speaking thirty different languages.

Missionaries have the privilege of talking from practical experience of the spread of the word of God throughout the world. Mr. Anderson sketched the triumphs of the Bible in accordance with William Carey's famous motto, "To every man of every nation a copy of the word of God in his own language."

He gave some telling instances of the power of the Book to shine by its own light, and to reach and awaken the hearts of men. And every one may have a share in spreading the Book among the darkened nations of men.

THE EVENING MEETING.
The Temple.

Was it a sympathetic coincidence that caused the Sunday-evening meeting on "Christian Endeavor and Prison Reform" to be held in the open air, in the Pavilion, which, for some reason, was totally dark? — an indication, possibly, of the condition of some prisons.

Meantime, to the strains of "Onward, Christian soldiers," the audience marched fifty yards further on to the Temple, where the meeting was conducted in the light. Probably also a prophecy.

Judge Warner, superintendent of the Connecticut Christian Endeavor prison work, handed out printed slips containing a weekly prayer-cycle for prison reform. The idea, and it is a splendid one, is to have everybody pray for the prisoner — the only method of real success.

Judge Warner when in the city court aimed, he said, to use the probation system rather than send boys to the reformatory. He gave one instance of a boy that had stolen (and eaten) two chickens. He was sentenced to two years' imprisonment, but Judge Warner got the sentence suspended and a place found for him on a farm. In the autumn this boy gave $1.50 to home missions, and to-day is an employer of labor in New York State. Surely it pays to save the boys!

One interesting incident was brought out by Rev. E. A Fredenhagen, the leader of the meeting. He read a letter from Harry Orchard, the star witness for the State in a famous Western murder trial. Since entering the Idaho State prison this man has found Christ, lives a true Christian life, and is president of the prison Christian Endeavor society!

Bishop Fallows spoke with his usual lucidity and force. For twenty years he has been connected officially with the Illinois State Reformatory, and knows his subject from the practical side.

The bishop's message was one of hope. He has had a hand in paroling 8,000 boys and young men from the State reformatory. Every time a wave of crime swept over Chicago, officials claimed that the cause was the large number of paroled prisoners who in reality were criminals. An examination was made, and it was denomstrated beyond doubt that eighty per cent of Chicago's paroled prisoners were on the high road to good citizenship. A further examination of all reformatories and prisons in the United States proved indisputably that eighty per cent of the paroled men make good.

Take a case. A pitiful letter came from a Jewish rabbi. It said: "I have a boy, and somehow he has gone astray. He is in your institution. Do what you can for him." The bishop investigated, and the young man was paroled.

Two or three years later, at a G. A. R. gathering, a young fellow, bright, sharp, eager, stepped up to him and said, "You do not know me." "Yes, you are —." "Yes," he said, "I am. I am correspondent for *The New York World.*"

He had fallen — that was all. He was not bad. Stranded in Chicago, he had helped himself to something that did not belong to him. Prisoners are men to be met not with averted faces, but as brothers.

"Christian Endeavor," declared the bishop, "has been and is one of the great forces for bringing Christian principles to bear upon our brothers in bonds."

Mr. Spooner, of Connecticut, followed with a plea for the young ladies to seek and to save girls that were going wrong for lack of opportunity and proper help.

CHAPTER IX.

DENOMINATIONAL RALLIES.

THE MILLION-DOLLAR PIER AND THE CHURCHES OF THE CITY MONDAY AFTERNOON, JULY 10.

African Methodist Episcopal and African Methodist Episcopal Zion Rally.

The rally of our colored brethren, which was conducted by Rev. Julian C. Caldwell, D.D., General Secretary of the Allen Christian Endeavor League, assisted by Bishop Alexander Walters, D.D., New York, was one in which enthusiasm flowed at flood-tide. Splendid addresses, full of hope and encouragement, were delivered. A symposium on Christian Endeavor serving — in the home, in the church, and in the world — proved helpful, while Bishop Walters conducted an open parliament dealing ably with Christian Endeavor problems.

The rally gave in cash and pledges $71.61 to help to swell the funds of the International Christian Endeavor Headquarters in Boston, another proof, if one were needed, of the willingness of our negro friends to help on this good work.

The Baptist Rally.

Other rallies may have had larger numbers, but the Baptist certainly was the breeziest, as it was held in the Pavilion on the pier, and was swept by all the ocean winds that happened to be blowing. The seats were filled and the time was fully occupied until five o'clock. The singing was led by Mr. Percy Foster, who is as much a favorite with his own Baptist Endeavorers as with all others.

The programme was wholly informal, designedly so, as the purpose was to have an open discussion of "The Young People's Work of the Baptist Denomination and How it Can Most Effectively Be Prosecuted." The result was interesting, although the presence of a number of missionaries from foreign lands gave a distinctively missionary cast to the afternoon, to the profit and pleasure of all.

The opening prayer was offered by Rev. Dr. Powell of Philadelphia. The leader said, by way of introduction, that the one desire of all was that the Baptist young people should work in perfect harmony and seek together to do a constructive and fruitful work. If different names were borne, that constituted no reason for either rivalry or faction. As Baptists they were one, one in interest in the broad denominational movements. There was no reason why the denominational aims should not be furthered and at the same time the interdenominational fellowships and relationships, which many had found so helpful and delightful, be enjoyed and maintained.

Dr. Clark was introduced and warmly welcomed. By request of the leader he spoke upon the Baptist Endeavor societies as he had seen them in his trips around the world, especially in Burma and the Far East. He expressed the hope that a close federation of all young people's societies was coming, and told of the aid these societies of Endeavor had been to the missionaries.

The general secretary of the Baptist Young People's Union, Rev. George T. Webb of Philadelphia, who is just laying down that office to become associate editor of Baptist Sunday-school periodicals for the Publication Society, spoke upon the subject of the afternoon, showing that there is a special denominational educative work that can be done more effectively through the denominational agencies, but without disturbing in any wise the existing affiliation of societies, or involving any change in name or relation. The vital thing is that young people in the denomination should know what their denomination stands for, be interested in its history and work, and keep in touch with the great movements such as the Northern Baptist Convention. As for Christian Endeavor, he said there could hardly be any feeling of unfriendliness or unfamiliarity, for it had happened that from the first general secretary of the Union down to the present the occupant of the office had been a member of an Endeavor society. This was a fine tribute to Christian Endeavor training. Mr. Webb echoed the leader's sentiment that our young people should work in perfect harmony of spirit, and federate most closely in all ways of service. There is a larger denominational life and spirit into which all should enter.

He spoke also of the World Alliance in Philadelphia, its significance, and how the Baptist young people are organizing for world-consciousness and effectiveness.

Rev. Herbert Anderson, English Baptist missionary to India, told of the great help Christian Endeavor has been to the work in India, as in all mission lands. Other missionaries that gave cumulative testimony on this point were Rev. C. H. Heptonstall and Rev. H. J. Marshall of Burma, who described Endeavor societies as they found them on their tours, and showed what a missionary zeal possessed them, as illustrated by one society, which raised money to send a missionary to unreached tribes, and by the native young men Endeavor-trained, who went out preaching in the villages and reached multitudes.

Then there was a living object-lesson in the person of Miss Nellie Yaba, of Bassein, Burma, a young woman who came to this country seven years ago, and has earned her way through college and medical school, and is now going back as a missionary to her people. She is a remarkable scholar and personality and has a missionary ancestry, her father being a native missionary who was educated in this country, while her grandfather was among the first Karen chiefs converted and baptized by Adoniram Judson. After giving a thrilling story she sang a hymn composed by her father. She was in native costume, and her presence and words put a strong missionary impress upon the rally. None there will forget her saying, "I would rather be a heathen in a heathen country than a heathen in a Christian country," a fitting answer when taunted with being a heathen by birth. There is a deal of truth in the words.

The meeting was brought back to the discussion by an admirable talk by General Secretary Chalmers, who is to succeed Mr. Webb. Mr. Chalmers is the right man for the work, and comes from a pastorate in Morgan Park, Illinois, where Christian Endeavor has been very strong for many years. He is broad-visioned, fine-spirited, and will make friends wherever he goes. He laid down a platform broad enough for all Baptist young people to stand upon. He stood for denominational training and interdenominational fellowship, with no stress laid upon names, with perfect freedom for each local society, according to Baptist principles and practice. All agreed that true denominationalism was not weakened but rather strengthened by the broader relationships, while the gain was great to the wider kingdom of God. The Endeavorers gave Secretary Chalmers a most cordial reception.

Rev. David Ross, of England, brought greetings from the loyal Baptist Endeavorers there, who have received great good from the Society and been brought into contact with the world by it.

The Free Baptists were represented by a Free Baptist pastor who expressed his pleasure at the union in process of consummation beteen his people and the Baptists, and told of the strong Christian Endeavor work of the Free Baptist young people. Canada and the South were also represented, and the closing words were by Dr. Brooks of Washington, who spoke for the negro Baptists and their rapidly developing young people's societies, which are solidly Christian Endeavor. A goodly number of them were present.

The Brethren Rally.

More Endeavorers of the Brethren Church were present than at any previous rally. After the devotional service a brief address on "Some Personal Convictions about Christian Endeavor" was made by Rev. H. M. Oberholtzer, of Allentown, Penn. An interesting paper on Junior work, written by Miss Ruth Blue, was read by Mrs. Dr. Laughlin, of Philadelphia.

A round-table conference followed, and was a most helpful part of the programme. The hopeful sign in Christian Endeavor in the Brethren Church is the increasing number of societies and of district organizations, several of which are holding summer conferences for the study of Christian Endeavor methods.

The Christian Convention.

At the rally of the Christian Convention, where Rev. E. A. Watkins presided, it was decided that some definite objective must be a vital factor in the work for the future. Field work will also receive more attention than before. Steps were taken for a more effective organization of mission-study classes and missionary reading-courses. The problem of the rural society was considered at length.

Interest in Christian Endeavor is growing among these churches, and the rally will result in much good.

The Congregational Rally.

Owing to the illness of Rev. S. H. Woodrow, D.D., the large rally of Congregationalists in Auditorium Williston was in charge of Secretary Shaw, who kept things moving at a good pace and every one in good humor.

In token of Christian Endeavorers' loyalty to their denomination it had been arranged that each of the denominational boards should be represented by a speaker to tell of its objects and needs.

For the American Board the president, Hon. Samuel B. Capen, LL.D., told of the opportunity and the obligation in regard to the foreign field and of the economy with which the work is conducted.

Rev. Frederick H. Page, president of the Sunday-School and Publishing Society, urged the young people to take hold of the movement for religious education and to help it forward.

The secretary of the Congregational Education Society, Rev. Edward S. Tead, D.D., referred to the fact that his society's initials and those of the Christian Endeavor Society are the same, and mentioned some of the products justifying the emphasis that has been put by the denomination on education.

THE CLASSIC ENTRANCE OF THE TEMPLE, ON THE PIER.
Here were held the meetings of the United Society and the Board of Trustees.

A BOARD-WALK CROWD.

Rev. Charles H. Richards, D.D., witnessed to the interest that the Endeavorers had shown in the Church Building Society as manifested by their gifts.

Rev. R. L. Breed, in charge of the immigration exhibit at the Convention, spoke for the Home Missionary Society and of the need of definite work, alike religious and patriotic, for young people's societies.

For the American Missionary Association Rev. F. Q. Blanchard said that its aim is to raise men, and its success depends on the young people's doing their part.

Rev. William Rice, D.D., showed the necessity for the work of the Board of Ministerial Relief, and echoed the suggestion of Mr. Shaw that each society should send a gift to that board near Christmas or at some time each year.

Secretary Shaw asked whether any Williston Endeavorers were in the audience, and the two young ladies that responded were asked to come to the platform, and were introduced as "chips from the old block."

On a suggestion from Mr. William I. Jones, field secretary of the Kansas Union, heartily seconded in remarks by several others, it was unanimously voted to appoint a committee of seven to memorialize the Committee of Nineteen of the National Council of Congregational Churches for the appointment of a committee on Christian Endeavor work who shall be sympathetic with the movement and promote its interests in Congregational churches.

The committee appointed was Rev. S. H. Woodrow, D.D.; Samuel B. Capen, LL.D.,; President Henry Churchill King; Rev. Jesse Hill, D.D., Paul C. Brown, William I. Jones, and Rev. Edgar T. Farrill.

The Cumberland Presbyterian Rally.

The Cumberland Presbyterians held a most interesting denominational rally at the Young Men's Christian Association Building. Rev. J. S. Stiles, of Rutherford, Tenn., conducted the services of praise. Rev. T. Ashburn, of Knoxville, Tenn., addressed the meeting on the subject, "Opportunities Before Young People of To-day," discussing opportunities for the preparation for the great battle of life, opportunities for service in State and in church.

A most helpful paper was read by Miss Nannie Davis, of Knoxville, Tenn., on the subject "Ideals for the Local Society." This was followed by an open conference, in which many practical suggestions were brought out for making the best of the local work.

Mr. A. S. Wilson, Jr., of Nashville, Tenn., discussed the

topic, "How to Promote Christian Endeavor in Our Denomination," giving emphasis to the fact that the great thing needed is information about Christian Endeavor; and speaking of its place in the church, what it stands for, what it is doing, what it proposes doing.

The Disciples' Rally.

The Disciples' rally was held in the First Baptist Church. The programme was arranged by the National Board of Christian Endeavor and Rev. Claude E. Hill, who for nearly five years has served as national superintendent for the Disciples.

Although Atlantic City is away from the centre of Disciple strength, the meeting was largely attended, twenty-nine States being represented, the delegates filling the auditorium of the church. It was an earnest and enthusiastic as well as a representative gathering of this great and growing body.

The meeting was called to order by Mr. Hill, who introduced Mr. G. Evert Boker, president of the Oregon Union, who conducted the devotional service. Dr. Earl Wilfley, pastor of the Garfield Memorial Church, Washington, D. C., was presented, and presided over the meeting. Dr. Wilfley is the successor of the late Dr. F. D. Power, both as the pastor of the great Washington church and as a trustee of the United Society.

Rev. L. N. D. Wells, of East Orange, N. J., welcomed the Disciples to New Jersey, and Rev. R. P. Anderson of THE CHRISTIAN ENDEAVOR WORLD spoke on "The Debt of the Disciples to Christian Endeavor." Irving S. Chenoweth of New York spoke on "The Debt of Christian Endeavor to the Disciples."

Mr. Hill spoke briefly on the work of the National Board of Christian Endeavor. Rev. H. A. Denton, of Troy, N. Y., another trustee of the United Society, spoke of the duty of Disciple Endeavorers to extend Christian Endeavor, urging particularly the support of the Board of Christian Endeavor. It was brought out that the Disciples stand second in number of societies among all religious bodies and that during the last two years fully two thousand new societies have been organized.

The meeting was concluded with a consecration service led by Rev. O. L. Smith, president of the Kansas Union.

The rally was one of the most successful ever held, and was marked by a deep spirit of devotion. The Disciples have always been enthusiastic in their attitude toward Christian Endeavor, and if this meeting was any indication, the next two years will be the best in all the history of Christian Endeavor among these people.

The Friends' Rally.

The Friends' Rally, held in the Friends' Meeting-House, was opened in the true Friendly spirit, with a season of waiting on the Lord, in which He spoke to the hearts of those present.

Richard R. Newby, superintendent of the evangelistic work of the New York Yearly Meeting, sat on the facing seat. Henry Bartlett, of the Philadelphia Yearly Meeting, welcomed the company, and told of the increased activity of the young Friends of Philadelphia.

Rev. Robert E. Pretlow, of Brooklyn, trustee of the United Society, for the Society of Friends spoke of how leading men of other denominations are accepting the principles for which Friends have so long stood, not only with regard to peace and reform, but also on the questions of spirituality of worship and the non-necessity of outward forms. He said that church unity will be reached only when the Christian world accepts Quaker principles as a centre around which to crystallize.

A paper was read for L. Oscar Moon, of Baltimore, in which he urged young Friends to master the principles of constructive discipline and to labor for unity in worship of Christ and unity in service for Christ.

Miss Lillian E. Hayes, of Indiana, international superintendent of Junior Christian Endeavor work, told of the concern the Lord laid on her heart for a school in which young Friends may "study to show themselves approved unto God, workmen that need not to be ashamed," and the establishment of the Summer Assembly for Young Friends of America at Winona Lake, Ind.

Mrs. E. L. Condon, superintendent of Junior Christian Endeavor work of the Iowa Christian Endeavor Union, and Miss Ruth Farquhar, superintendent of Junior Christian Endeavor work of Wilmington Yearly Meeting, Ohio, spoke of encouraging signs among the boys and girls.

It was a pleasure to have the presence of S. Edgar Nicholson, of Washington, D. C., national secretary and legislative superintendent of the Anti-Saloon League, and Herman Newman, editor of *The American Friend*, who urged the study of the needs of the group, not only of those about us, but also of the individuals we do not see.

The missionaries present were Miss Alice Gifford, of New England, who is under appointment of the Philadelphia Yearly Meeting for Japan, who brought the greetings of the New England Christian Endeavor Union; Miss Clotilde Pretlow, from Cuba, who brought greetings from that field, and said that Christian Endeavor is a great boon to their work. Sada F. Stanley, president of the Friends' Christian Endeavor Union in Jamaica, and Jefferson W. Ford, president of the

Christian Endeavor Union for all Jamacia, told how Christian Endeavor is accomplishing the object of its existence in training young Christians in effective service for the Master.

A brief extract from a letter was read telling of an awakening among the young Friends up and down England through the earnest efforts of Elliot Thorp and others there.

Eight Yearly Meetings that have Christian Endeavor organizations were represented, and individuals were present from two Yearly Meetings in which Christian Endeavor is not recognized.

The key-note of the meeting was unity first among ourselves and then with others in the Master's business.

The Lutheran Rally.

The Lutheran Rally was held in St. Andrew's Lutheran Church, Atlantic City, Rev. Theodore Buch, pastor. The church was full to everflowing, and was one of the best ever held.

Rev. P. H. Heilman, D.D., of Baltimore, presided. Addresses were made by Rev. Friedrich Blecher of Berlin, Germany, Rev. L. B. Wolf, D.D., our foreign-missionary secretary, Rev. S. Stall, D.D., Rev. R. G. Bannen, D.D., Williamsport, Penn., Rev. F. W. Meyer, D.D., of Baltimore, Prof. A. B. Van Ormer, D.D., Shippensburg, and Rev. A. Pohlman, D.D., Philadelphia.

Enthusiasm inside the meeting equalled the temperature outside. The motto adopted for the ensuing two years was, "A Young People's Society in Every Lutheran Church in Our Country." New officers were elected: Rev. R. B. Peery, Ph. D., of Denver, Colorado, president, and Rev. H. J. Weaver of Los Angeles, Cal., secretary. Rev. P. A. Heilman, D.D., of Baltimore, was elected a member of the Christian Endeavor Board of Trustees.

The Mennonite Rally.

The Mennonite denomination held its rally at the Chelsea Baptist Church.

The meeting was conducted by Rev. N. B. Grubb, D.D., of Philadelphia.

A message was read from Rev. E. Grubb, of Los Angeles, Cal., who admonished the Mennonite people to maintain the blood-bought principles of their forefathers.

This was followed by a brief message from Rev. H. J. Krehbiel, of Reedey, Cal.

Then followed a message from Rev. N. C. Hirschy of Redfield, S. D.

He said in part: We must go forward. It is not so much what we do for ourselves as what we do for others that counts, A Christian Endeavor society must be progressive, or it will not accomplish what it should. Not moving forward means to go backward.

A paper by Rev. Annie G. Allebach, of New York City, was read, the subject being "Winning Forces in Christian Endeavor."

Some of the forces named were love for God, love for souls, love for humanity, tact, patience, perseverance, faith, and consecration.

This was followed by a very earnest discussion for and against modern methods in church-work.

The Methodist Rally.

At St. Paul's Methodist Episcopal Church a goodly company of Methodist Endeavorers of the three great denominations, the Methodist Church of Canada, the Methodist Episcopal Church, South, and the Methodist Episcopal Church, gathered with characteristic enthusiasm that even the torrid heat of Monday afternoon could not abate.

Rev. Charles Roads, D.D., of Philadelphia, former president of the Pennsylvania Union, and now pastor of Cumberland Street Church of Philadelphia, presided.

Dr. Roads opened the meeting with an address on the striking points of similarity between the spirit of early Methodism and the Christian Endeavor movement in Christly enthusiasm, wisely directed personal work; the raising of the average Christian to efficiency, larger vision, richest fellowship; and team work for Christ's kingdom in thorough organization. Methodism is Christianity with methods touched with enthusiasm and the power of the Holy Spirit. Especially in the development of the unused assets of the local church is Christian Endeavor to find its mission now. Not less personal work, but much more team work, the church now with one accord praying for such a Pentecost as came to Wales in 1904.

The Methodists heartily welcomed Rev. Dr. W. F. Wilson of Toronto, Canada, who emphasized the value of old-fashioned Methodist expression of religious life, the importance of the union of all the great Methodist bodies in America, and the essential oneness of Canadian and American Methodist peoples. He described the splendid form of the Canadian Endeavor societies as Epworth Leagues of Christian Endeavor, both denominational and united with all Christians. With keen wit, delightful humor, and finest illustrations he deepened the earnestness of all who were present, and received "the white lilies" of a great Chautauqua salute as he sat down.

Then came a delightful surprise in the address of Mr. Enos Bacon, the Wesleyan of England, whose very wonderful singing was a feature of Atlantic City meetings. The workers had heard his "two voices" with great pleasure, and now heard him in a third voice of equal richness in hearty appeal to all Endeavorers to restore the Sabbath day to the church and to the world, to make much of the church and the home for God.

President A. R. Walkey of the Manitoba Christian Endeavor Union, represented western Canada in a forceful, hope-inspiring, and deeply spiritual address, which was greatly appreciated.

Rev. Dr. Gilby C. Kelly of the Methodist Church, South, was detained from the meeting; but came in just at the close, and was greeted warmly by many.

The guest of honor of the rally was that distinguished statesman and honored Methodist layman, Hon. Charles W. Fairbanks, recently vice-president of the United States. He was received with great applause by the standing congregation, and soon put every one at ease by his beautiful simplicity of manner and deep sincerity. He joined in earnest advocacy of the Christian Sabbath, pointing out its vital relation to the prosperity of the nation, the best interest of the home and of the church. He strongly emphasized the value of the godly home in an eloquent and impressive passage of his address. He reminded those present that he had earnestly advocated union with the church, South, now that the cause of separation had passed away, and told how he had urged such union when he went as delegate from the Methodist Church to the Southern General Conference. He told of his visits to missions all over the world on his recent tour, and especially of a trip to a Friends' School in Palestine, which he had greatly admired. In all the address Vice-President Fairbanks was simply the earnest Christian man talking to fellow Christians upon the great and ever-developing work of the kingdom of God. In another eloquent passage he was pleading for great respect to be paid to all pastors and for earnest co-operation with them.

Dr. Roads reminded the company present of the inspiring statement in Dr. Clark's report that even now Methodists in all the world have the largest number of Endeavor societies in any denomination, and expressed the hope, which was warmly received, that by a union of all Methodisms in America there might come the adoption of Christian Endeavor with the Epworth League that would soon make the Methodist Endeavorers of the United States the largest number at all the interdenominational conventions.

Rev. Dr. G. J. Burns, of Pennsylvania, offered the closing prayer, and an impromptu reception to Vice-President Fairbanks closed the rally.

The Moravian Rally.

Moravian Endeavorers from New York in the East to Wisconsin in the West attended their denominational rally. The presiding officer was Mr. James E. Grunert, treasurer of the First District Moravian Union. Distinctively Moravian hymns were sung as well as others from the official programme.

After an opening prayer by Rev. H. E. Stocker, greetings were received from Dr. William H. Vogler, former trustee of the United Society; and from Rev. F. W. Stengel, the Moravian young people's secretary of missions, who included in his message an earnest plea for the forming of mission-study classes.

Then came enthusiastic, inspiring, and helpful addresses from Rev. Edward S. Wolle, Rev. F. R. Nitzschke, and Rev. F. W. Wantzel. The remainder of the afternoon was given to social conversation, and a photograph of the Moravian delegates was taken.

It was suggested at this rally that a union be formed of the Endeavorers of the Second District — Philadelphia, western Pennsylvania, southern New Jersey, and Maryland. The First District Endeavorers — those of New York State, northern New Jersey, and eastern Pennsylvania — have for their special work the support of missions among the Indians in southern California.

The Presbyterian Rally.

More than a thousand Presbyterian young people gathered in Auditorium Endeavor on Monday afternoon, and a finer set of young folks it would be impossible to find.

The presiding genius of the hour was the well-beloved Superintendent Gelston, who is doing so noble a work for Presbyterian Endeavorers.

After devotional exercises by Dr. Gilray and Mr. Wells, Rev. Elliot Field, former field secretary of the New York State Union, gave a fervent address on mission study. Study missions, he urged, not as medicine, but as candy. It is the widest of educational training. There are no political problems in all nations that are not bound up, warp and woof, with the missionary problem. Further, we can hardly know the value of Christ, even to ourselves, unless we know the value of Christ to other men. The study of missions is a vitalizer of impotent Christianity.

A show of hands disclosed the encouraging fact that more than half of those present had studied in mission-study classes, and many had organized and led such classes. Large numbers are not necessary. Mr. Field's least successful class was one of 102 members; his most successful class was one of only seven members.

The leader need not be a brilliant expert. Mr. Field told

of a girl in New York who once declared that she could *never* lead a mission-study class, but she has led fifty-five of them during the past years.

One of the most helpful of Presbyterian workers is Miss M. Josephine Petrie, who told about the young people's department of the Board of Home Missions, the helps they give so freely on the missionary topics, the mission-study classes they help to organize, the information they are quick to supply on demand.

Miss Petrie told of a recently organized New Jersey correspondence course in poultry-raising which has already enrolled 1,200 members. The mission boards of the church, charging no fees and dealing with the most important of all topics, should enroll correspondents by the scores of thousands.

Mr. Gelston's associate, Rev. William Ralph Hall, a former treasurer of the Michigan Union, told about the work of the Young People's department. They seek to organize societies in the third of Presbyterian churches that have no young people's organization except the Sunday schools. They labor to better the organization of the four-fifths of Presbyterian societies that are not well organized. "Some talk about churches that are 'organized to death,'" said Mr. Hall; "but I have yet to find a single church that has been organized to death, while I can easily find hundreds of churches that have been organized to life."

The Presbyterian rally was packed with practical points. Helpful circulars were distributed. Mr. Gelston threw himself and his big crowd heart and soul into the plans for the Efficiency Campaign. Presbyterians will be at the fore in this as in all other good works.

The rally closed with addresses by two distinguished leaders in the Presbyterian Church. The first was Dr. William H. Roberts, stated clerk of the General Assembly, its ex-moderator, and chairman of the executive committee of the Federal Council of Churches in America. He reviewed the splendid course of Presbyterianism in America, especially its strong stand for popular liberty and its many contributions to national welfare. Dr. Roberts paid a very earnest tribute to Christian Endeavor, and declared that day by day he is thankful for what it is doing for the country.

The closing word was by Dr. Darby, who spoke of "the youngest baby of the Board of Trustees" — home-mission work among the colored people of the various denominations in the South. A new department to further the formation of Christian Endeavor societies among colored churches has been established by the trustees, and a committee of Southern trustees

Hon. Chas. W. Fairbanks, Indianapolis, Ind.

Judge Ben. B. Lindsey, Denver, Col.

Hon. Champ Clark, Washington, D. C.

Rev. George B. Stewart, D.D., Auburn, N. Y.

Rev. Floyd W. Tomkins, S.T.D., Philadelphia, Pa.

Rev. Sam'l H. Woodrow, D.D., Washington, D. C.

Rev. T. D. Lewis, D.D., LL.D., Westminster, Md.

Rev. Russell H. Conwell, D.D., LL.D., Philadelphia

Rev. J. Wilbur Chapman, D.D., New York.

has been placed in charge of it. This will mean the increase of our fellowship by thousands of new societies.

The Church of England and Protestant Episcopal Rally.

This rally was held at St. James's Church, Rev. Floyd Tomkins, S.T.D., of Philadelphia, presiding. After hymn and prayers the chairman called upon Rev. Mr. Keiffer in the absence of the rector, Rev. Mr. Blatchford, who is in Europe, to give an address of welcome. The chairman responded, speaking of Mr. Blatchford's successful work at St. James's Church for fourteen years, The chairman also gave an extended address on Christian Endeavor in the Episcopal Church.

Rev. F. J. Horsefield, president of the Church of England Christian Endeavor Union, spoke of the work in England, with some two hundred societies and four bishops and patrons. Most interestingly Mr. Horsefield spoke of the spirit of Christian Endeavor as demanding knowledge of the Master, the mission, and the message, with a determination "to grow and glow and go."

The Rev. Archdeacon Richardson of London, Ont., spoke of the Young People's Union in Canada, which has all the elements of Christian Endeavor, with a pledge and committee, and expressed the hope that it might be affiliated with Christian Endeavor.

Rev. C. J. Palmer, of Massachusetts, spoke helpfully of the work. Mr. Palmer has attended every Convention for twenty-nine years and has been ardently interested from the first. He estimated that there are some twenty thousand Christian Endeavorers in the Episcopal Church, and told of a model society.

Adresses were also made by two Endeavorers from Texas.

It was altogether a most encoraging meeting, the best "rally" the denomination has ever had; and some seventy-five were present.

The Rally of the Reformed Church in the United States.

The dominant note of the enthusiastic rally of the Reformed Church in the United States was the unanimous expression of approval of the proposed action of the Missionary and Sunday-school Boards to establish a department of Young People's Work, and to elect a secretary to give his entire time to the work.

The representatives of societies from Indiana, Ohio, Pennsylvania, etc., present, pledged their support to the plan. Mr. H. E. Paisley, ex-president of the Philadelphia Christian Endeavor Union, conducted the round table on the subject. Mr. A. J. Shartle, a member of the Reformed Church, and business manager of the Publication Department of the United Society of Christian Endeavor, pointed out the work of the secretary. The other speakers, Dr. C. E. Schaeffer, general secretary of the Board of Home Missions, Prof. Paul Gerhard, Sendai, Japan, spoke on the mission-study class, and the presiding officer, Dr. Rufus W. Miller, gave their emphatic indorsement to the plan.

The Rally of the Reformed Church in America.

A representative company gathered in the First Presbyterian Church with Mr. H. A. Kinports as the presiding officer. Devotional exercises were conducted by Rev. Jasper S. Hogan of Jersey City, Then followed a brief introductory period. It was found that delegates were present from as far west as Orange City, while the eastern section of the church was largely represented.

The president of the General Synod, Rev. Dr. P. T. Pockman, stirred the delegates by his enthusiastic address on "Denominational Loyalty." The work of the several mission boards was presented by Mrs. R. H. Morris and Secretaries Demarest and Chamberlain. The practical side of the young people's work was covered in brief addresses by Miss May Osborne on "The Advantages of Mission Study" and by Mr. W. T. Demarest, on the "Use of Literature." Brief conferences followed.

Rev. Dr. A. DeW. Mason, the organizer of the Christian Endeavor Missionary League, was presented to the conference, and spoke briefly.

The closing address of the afternoon was given by Rev. Edward Dawson, pastor of the First Church of West Hoboken, on "The Price of Victory." It was a heart-searching address full of power.

A brief social hour followed. It was good to get together in this family reunion.

The Reformed Presbyterian Rally.

The Reformed Presbyterian rally was held in the Chelsea Presbyterian Church. The pastor, Rev. Dr. Rundall, led in prayer and took part in the discussion. The psalms were used exclusively in the service of praise and worship. The chairman, Rev. Samuel MacNaugher, spoke of two great tendencies in the Church of Christ, the tendency toward organic church union and the reactionary tendency toward sectarianism. On the whole, the friends of progress have great reason for encouragement.

Dr. T. P. Stevenson spoke on the subject, "Modern Advance in the Kingdom of God." This was a very hopeful message, as he reviewed the stages of progress and the present advance.

Rev. James S. McGaw spoke on "True National Patriotism." True and false patriotism were both clearly defined. He closed his remarks by appealing to us to enlist in the cause of Christ and country.

The meeting closed with a Christian Endeavor testimony meeting, with the call of the roll, and a period of social fellowship. It was a good meeting, and well worth while.

The Seventh-day Baptist Rally.

The Seventh-day Baptist rally was a delightful two hours to those present, notwithstanding the fact that some of those that were to address the rally were unable to attend the Convention.

After the opening service and introductory remarks by the leader, Rev. M. G. Stillman of West Virginia gave word-pictures of men and conditions thirty years ago, Mr. Lloyd R. Crandall of Rhode Island led up through the avenues of the Bible and philosophy to the presence of God, Rev. J. L. Skaggs of New Jersey went into the very heart of Christian Endeavor, the prayer meeting, and Rev. E. A. Witter of New York gave a vision of the grand service to which Christian Endeavorers are called.

Each speaker had been asked to bring the message that was in his heart. This they all did. The addresses were followed by a general discussion, in which several participated, and at the close a few minutes were spent in introductions and renewing acquaintances.

The United Brethren Rally.

The United Brethren rally, which was the most enthusiastic that has been held for a number of years, was attended by more than fifty delegates, representing States from Iowa eastward. Rev. H. F. Shupe, D.D., editor of *The Watchword*, presided. Miss Blanche Stauffer was elected secretary.

A message from Rev. W. L. Bunger, Christian Endeavor secretary of the United Brethren Church, was read by Rev. C. W. Winey. The message was a plea for increase and efficiency.

Reports of good work done in societies and local unions, with effective plans carried out and suggestions for future work, were presented by more than thirty persons. The spirit of fellowship was delightful, and confidence in Christian Endeavor unbounded.

The rally heartily adopted resolutions commending to United Brethren Endeavorers a campaign for evangelism, for efficiency, for great societies in college centres, and in favor of peace among nations.

The United Presbyterian Rally.

The rally of the United Presbyterians was distinguished by great enthusiasm and an eager desire to have the denominational society merged in the wider fellowship of Christian Endeavor. Under Rev. Huber Ferguson, Ohio's State President, the following resolution was unanimously adopted and forwarded to the Board of Trustees:

"The Christian Endeavorers of the United Presbyterian Church assembled in denominational rally at Atlantic City, July 10, 1911, taking into consideration the loss in Christian fellowship and in training for service that is sustained by many of the young people of our denomination, by reason of the fact that they organized in a denominational society and not in Christian Endeavor, earnestly petition your honorable body to extend to the young people of our church an invitation to join the wider fellowship of Christian Endeavor.

The Young People's Christian Union — which is the name of our denominational society — will meet in annual convention in Baltimore, August 3-8, 1911, which fact gives opportunity for the immediate presentation of an invitation.

"This petition is sent with the very earnest prayer that it may lead to the rich blessings in all of the societies of our church, that some of us have enjoyed."

The German Rally.

The German-American rally opened with an address of welcome by the pastor of the church, Rev. William Kliefken, after which Rev. Albert F. Hahn, president of the Atlantic District German Christian Endeavor Union, took charge.

After a short song service an address was given by A. Fismer, Ph.D., D.D., of Bloomfield, N. J., who skilfully defined the word "Endeavor," giving a noble Christian quality for each letter — Enthusiasm, Nobility (service), Devotedness (consecration) Energy, Ambition, Vigilance, Obedience, Reliability.

A selection entitled "Am Meeresstrand," written for the occasion by Rev. C. H. Albrecht, D.D., was then sung, and Dr. Clark asked the members to sing it again at the meeting on Monday night (which was done).

Dr. Clark gave a short address. He spoke with appreciation of the work of the Christian Endeavor both in Germany and in this country. He further said that the German Endeavor had especially contributed a deep and abiding spirituality and a great missionary zeal to the movement. The president, Rev. A. F. Hahn, and the field secretary responded to the address.

Rev. Friedrich Blecher, secretary of the German Christian Endeavor Union, spoke of the necessity of leading a wholly consecrated life.

The following resolution was passed:

"We German Christian Endeavorers in the United States of America and Germany, heartily recommend that the proposed peace treaty between the United States and Great Britain be also accepted by the German Empire, this resolution to be introduced to be accepted by the International Convention and to be sent both to President William Taft and Emperor William."

The Welsh Rally.

Endeavorers from ten States were present at the Welsh rally and enjoyed the splendid singing of Mr. John T. Richards and Mr. William Morgan of South Wales. Mr. Morgan was converted during the great Welsh revival under Evan Roberts.

Rev. F. T. Roberts, Scranton, Penn., spoke in both Welsh and English on "Youth and Religion." He said:

"There are many reasons why the youth of our country should be early seekers after God. The first is that God has given to youth special frequent and powerful injunctions to do this. 'Remember now thy Creator in the days of thy youth.' 'Those that seek me early shall find me.' God wants you to accept Him in the morning of life. To believe otherwise is to believe that God is willing that you should spend your life in dishonoring Him and His church until you are unfit for service."

The congregational singing, which was in Welsh and English, was rousing and enthusiastic. Dr. W. H. Roberts of Philadelphia was a speaker, and delivered a most helpful address.

The United Evangelical Denominational Rally.

At the rally of the United Evangelical Church a good representation from Nebraska, Iowa, Illinois, Ohio, Pennsylvania, and China was present. It was an enthusiastic company. Field Secretary D. A. Poling directed the service. Addresses were delivered by Rev. Mr. Evans of Nebraska, Mr. Munday of Chicago, Rev. Mr. Ramige of Iowa, Rev. Mr. Harpster, ex-president of the Ohio Union, Rev. Mr. Slagel, Bishop U. F. Swengel, Rev. L. C. Hunt of Pennsylvania, and Rev. W. I. Shambaugh, missionary on furlough from China. The educational and missionary interests of the church were discussed. The erection of mission buildings in Siangton, China, by the Keystone League of Christian Endeavor was enthusiastically indorsed. A new departure, the electing of a field secretary in the person of Rev. D. A. Poling, for Christian Endeavor and Sunday-school interests, was hailed with delight. A delightful social hour followed the literary exercises.

The Reformed Episcopal Rally.

The Reformed Episcopal rally was held in St. John's Church by the Sea, and was attended by numerous Endeavorers, especially from Philadelphia and neighboring cities and from Chicago.

Bishop Samuel Fallows presided, and Mr. H. Fleming of the Theological Seminary acted as secretary.

Rev. William Tracy, D.D., of Philadelphia, made the first address. He referred with great earnestness to the grand work of the Christian Endeavor Society among the young people of the Refomed Episcopal churches. He stated that nearly all the young men who have gone into the active ministry in recent years from the Theological Seminary had received their impetus and inspiration from Christian Endeavor. The members of the vestry of his church and the officers and teachers of the Sunday school have come from its ranks. This great Convention, he said, is simply the exhibition of the real work done in the societies at home — surrender of self, loyalty in service, and constant endeavor.

Rev. Augustus Burnett, D.D., emphasized forcibly the importance of the three notes sounded in the Convention. Mere creed, or a religion without close relation to Christ, is worth nothing. Religion is an inspiration. Religion is a programme for the present, not a life insurance for the future.

Bishop Fallows placed special stress upon the important place the Christian Endeavor movement has in the entire Reformed Episcopal Church. Although this church cannot compare with some of the great Christian organizations in the number of its societies or members, yet it recognizes its position as an integral portion of the one universal church to which Christian Endeavor belongs.

He declared that the individual Christian Endeavor society is the right arm of the rector in his parish work. He referred in particular to the great field of activity it opens to woman in social and religious life. He averred that the Christian Endeavor movement has given the world the true idea and exemplification of Christian unity, and that all plans and methods in the future for such unity must be based upon its imperishable principles — unity in diversity, supreme loyalty to Christ, and loyalty to the individual church built on Him.

Encouraging responses were made by members of the various societies present, and pledges of greater consecration to Christ and His church were given.

Among those in attendance was Rev. Frederick H. Neals, secretary of the China Inland Mission.

CHAPTER X.

INTERNATIONAL BROTHERHOOD AND GOOD CITIZENSHIP.

Auditorium Endeavor, Monday Evening, July 10.

The Twenty-fifth International Convention will go down to history on moving-picture films.

Christian Endeavor knocked out a certain class of pictures not long ago, and now, as a kind of compensation, the movement itself is being put on the screen!

Mr. Edison had desired to have pictures of the Convention taken, and Secretary Shaw's announcement of this fact at the Monday evening session in Auditorium Endeavor was received with enthusiasm. This will be the first Christian Endeavor convention ever transferred to and perpetuated upon moving-picture films.

After the inspiring choral singing led by Mr. Lincoln, the sweet and tender rendering of "The Homeland," by Mrs. Edna Cale, of Atlantic City, who is consecrating to the Master's service a voice of remarkable caliber, power, and winning vibrancy, awoke tender memories in many minds.

The Harrisburg chorus, led by Mr. E. O. Zarker, made a fine impression by its careful and tasteful rendering of the hymns it sung, always a proof of intelligent training.

When Dr. Clark stepped to the front, he held in his hand a sheaf of telegrams.

From Los Angeles came this message:

LOS ANGELES, CAL.

Los Angeles County executive send greetings to the Atlantic City Convention. We are overjoyed that the Convention of 1913 comes to Los Angeles. In plan, purpose, prayer, and results may it be the best yet. Leonard Merrill, Dr. John Willis Baer, and Rev. Hugh K. Walker join with us in this large vision.   R. E. SMALL, *President*.

Last year the Disciples of Christ added 2,000 new societies to their number. This denomination was holding its national convention at Portland, Or. It stands four-square for Christian Endeavor, and showed its interest in the Convention by sending the following telegram:

PORTLAND, OR.

The International Convention of Christian Churches greets and congratulates Christian Endeavor on thirty years of splendid achievement. We join hands with you for the study of the Word, the unity of all Christians, the abolition of the liquor traffic, universal peace, and the evangelization of the world. One is our Master, and all we are brethren.

GUY WITHERS.

Everybody knows that Germans are both poetical and musical; so no one was surprised to know that the German delegates had written a song in German and were prepared to sing it in their native tongue. Field Secretary Rottmann, who interpreted the song, called upon those of German descent in the audience to rise. What a crowd of splendid men and women sprang to their feet—perhaps a fourth of all present! Surely a remarkable showing!

The singers made a fine showing, too. Among them were Secretary and Mrs. Blecher, of the German Union, Secretary Rottmann, and Karl Lehmann.

At the German rally earlier in the day this resolution was passed:

The German-American Christian Endeavor members attending the Twenty-fifth International Christian Endeavor Convention at Atlantic City heartily recommended that the proposed peace treaty between the United States and Great Britain be accepted also by the German Empire.

Committee:

G. WIDMAN.
CARL ROHDE.
E. ENGELMAN.
A. ARCHINAL.

Dr. Clark is never more happy than when introducing a speaker; he was particularly felicitous in presenting Rev. F. J. Horsefield, president of the British Christian Endeavor Union. Mr. Horsefield is the first Church of England clergyman who has held this high office. Around his neck, according to the custom of British mayors, he wears a golden chain of office, for British Endeavorers think their president as important as any mayor. This chain grows by one link each year; a new link is added for each new president.

"Mr. Horsefield has been in this country before," said Dr. Clark. "In fact, he is said to be the only man that ever *brought down the house* in a Christian Endeavor Convention. While

THE CALIFORNIA HEADQUARTERS,

Brilliant with purple and yellow, and "boosting" Los Angeles for the next Convention.

Used by permission   ON THE BOARD WALK.

he was speaking at the Denver Convention a cyclone came up, and the great tent fell upon the audience. Nobody was hurt, and no one, after it was over, would have cared to miss the experience, although it put a sudden and effectual period to Mr. Horsefield's address."

Mr. Horsefield won the hearts of his audience by his opening words. "At one of our London conventions," he said, "many mottoes were hung upon the houses, and it is said that above a police station the men had erected a card with the word, 'Welcome.' One may doubt the warmth of the welcome given in that place, but there is no doubt about the generosity and the kindness of my welcome to your shores."

His theme was "Our International Brotherhood." (For address see chapter 17.) "Endeavorers have dreamed of the day," he said, "when war shall be no more. This is no Utopian idea, it is not the vain imagining of a visionary. It is something that we shall realize some day.

"A girl went into a druggist's shop and asked for five cents' worth of 'glory divine.' The druggist was amazed. 'Glory divine?' he asked; 'whom is it for?' 'It's for mother,' said the girl. 'My mother spreads it in bad places to make them sweet.' 'O, I see,' said the druggist. 'She wants *chloride of lime.*' Endeavorers have got a glimpse of glory divine, and they are seeking to spread it upon the bad places of the earth in order to make them sweet and beautiful."

Mr. Horsefield went on to speak of the cost and curse of war, bringing a strong message from British Endeavorers urging upon American Endeavorers the need of the establishment of a peace treaty between Great Britain and the United States. He expressed in their name gratitude and admiration for the magnificent lead that President Taft has taken in showing the way to realize this ideal.

Hon. Champ Clark, Speaker of the House of Representatives, had by that time entered the building.

"Never was there a convention," said Dr. Clark, "so honored as this one. We have had an address by the President of the United States. Now there comes to us one who is second in power in this country. To-morrow evening a former Vice-President of the United States will speak to us. We have never before had a speaker of the House of Representatives as our guest. He takes his pastor's place in the pulpit occasionally. He taught a Bible class of lawyers in his home city. We honor him, not only because of his high office, but because he is a Christian and a brother."

Champ Clark is slow in his movements, deliberate, cautious. But beware! It is only the heavy litheness of the lion. When he launches himself into his address (for that is just what he does), his wit flashes like a rapier. He is the kind of man one does not want to have as an opponent.

"I have never been ashamed" (for address see chapter 17), he began dryly, "or afraid to stand up and be counted with any crowd I belonged to, religiously or politically." It was said in a manner that defies description or reproduction; but it set the audience laughing. They recognized the first snort of the war-horse.

"I have only one objection to making a speech on this kind of occasion, and that is that half the papers in the United States to-morrow morning will declare that I have gone to preaching. Well, I have not, though a man could do worse than that. I believe about the only qualification I have for being a preacher is my personal appearance. Senator Tillman always calls me 'Bishop.' I was down in Pittsburg once, and a young Irishman standing on the corner said, 'Good morning, father.' Thackeray says that George IV. during the Napoleonic wars knighted so many officers and wore so many kinds of uniform that he finally came to believe that he fought battles himself. I have been so much in the company of preachers that I have come to feel myself as one them."

Champ Clark cannot help making jokes. He sees the funny side of things. But there is wisdom in his wit. His real text for the evening was a saying he attributed to Emerson: "We live in a new and exceptional age. America is another name for opportunity. Our history seems like a last effort of divine providence on behalf of the human race."

One strong point he made was that the civilization of a country is to be measured by the estimation in which its women are held. This led to a reminiscence of Professor Pickett, one of his old teachers, who was travelling in Europe many years ago. A Dutch princess said to him, "I am astonished at your politeness, since you live in a country where there is no queen." "In your country, your highness," replied the professor, "there is one queen, while in my country every woman is a queen."

He went on to trace some of the signs of progress in the nation, applying two universally accepted tests, increase in population and increase of wealth. This gave occasion for many interesting contrasts between the condition of things a century ago and the conditions to-day.

"This nation," he continued, "stands for an ideal, the ideal of representative government. When our fathers founded this republic there were only two other republics on the earth; now there are twenty-seven, *and we made them, we made them every one.* We did it, not by force of arms, but by the force of example. Mark Twain," he added, with evident purpose, "said, 'Blessed is the man that bloweth his own horn, lest it be not blown.' "

At the same time, horn-blowing or not, one could see that Champ Clark meant what he said. The influence of republicanism in the United States has been very great over all the world.

Nevertheless Champ Clark is not blind to the defects in our system. He even admitted that Great Britain has some things that are good. For example, the cabinet ministers are members of the House. That is good, because the other members have them at short range and can question them. "And they have no time to sit down for two weeks and study out a lie," he added with bitting sarcasm.

The entire address was a pæan of optimism. The world is growing better. If it is not, then the school system is a failure. Worse than that, the plan of redemption is a failure. But we know that this is not true. We are marching with our faces to the light.

CHAPTER XI.

THE BEST IN CHRISTIAN ENDEAVOR.

The Million-Dollar Pier, Tuesday Afternoon, July 11.

After a very inspiring opening service based on the Twenty-third Psalm, by Dr. C. A. Heilman, the Auditorium Endeavor meeting of Tuesday afternoon passed at once, under Dr. Clark's leadership, to answer the question, "What is the best thing that you have seen in Christian Endeavor?"

It was indeed what the programme called it — a "rapid-fire" meeting. The replies were made in most cases by the presidents of the State unions, though sometimes they sent representatives. The first half, alphabetically, spoke in Endeavor; the second half, in Williston. Here is the substance of these golden testimonies:

Alabama. Christian Endeavor sets the young people to work for Christ very early, and so saves an enormous amount of life. If in each case ten years is saved, how much it is when multiplied by four million Endeavorers!

California (A. W. Johnson). Three hundred and one children confessed Christ in California last year as the result of Junior Christian Endeavor work. During the year 1,248 young people accepted Christ as the result of Intermediate work. At the last State convention 100 accepted Christ.

Colorado (Secretary Jaeger). President Fisher telegraphed his message, that the best thing in Christian Endeavor is the efficient training of young people for larger church activities.

Connecticut. President Bidwell told of a union whose presidents had left to become ministers before their terms of office had expired, the chairman of the citizenship committee has been chosen to lead the Men and Religion movement in Connecticut, and another officer to lead the same movement in Baltimore. Thus Christian Endeavor is always giving of its best to other work.

Delaware. President Litsinger told how, after weeks of delightful work with his Juniors, he urged upon them the claims of Christ; and fourteen of them, between the ages of ten and fifteen, came to him, and with tears in their eyes knelt with their pastor and definitely accepted Christ.

District of Columbia. Since Secretary Lehmann's lively visit this union has graduated 65 Christian Endeavor specialists, and the Increase Campaign has kept them wide-awake for new plans.

Florida. Christian Endeavor has brought an awakening from religious apathy through prayer and Bible-reading.

Idaho sent a telegram to the Convention, and its two delegates rose and were greeted with applause.

Illinois. President Dyer told how the citizenship workers had agitated so successfully as to a minimum of Sunday post-office work in Chicago. Also he told how the Illinois House of Representatives had passed a bill legalizing sparring-matches; then the chairman of the citizenship committee stepped into the ring, and by letters and telegrams so worked upon the Senate that they killed that bill.

Indiana. Secretary Lanham told how the Increase Campaign in her State came to be such a glorious success — just because the societies went out and organized other societies.

Iowa. Mr. Hardcastle asserted that Iowa young people are as faithful to their pledge as the older Christians to their church covenant. One little society in Iowa Falls sent six members to the mission fields last year.

Kansas. President Smith rejoiced to see that Christian Endeavor is doing for the young people of the present generation just what it has been doing for the young people of the past thirty years—it is teaching them to do by doing. Kansas has enjoyed a wonderful revival in Christian Endeavor. Her goal in the Increase Campaign was 400, and she organized 477 new societies. The cause? Kansas Endeavorers had faith enough to get a field secretary, and he made good.

Kentucky. The best endeavor of this State is prison work—four societies, two colored and two white, in its two State prisons, and an aggregate of 600 members.

Maine. The best thing in Maine Endeavor is its vision of fellowship—among nations, denominations, and citizens. There is power enough in the prayers of our fellowship to retain Maine in the prohibition column.

Maryland. Its best is its fresh-air work, taking children from the slums and giving them a taste of the country.

Massachussetts. Its best is its summer Christian Endeavor institute at Sagamore Beach. More than once a delegate of one year has stayed home the next year in order to let some one else take a turn at the great privilege.

Michigan. Dr. Hubbell told of a Western postmaster who put up this notice: "The post-office has moved from where it was to where it is." That notice would always fit Christian Endeavor. Michigan has made its quota of societies in the Increase Campaign. It has just held its best convention, raised last year three times as much money as ever before, is sending two workers into the field. One convention delegate was a penitentiary prisoner, released on parole for that purpose.

Minnesota. President Brack told of one little society from which three missionaries have gone and two ministers, while two more young men are in training for the ministry. That society, living on an electric line with only two cars, chartered one of them and went forty-five strong to Minneapolis to hear Dr. Clark.

After one of Mr. Bacon's sweet songs we heard some rapid-fire replies to the question of the afternoon by representatives of other lands. Mrs. Hubbard, who with her husband established the first Christian Endeavor society in China, appeared in a lovely Chinese costume, and began with a greeting in the Chinese language. She showed the banner sent from Foochow as a greeting to our Convention.

Scotland spoke well in the person of D. N. Walker. "Please," he requested, "do not call us Britishers foreigners, for we are not." In Scotland, he said, prayers of from fifteen to thirty minutes used to be common in prayer meetings, and only the minister and a few of the older men would dare to take part. But Christian Endeavor is changing all that.

Rev. G. Fukuda, vice-president of the Japan Christian Endeavor Union, was received with especially hearty applause. He gave a finely thoughtful message in which he declared that "Christian Endeavor has no greater duty than to advocate peace and righteousness in international relations. Japanese Christian Endeavor holds two great ideas: world-peace, and the union of all Christians during this century."

Burmese Christian Endeavorers were represented by the Baptist missionary from that country, Rev. H. I. Marshall, who contrasted Christian Burma with Buddhist Burma, and especially pictured the stirring scenes at the Agra Convention as veritable foregleams of heaven.

That popular Chicago Endeavorer, Rev. George W. Wright, missionary to the Philippines, told how the Filipinos are becoming Americanized, and what great work Christian Endeavor has to do in furnishing in hundreds of places the beginnings from which churches will spring.

Mexico, represented by Mr. Loder of Chihuahua, told how a Mexican Endeavor society had paid the expenses of one of its number in attendance at a distant school; how he had come back, carried through a successful revival, and now was pastor of a native church in Guadalajara, the second city in Mexico. Mexican Endeavorers are seeking to evangelize their country, especially in this new political regime.

President Horsefield, of the British Christian Endeavor

Union, told of the marvellous permanent results of a young people's revival throughout England early this year; hundreds were brought to Christ. British societies are trained for evangelizing at home and abroad. A little society in Ireland had an "S. S. S. committee"—"Secret Soul-Saving committee," and scores have been brought to Christ by their work. "Endeavor does not mean a garden for growing faddists and idealists, but a society for training workers for Christ."

The close of this crowded session was the most crowded part of all, for it was led by Secretary Shaw, and was a season of splendid giving to the Headquarters Building. Gifts from five hundred dollars (by Dr. Sylvanus Stall) to one dollar were shouted from all parts of the house. It was as swift and as bewildering as the popping of corn over red-hot coals. The total of Endeavor and Williston Auditoriums was more than $8,000, and that is magnificent when we remember how many of the Endeavorers present at the Convention have given to this cause already, and more than once. How easily the Building might be erected if every Endeavorer would do only one-tenth as well as these leaders!

In Auditorium Williston the pastor of Williston Church, Rev. Jesse Hill, as presiding officer, called out those that took part in the rapid-fire replies, every one of which hit the target squarely.

For Missouri President Cree J. Henderson cited as the best thing he had seen in Christian Endeavor the Intermediate society. He spoke from experience with one such society organized about four years ago, about to be transformed into a Young People's society and to be replaced by another Intermediate society.

Nebraska's representative pointed to Christian Endeavor's power to develop Christian workers as illustrated, for instance, in the case of one young man awakened to an ambition to become an expert in Christian Endeavor.

President Collins of New Hampshire told the story of a mission organized by a Keene society about eighteen years ago, who have since sustained the work, which has resulted in many conversions.

New Jersey's president, Mr. John T. Sproull, was cordially welcomed as he spoke of the spirit of loyalty that he regards as Christian Endeavor's predominant feature.

Mr. Hill next introduced as one of the finest illustrations of loyalty Mr. John R. Clements, New York's vigorous and popular president, who announced as their watchword for the year to come, Organization. Two deeds worth while are societies among two groups of soldiers and societies in prospect among Indians and in the George Junior Republic

The roll of State presidents was at this point interrupted to make way for representatives from foreign lands. The first of these was Rev. Friedrich Blecher, Germany's indefatigable worker, for whom Dr. Bernard Clausen acted as interpreter. There were at first many suspicions of the Society in the Fatherland because it came from America. A man that had written an article telling why the movement was unnecessary in Germany was brought to the point of asking Mr. Blecher to write an article on it. In Mr. Blecher's judgment the best thing about Christian Endeavor is that young people dead to Christ are now alive in Him, that those that could not find their way to Jesus Christ have found their way, and are bringing others with them.

"Victory to the living Jesus" in one of India's tongues was a phrase that Rev. Herbert Anderson of India taught the audience to repeat after him as the key-note of his remarks.

He put as Christian Endeavor's outstanding characteristic personal devotion to Jesus Christ, illustrated by a little girl dying of consumption, who spent the last weeks in making lace to be sold to help build a church.

Japan's representative, Mr. Y. Baba, a theological student in America, spoke of the uniting of denominations in his land and of Christian Endeavor as standing for practice and training. In closing he asked the audience to join him in the Japanese form of cheering, saying, "Christian Endeavor banzai! America banzai! Japan banzai!"

Rev. David Ross of England mentioned as an example of the faithfulness to death that is a fruit of Christian Endeavor the devotion of the mother of Christian Endeavor in the district he represents. As she neared the end of life, she worked for the cause, and wished that greetings from her home should be carried to Atlantic City.

Rev. J. W. Ford from Jamaica declared that the best thing in Christian Endeavor is to be seen in the individual baptized with the Spirit of God and with the power of God working in him. Twelve Juniors invested each a penny, and as a result raised five dollars for missions. Excellent work has been done by an open-air band and a Sunday school organized by Endeavorers.

The responses were suspended for a time in order that the situation in regard to the Headquarters Building might be presented. After strong addresses by Rev. Daniel A. Poling and Mr. Karl Lehmann an opportunity was given to share in making up the sum needed to finish the undertaking. Nebraska led off with the splendid pledge of a thousand dollars, followed by Ohio and New York, each of which promised a like sum. Manitoba added five hundred dollars to what it had before

 Rev. Daniel A. Poling, Columbus, Ohio.

 Mr. Walter L. Jaeger, Colorado.

 Mr. Karl Lehmann, Boston, Mass.

 Rev. H. H. Rottmann, Wisconsin.

 Mr. John R. Clements, Binghamton, N. Y.

 Mr. W. I. Jones, Kansas.

 Mr. Paul C. Brown, Los Angeles, Cal.

 Mr. E. P. Gates, Chicago, Ill.

 Dr. Bernard Clausen, Binghamton, N. Y.

given. From Brooklyn came three hundred dollars; New Jersey followed with five hundred, Indiana with five hundred, Oregon with two hundred, Germany with fifty. In the mean time individual gifts of various sums had been pledged, and blank pledges had been circulated through the audience, filled out, and collected.

Rev. George H. Hubbard, a Christian Endeavor pioneer in China, exhibited what stood for some of the best things he had seen connected with it there. One was Mrs. Hubbard in Chinese costume; another was a banner first shown in the Nankin convention; another is the present progress represented by Mr. and Mrs. Strother engaged in extending the movement in the Celestial Empire. Mr. Hubbard showed coins given for the new building by one Chinese Endeavorer, representing a day's wages, and an elaborate banner sent for presentation at the Convention.

Rev. Huber Ferguson of Ohio spoke of being impressed with the training of a single Endeavor girl in Christian service, passing from indifference to a career of helpfulness as a teacher among the children of foreigners.

The unconscious development of members by doing little duties in the society was noted by Mr. Ray A. Worthington from Oklahoma.

President Baker of Oregon told an incident about a girl in the graduating class of a high school, who told her classmates that because she was an Endeavorer she could not join them in a ball they were planning. The result was that the ball was changed into a beautiful reception.

Power to attract and hold the young people in the service of Jesus Christ, giving them a joy that otherwise would never have been known, was the feature especially impressing Pennsylvania's president, Rev. William A. Jones, D.D.

Rev. W. W. Deckard, Rhode Island's president, spoke of the efficiency plan suggested by Dr. Clark, and the boys and girls transformed into efficient workers in the Master's cause.

South Carolina's spokesman compared the value of a literary training with the inestimably strong personal training won through service in a society.

Tennessee's representative touched on the training to witness for Christ in public to which pastors bear witness.

Miss Wilkinson, the field secretary of Texas, commented on three fruits of Endeavor, fellowship, training, and loyalty to Christ, or love, the greatest.

A delegate from Vermont observed that the best church-members in the State are Endeavorers, and they are doing good work in small places without pastors.

The Seattle spirit is proverbial, and one from that city finds in Christian Endeavor a religious spirit that keeps pace with the commercial, and is displayed in definite forms of service.

The diminishing if not destruction of denominational differences through Christian Endeavor influence had impressed the speaker for West Virginia.

Rev. Edgar T. Farrill, the president of Wisconsin, referred to the old stone face of the White Mountains as God's witness to America's business to turn out the finest manhood and womanhood, while a striking point about Christian Endeavor is its power to help realize God's idea of manhood and womanhood as seen in the face of Jesus Christ.

Manitoba's president, Mr. A. R. Walkey, claimed that as coming from a foreign country he was entitled to the eight minutes allowed foreigners instead of the minute and twenty seconds to which others were limited. Referring to the remarkable movement toward union among denominations in Canada, fostered by Christian Endeavor, he told of a society in one small town where four denominations unite harmoniously.

Quebec was represented by a lady, who told of the training given by the various forms of activity connected with a society that has worked through a mission-study class, visiting city missions, and holding open-air meetings.

Speaking for Ontario, Rev. Alexander Gilray, D.D., spoke of new life manifest there in the appreciation of Christian Endeavor's advantages and the enthusiasm with which new societies are organized.

A representative from Saskatchewan told of the large field for Christian Endeavor there, referring especially to the opportunities for missionary and temperance effort.

The two hours of testimony to Christian Endeavor's achievements were thus packed with an impressive array of varied and strong witness to its value and possibilities.

CHAPTER XII.

TRAINING IN INTERDENOMINATIONAL AND INTERNATIONAL FELLOWSHIP.

Auditorium Endeavor, Tuesday Evening, July 11.

Interdenominational and international fellowship was the general theme of Tuesday evening's meeting over which Bishop Samuel Fallows, D.D., presided. The devotional service was beautifully and ably conducted by Rev. W. T. Johnson, D.D., of Richmond Va., our colored Baptist trustee.

Although not on the programme for this meeting, Hon. Charles W. Fairbanks, ex-Vice-President of the United States, was the first speaker. Mr. Fairbanks, tall, deliberate in action, and thoughtful, is a powerful speaker. For years he has been an active and ardent supporter of Christian Endeavor, always ready to respond to any call for service, and willing to serve even at the cost of great personal sacrifice. The first words he uttered, after the ovation with which he was greeted had subsided, struck a sympathetic note:

"I am gratified to be with you this evening. It has become a second nature with me to attend Christian Endeavor conventions. I do it for my own good, and not for theirs. A Christian Endeavor convention is a good place to be in.

"Christian Endeavor is one of the greatest forces for good, not only in America, but to the uttermost parts of the earth. I know something of its work, and the more I know of what it stands for and what it accomplishes, the more I yield to it my admiration and encouragement.

"The problems of the future are not to be determined and settled in the halls of the legislature; they are to be settled in the churches of America. Our State laws will not be worth the paper on which they are written if they are not founded on the moral law that is inculcated in the churches of the country."

Mr. Fairbanks, as all who know him realize, is a man of strong convictions. He means what he says. Endeavorers were pleased to hear his strong commendation of Christian Endeavor.

"The great Christian Endeavor societies of America," he said, "are a powerfully wholesome influence in American life. It is gratifying to see this great order growing greater and greater in numbers, and performing better and better the work committed to its charge.

"I trust," he added, "that the numbers of Christian Endeavor societies will grow larger than they are at present. I believe that the past and present growth of the organization is prophetic of what is yet to be. Christian Endeavor is not an accident; it has come forth in response to a world-wide need."

Mr. Fairbanks went on to speak of the advance that is being made in moral life, and expressed his conviction as to the happy outcome of God's providential leading

A splendid, stirring young people's address was delivered by Rev. W. H. Roberts, D.D., the chairman of the executive committee of the Federal Council of Churches of Christ in America. His subject was "The Value of Federation." He emphasized the fact that Christians are getting together, and this is true of Christians in America more than in any other land. Denominational differences are vanishing.

Dr. Roberts sketched some of the great unities that are attracting Christians to each other. First, the unique and supreme place given by all Christians to Jesus Christ as Lord and God. Second, the activity of the church, visible and universal. Third, the common belief in one test of admission to the church, namely, faith in Christ. Fourth, a general recognition of the word of God as the rule of faith and practice. And, finally, the unity of the whole human race.

A fine paragraph closed this strong address:

"I long to say to all Endeavor societies, 'Get together!' I am here in the name of the Federal Council to call upon you to take the initial steps that shall make all young people's societies *one*. We wait for you. We want to go in your name to the denominations in this land, and say to them, 'Christian Endeavor asks us to beg that the young people of all denominations stand together in Christian work.' If this were done, the day will not be far distant when the world will be won for its Saviour and its King."

"The Necessity of Interdenominational and International Fellowship to World-wide Evangelization" was the theme of a forceful address by Rev. L. B. Wolf, D.D., general secretary of the board of foreign missions in the Evangelical Lutheran Church. In opening he recalled one great reason for division among men, the setting of themselves apart as nations with certain customs and methods of thought. These customs and this mental peculiarity have been transferred into church life, so that Scandinavians and Germans coming to this country bring with them their national prejudices, and try to perpetuate their church life as in the mother lands. Nevertheless, God is casting all these things into the melting-pot, and forcing us to change our national prejudices into international conceptions.

He spoke of the work on the foreign field and the need of its being pushed in faith, trusting in the power of the Holy Spirit. We cannot force upon the Orient our Western ideas even regarding church organization. The Christianity of the East must not be a dead copy of that of the West, but a living growth of Eastern thought illumined by the Spirit of God.

Rev. T. H. Lewis, D.D., president of Western Maryland College, who has made a special study of Christian union, gave an eloquent and powerful address on "Words of Jesus on the Union and His Disciples."

"Some people think," he began, "that Christian union is a fantastic dream, and that Christ's prayer 'that they all may be one' is a figure of speech." Dr. Lewis believes that Christ meant exactly what He said. "The divisions of Christendom," he cuttingly remarked, "are not only to be deplored with that piety that lets them alone; they are sins, which should be grappled with and overcome. The great difficulty in the way of Christian union is the indifference of Christian people."

Dr. Lewis is a master of felicitous phrase. For example, he said: "Jesus Christ is the supreme unifying force in the universe. In Him is no division at all. He is the sum of all systems, and in Him all things hold together. He is the peace of all strife, the eternal harmony of the universe."

With wonderful insight Dr. Lewis proceeded to analyze the sayings of Jesus regarding division and union. He started from this axiom, that nothing that Jesus ever said or did was intended to divide his disciples from one another, His reconciliation of the apparent contradiction between two sayings of the Master, "He that is not with me is against me," and "He that is not against us is for us," must have proved helpful to many. The saying is an illustration of the truth that there may be differences among *allies*; they may work for the same cause in different ways. The other saying illustrated the truth that there is antagonism among *enemies*. "He that is not with me is against me."

Then came the application. "The churches, alas! often fight their allies, and let their enemies go with nothing more serious than a resolution." Men feel insulted when they or their beliefs are attacked; but when the enemies of Christ smite Him on the cheek, these same men sit silent, indifferent, and invertebrate. "This is a damning sin against which I will never cease to cry out."

Another fine passage was his remarks on the beautiful text, "Other sheep I have, which are not in this fold; them also I must bring." The din of denominationalism prevents us from hearing the Shepherd's voice. Yet He has spoken: "I must bring." This is the divine predestination of the unity of His people. "I *must* bring."

Nothwithstanding the lateness of the hour Dr. Lewis held his audience to the very end, a tribute to his eloquence, but a still greater tribute to the interest people take in the union of all believers.

CHAPTER XIII

WILLISTON'S GREAT MEETING.

Tuesday Evening, July 11.

Not through all the Convention up to that point had we had such a pandemonium preceding a meeting as that which reigned in Auditorium Williston for nearly an hour on Tuesday evening. The Endeavorers had come long in advance, to make sure of seats, and they put in the time with the jolliest racket imaginable: yells of every variety, and most of them worth yelling, too; bursts of beautiful songs, rapidly caught up by the crowd; and then an indescribable medley out of which it would be quite impossible to pick anything intelligible.

After a characteristically bright song service led by Professor Foster, and a most impressive devotional service led by Archdeacon Richardson, Secretary Rottmann sung a lovely song just written on the Pier by the Christian Endeavor hymn-writer, John R. Clements. It was to the beloved old tune of "Silver Threads among the Gold," and was written for that tune at Mr. Rottmann's special request. Here are the fine words:

> Saviour, Thou alone canst keep
> These Thy frail and erring sheep;
> Sheltered in Thy fold of grace,
> Make for each a helpful place.

CHORUS.
> Jesus, precious Friend of mine,
> Keep me in this fold of Thine,
> Till life's latest sunset ray
> Points me to the land of day.

> Saviour, make my life to be
> Of some lasting worth to Thee.
> Never let my footsteps roam
> From the path that leadeth home.

> Saviour, hear my heartfelt prayer;
> Guard my life with loving care;
> Keep me from enticing sin;
> Make me pure, without, within.

The programme of the evening was a rich one, with three remarkable speakers. The first was Dr. Julian C. Caldwell, who took the late Bishop Arnett's place on the board of trustees.

With his superb voice, his ready wit, his fine choice of words, and his inspiring thought, he is indeed a magnificent illustration of the oratory of the colored race.

His theme was "The Open Door of Opportunity." (See Chapter 17.)

When Dr. Caldwell finished, he was given a salvo from the Florida delegation. Just then the audience rose *en masse* to receive former Vice-President Fairbanks. The well-known tall form was immediately recognized by all, and we began to sing "America," with the rhythmic waving of thousands of handkerchiefs. The happy Indianapolis delegation further signalized Mr. Fairbanks's entrance with their vigorous "yell," followed by the "Hoosier" yell, unique and pointed and evidently enjoyed by Mr. Fairbanks.

Next on the programme was a universal Christian Endeavor favorite, President Ira Landrith. "The Call for Fellowship in Service" was his subject. His key-note was the opening sentence: "It is not shouting our shibboleths that postpones the millenniums; it is rather our hateful disposition to swat in the mouth the other shouters." The address is so sensible, so pointed, and so carefully prepared (it was read from manuscript, and heard with no less interest because of this) that we print it entire, on another page of this report. (See Chapter 17.) Almost every sentence had applause for its period.

"There is an eminent statesman," said Dr. Clark, "who peculiarly endeared himself to Christian Endeavorers by going clear across the continent, when he was vice-president, to address our Seattle Convention. He was to address the World's Convention at Agra, India; and, when prevented from attending, he *telegraphed* fully a thousands words of the address he had intended to deliver."

The Endeavorers rose once more to receive the honored Christian statesman, who began his fine address by saying: "It is a fact very gratifying to me that I have attended a number of your Conventions. I am not to blame for it; I simply could not help it. I have got into the habit of accepting your invitations; my record is unbroken to-day; and I assure you it will not be safe to extend to me any invitations in the future unless it is intended that I shall accept. Christian Endeavor is not the expression of a moment. It came in response and it lives in response to a need as wide-reaching as the human heart; and for this reason it will continue a vital and energizing force for centuries and centuries to be."

This address also must be printed in full, and appears elsewhere in this report. (See Chapter 17.) Mr. Fairbanks was at his very best on that evening, and that best is wise and witty, eloquent and thoughtful. His speech was one of the chief de-

THE MINNESOTA DELEGATION.

GROUP OF IOWA DELEGATES.

lights of a Convention where oratory often touched a very high plane.

The reading of convention resolutions is usually a bore, but on this evening the presentation by Dr. Grose of an exceptionally long series of resolutions was really a climax of one of the finest sessions Christian Endeavor has ever enjoyed. Read those resolutions (in Chapter 19), and you will not doubt that the applause rose with every ringing sentence, and that enthusiasm mounted high long before the end was reached.

Still one more surprise — the Fisk Jubilee singers; and never did this famous quartette sing more sweetly. The Endeavorers hugely enjoyed them, and wanted to keep them singing half the night.

CHAPTER XIV.

CHRISTIAN ENDEAVOR IN CONFERENCE.

On the Million-Dollar Pier and in Many Churches.

No convention ever held has done more fruitful conference work than the great Oceanic Convention. Every morning about one dozen conferences were held, every one of them under the leadership of a Christian Endeavor specialist. Workers from all parts of the country had thus a unique opportunity of learning the best and most up-to-date plans for Christian Endeavor work along all lines, and of presenting their own difficulties. State officers' problems were discussed, and all kinds of committee plans were dealt with, so that the following pages are sure to suggest some fruitful idea in one line of work or another.

A new feature was the Consultation Hours conducted by Mr. John R. Clements, Dr. Clark, and Secretary Shaw. They proved exceedingly helpful to the workers present.

Christian Endeavor Methods.

A big churchful attended Secretary Lehmann's conference on Christian Endeavor methods, and many note-books were in evidence. The Endeavorers took part freely, as many as a score being on their feet at a time ready to tell about successful methods.

The leader warned against spasmodic ways of getting new members which leave the new recruits practically without after-help. Every contest should be followed by other methods for keeping up interest and preventing indifference or backsliding.

Here is one good plan suggested. A president has a president's aid committee which helps the president in his work. Another suggestion: that associate members should be put on committees. Any committee except the prayer-meeting committee may have associate workers.

Christian Endeavor Methods.

Mr. Walter D. Howell, circulation-manager of THE CHRISTIAN ENDEAVOR WORLD, introduced those who attended his conference on Christian Endeavor methods in the First Presbyterian Church by making them shake hands, Chinese fashion, with themselves. First, they were told to raise the right hand; then the left, clasping hands above the head; finally, shake. That broke the ice, and, for that part, loosened the tongue.

Many questions were asked and answered, such as how to lead young Endeavorers from the slip-reading stage to giving their own thoughts in their own words. Personal work in the shape of guidance and assistance given by older Endeavorers is the best way to overcome this difficulty. Beginners may be encouraged to read slips at first; then to write their thoughts at home, and read them in the meetings; finally to express their thoughts in their own words.

An interesting discussion was started on the question whether it is not better to dispense with printed topic-cards that give the name of leaders, so that more of the element of surprise may be introduced. The meeting seemed to think the old way best, leaving room for surprise by announcing special meetings.

Junior Christian Endeavor Methods.

The First Baptist Church was beautifully decorated with flags, Christian Endeavor monograms, and bunting; and here met the Junior methods conference, conducted by Mrs. Charles Hutchison, Junior field secretary for Ohio.

A show of hands made it clear that almost all the large number of women present were Junior workers, a fact as creditable to the women as it is discreditable to the men. Why is it that men are blind to the possibilites of Junior work?

The Pledge in Junior Christian Endeavor was the theme. The following suggestions were given on presenting the pledge: Recite the pledge in unison; sing the pledge at each session; repeat the Apostles' Creed, followed by the Junior pledge, showing the connection between the two; the pledge is to the society what the flag is to the nation; as we stand to salute the flag, so should we stand to repeat the pledge; give to each Junior a copy of the Daily Readings when they have memorized the pledge.

Regarding the matter of signing the pledge, do not urge this until both child and parent understand it, and both are willing to try to keep it. Present the pledge to the boy as a heroic act, and he will endeavor to keep it. The Juniors should be given Junior pins to remind them of their obligations.

The question of missions was discussed, after which the vital question of getting Junior superintendents came up. Three suggestions were made: first, let the Young People's society appoint them; second, have a Junior committee in the Young People's society for the purpose of training superintendents; third, interview the pastor, and secure his co-operation.

Junior Christian Endeavor Methods.

A conference on Junior methods was held in two sections presided over by Miss Lillian E. Hayes, of Indiana, and Miss May Hice, of New Jersey. The subjects discussed were how to organize, how to conduct a society, and when to hold Junior meetings, while Miss Hice dealt with the boy problem.

Miss Edna Kelley spoke on Junior graduation exercises, and Miss Hayes dealt with the Junior pledge, when and how to use it.

Miss Margaret Koch of Maine said: "There are two points to make known to children with whom we work: their bodies and their wills. These are the tools with which, for the most part, we labor. If you build a house, you naturally employ the best carpenter you can find, and he must have sharp tools to work with. So we must understand our methods, know what we are trying to do, and how to accomplish our ends."

This talk was followed by a demonstration, Miss Koch putting the "Junior delegates" through a physical-culture drill.

Intermediate Christian Endeavor Methods.

The Intermediate methods conference, which was led by Mr. Tom Hannay, Jr., assistant evangelistic superintendent of California, was prefaced by a talk on physical culture by Miss Margaret Koch, of Maine.

Miss Koch knows how to put an audience at its ease and make people do things. She urged the physical side of pleasantness, and soon had her hearers rubbing their faces upward, instead of downward, in order to rub out the lines of depression and grouch. She showed them how to breathe properly, how to shake hands and put "soul" into the act, how to carry the body properly, how to place the voice in speaking — in the fore part of the mouth; how to give the lazy muscles of the lips helpful work to do, and so on.

Mr. Hannay, following, told about Intermediate work in California, especially among high-school boys and girls. He emphasized the fact that Christian Endeavor lays great weight on the spiritual side of boys' and girls' natures, and urged the elimination of silly things, especially from socials. Every social should be carried on so that it may be closed with a prayer meeting.

Answering rapid-fire questions, he said that in his State Intermediate work is done largely through the pastors, whose interest was first enlisted. No need to wait for numbers; five boys are enough to begin a society. The superintendent or leader should keep very much in the background. Intermediates are not Juniors: they may be guided, but not driven.

Call the superintendent an "adviser." Don't imitate the Young People's society; let the Intermediates imitate.

Christian Endeavor Union Methods.

The German Presbyterian Church was the rallying-point for about one hundred workers, where a rapid-fire union workers' conference was conducted by Mr. A. J. Shartle, publication manager of the United Society.

The subjects under discussion were organization, statistics, work. Many excellent and practical methods were jotted down by the delegates. One country union, for example, organized a pastor's aid committee whose duties were to keep in touch with pastors and help them in their clerical work, manifolding circulars, and such matters. This committee has won pastors over to Christian Endeavor.

This conference was alive, delegates from nearly every State in the Union being present, many of them taking part.

Christian Endeavor Union Meetings.

"The Kind to Have" and "How to Advertise" were the two heads under which the conference on union meetings, conducted by Rev. D. A. Poling, Ohio's field secretary, were discussed. The church was crowded, and the participation of the delegates was ready and vigorous.

There was general agreement on the position that the inspirational mass-meeting and the executive business meeting must not be combined. Most unions hold business meetings monthly and mass-meetings quarterly. These meetings should be Christian Endeavor meetings distinctively so, and not merely rallies that have nothing to mark them as Christian Endeavor.

Four methods of advertising were suggested. First, personal visitation of societies with a loving invitation and appeal, preferably made by a member of another society. Second, the newspapers. Third, the printed letter, made as personal as possible. Fourth, the display poster, "the eye-catcher," well adapted to arouse curiosity. Union officers should make the acquaintance of editors and reporters and thus pave the way for publicity.

Evangelistic Endeavor.

Evangelistic Endeavor was the theme of Secretary Rottmann's conference. Mr. Rottmann is an adept at making an audience sing without books, in itself an important lesson in evangelistic methods.

Instances were given of the power of prayer in the conversion of practical business men as well as of sin-burdened, fallen women.

Philadelphia Union and Cleveland, O., are organizing personal workers' classes. One delegate reported fifteen societies that are training workers.

The topically marked New Testament, which is sold by the United Society, is a great help in this work.

Christian Endeavorers, because of interdenominational connections, are able to unite churches in city or country in simultaneous evangelistic campaigns, a form of work heartily recommended.

Evangelistic Endeavor.

Some of the points brought out at Mr. Paul Brown's conference on "Evangelistic Endeavor" were: Christian Endeavor was first organized for young people of high-school age, and even to-day is best adapted for those who are passing through the adolescent period. It should, therefore, make a strong bid to reach high-school students through Intermediate societies. It takes a student to win a student; boys work best with boys, and girls with girls.

Christian Endeavor high-school students should form prayer circles and conduct quiet campaigns for winning their associates. Sydney A. Clark, of Dartmouth College, gave a splendid talk on college evangelism, telling of fine work done by college evangelistic teams, who are introducing sound, practical methods in many preparatory schools. Mr. Clark related some of his experiences as a member of a team of six from Dartmouth.

Missionary Endeavor.

The growing interest of Endeavorers in missionary work ensured an audience at the missionary conference led by Mr. E. P. Gates, Illinois field secretary.

Suggestions rained thick and fast. First, the committee should be organized, each member having a definite task to perform under the leadership of an enthusiast.

After organization the important matter is education. A mission-study class for the committee members only may be arranged. If people won't read missionary books, boil a pamphlet or book down to a few sentences, and get them to read that.

Then, interest the members through missionary reading-contests, prayer-circles, study-classes, and so on. The meetings may be advertised by mail, and a "follow-up" system should be employed. Plan to reach the non-interested more than the interested. Get the members to do definite home-mission work, and thus produce larger interest in foreign mission.

Missionary Endeavor.

About one hundred and fifty gathered in the missionary conference, which was in charge of Miss Emma Ostrom Nichols, president of the Massachusetts Union, an ideal and thoroughly practical leader.

Thought was directed to mission-study classes, in which knowledge dispels indifference. The limited class was insisted upon, not larger than six or eight members. Leaders of classes should first of all send their names to their denominational boards, in order to be put on the mailing-list, and thus get notices of missionary helps regularly.

Talk about missionary literature followed the discussion of classes. One union gives as an attendance prize at rallies a missionary library instead of a banner. To the person least interested give the most interesting and the *smallest* book.

Work with immigrants was the next theme. The fundamental task that many a society may undertake is to teach English to immigrants.

Finally missionary living was discussed, and tithing was recommended as the way that always keeps the missionary envelope full.

Sunday-school Endeavor.

A new feature of the Atlantic City Convention was three conferences on the relation of the Sunday-school to Christian Endeavor, conducted by Rev. C. H. Hubbell, secretary of the Board of Young People's Work of the Methodist Protestant Church.

The first conference discussed how Christian Endeavor may help the Sunday-school. Have a live Sunday-school committee. Pray for the school; come ahead of time, with a liberal offering and a "predigested" lesson. Be a "minute-man" for the superintendent. Help on special days, Easter, Rally Day, etc., make a canvass for new scholars. Provide substitute teachers. Follow up absentees.

Praise the superintendent and teacher. Did you ever say, "Thank you" to your teacher?

Bring flowers to the school and distribute them to the sick.

The second conference discussed how the Sunday-school may help the Christian Endeavor society. The superintendent can announce the meetings *heartily*. You can announce a meeting so as practically to annihilate it, if you want to. The superintendent and teachers may join the society. "Boost and Belong" is a worthy slogan. Teachers may secure new members by personal work. Canvass the whole school for prospective members. Use the Junior society as a special chorus in the school.

Repeat in the society meetings the best things brought out in the lesson. Publicly recognize the work of the society in the Sunday-school.

The closing conference discussed the co-operation of the Sunday-school and Christian Endeavor society for greater efficiency. The discussion centred about five A's: *Atmosphere* — Let it be hopeful, reverent, cheerful, helpful. *Ammunition* — A Bible-filled head and heart, lesson and topic prayerfully studied. Best helps procured and used. *Aim* — Prompt participation. A definite end for each meeting. Better Bible knowledge. Missionary instruction and giving. Evangelism, immediate decision for Christ. *Application* — Practise what you preach. Temperance. Missions. Enlargements of the school and society. Church membership. *Advocate* — We can carry it all out if we remember our divine Advocate.

The Sunday-school stands for impression, Christian Endeavor for expression. In the school the boy *soaks in* the Bible; for the society he *sweats it out*. We need both. Not competition but co-operation is the proper programme. The conferences were largely attended. A canvass showed that pratically every Endeavorer present was an active Sunday-school worker.

In a word, the conferences were snappy, substantial, stimulating, sunshiny, spiritual, successful.

Floating Christian Endeavor.

At the Floating Christian Endeavor conference, Rev. R. E. Steele, president of the North Carolina union, the leader, put emphasis upon the fact that Floating Endeavor and prison work provide the two greatest opportunities for Christian Endeavor.

On shipboard, where denominations are impracticable, Christian Endeavor meets the need and harmonizes all. The pledge supplies the basic principles of the Christian life, and therefore identifies, unifies, and segregates the Christians among the crew. Prison work is reformatory; Floating work is conservative. In this task, every society and denomination may have a part.

Inland societies can help by providing supplies, reading-matter, comfort-bags, and so forth; and they can correspond with Floating societies and with individual sailors.

The time seems to have come for men to give their whole time to this work. It opens up splendid missionary possibilities.

Rev. W. H. McMillan, D.D., Pittsburgh, Pa.

Rev. W. J. Darby, D.D. Evansville, Ind.

Rev. L. B. Wolf, D.D. Baltimore, Md.

Rev. W. T. Johnson, D.D. Richmond, Va.

Bishop Alexander Walters New York.

Rev. Julian C. Caldwell, D.D., Nashville, Tenn.

Mr. John T. Sproul, Arlington, N. J.

Prof. Percy Foster, Washington, D. C.

Rev. J. Spencer Voorhees, Massachusetts.

Clean and Strong.

The Y. M. C. A. gymnasium was well filled by "men only" to hear the famous author, Rev. Sylvanus Stall, D.D., on personal purity. In free and easy style the men took off their coats to listen in greater coolness.

A show of hands proved that only half a dozen of those present had been told by their parents in boyhood the facts about the origin of life, or had been warned regarding the results of evil habits. This all-too-common state of things formed the text of Dr. Stall's address, in which he outlined ways of teaching boys the facts about the mysteries of sex.

At the close the speaker answered a number of vital questions on the theme.

Temperance Conference.

The temperance conference conducted by Mr. H. H. Spooner, temperance superintendent of the Connecticut union, brought out the following points: Always have a temperance committee; put the care of temperance meetings upon this committee's shoulders; get up-to-date facts before the society; secure pledge-signers; petition town, city, State, and national authorities for good legislation and against bad; be alert on law-enforcement; educate young and old on this subject; fight your enemies, not your friends; use tact in prosecuting the cause; be definite in statement and conservative in claims; keep sweet, keep hopeful, and keep going.

Conference on the Boy Problem.

The hall was packed when Judge Ben B. Lindsey, who was introduced by his friend, Secretary Lehmann, opened his conference on "The Boy, and How to Handle Him."

Judge Lindsey is made up of nerves and backbone. He inspires; and this is doubtless the secret of his success with the boys.

He narrated some experiences with boys which first gave him a vision of what the boys might become, provided the conditions under which they live were changed. These revelations of the hearts of boys were touching in the extreme. Amused irony characterized the story of a boy who was dragged into court for stealing boards and boxes from a railroad, in order to build an elevated railroad in the alley in which he lived. This was the only case of stealing a railroad, said the judge, that he had ever seen in court.

He explained his probation system, which puts the boys on their honor. One lad, who had been hunted for two weeks by a posse, Judge Lindsey sent unguarded a journey of 250 miles to the penitentiary, with the injunction to run away and escape if he thought it was "square." The boy did not run away. Of 540 boys thus trusted only six ran away, and three of the six came back of their own accord.

The conference suggested many possibilities in work with boys.

Prison Christian Endeavor Work.

The conference on prison work, led by Rev. Edward A. Fredenhagen, Ph.D., national superintendent of the Society for the Friendless, was attended by a group of Endeavorers and a few others who are interested in the work. The informal nature of the conference made it perhaps more helpful than a larger meeting would have been. The subjects discussed were "Work in the Prisons," "Work for Discharged Prisoners," and "Prison Reform."

One of the speakers called attention to the intimate connection between cigarette-smoking and drinking and crime. The conscience of the church is not yet awake to the danger to the boys from this source.

Other points raised were the effect of the Christian work in prisons on convicts, many of whom are truly converted. In the East, it was pointed out, prison work is largely conducted on a humanitarian basis, Mrs. Booth, however, standing for the religious element. In the West the work is Christocentric.

Pastors should be interested in helping the criminal. Missionary addresses on this phase of evangelistic activity should be made in the churches at least once a year—not a large demand.

Presidents' Conference.

Bernard Clausen, M. D., New York's field secretary, presided over the largely attended presidents' conference.

Three classes of presidents were recognized: those that appreciate their positions, those that took office to accommodate, and those that took office without appreciating the position.

The president should always preside, and should always consult the pastor about any plan. He should preserve peace and harmony in the society.

The president should be assisted in all ways possible by the vice-president, who should consider himself an understudy for the presidency.

The president should realize that his service is for the Lord Jesus Christ, and should find his strength in Him.

Corresponding Secretaries' Conference.

An interested group of workers attended the conference for corresponding secretaries conducted by Miss Florence E. Lanham.

It was pointed out that the society must co-operate with the secretary, as a bored, listless expression while announcements are being made will dishearten the secretary. When there is occasion to give notice of a rally, or something similar at several successive meetings, it is well to enlist the services of the president, the pastor, and others, so as to secure variety and freshness.

It is a good plan to make the corresponding secretary a member of the information committee with a regular time for messages in the early part of the meeting.

Treasurers' Conference.

The treasurers' conference was led by Mr. A. R. Walkey. Much profit was gained from the discussion of ways to make the society's financial work a training for larger church-work. The points touched included the financing of the work of the local society, the county and the State, and of missionary undertakings together with the promotion of the Tenth Legion.

The system of pledged monthly offerings for missionary purposes was heartily approved, and a like system was recommended for the support of the State and county work. It was a general conviction that the adoption of tithing would make difficulties as to finances a thing of the past.

Lookout-Committee Conference

Miss Marion B. Crowell, field secretary for New Hampshire, was the able leader of the lookout-committee conference. It was pointed out that this committee is the gateway of the society; its aim is to secure and keep members.

To succeed, we should believe in Christian Endeavor and make others feel that our organization is worth joining. In looking for members, discover points of contact; make friends; improve every social opportunity; introduce variety into the prayer-meeting, that it may prove an inspiration for the whole week; look upon the Sunday school as a field of opportunity.

By means of a chart, Mr. F. F. Ballard, Birmingham, Ala., emphasized the fundamentals of the pledge; its appeal to young people; its reasonableness; its devotional spirit; and its call for definite Christian service.

Prayer-meeting-Committee Conference.

Members of prayer-meeting committees, and others interested, met in the Price A. M. E. Zion Church to consider their special work. Miss Tyler Wilkinson, field secretary of the Texas Union, was in charge of the conference.

She divided the theme into three parts: first, the preparation of the prayer-meeting committee; second, the part that the committee should take in the meetings; and third, the general or miscellaneous work done by the committee, the small duties that fall to its lot that are not embraced in its scheduled service.

Some suggestions: — Invite new and timid members to meet in a pre-prayer meeting, five minutes before the regular meeting, and there encourage them to take part in prayer. Have monthly committee meetings with all the leaders for that month. Discuss with them the topics, and prepare programmes. One society,. whose members are all engaged in Sabbath-school work holds committee meetings after the Sabbath-school services.

In the meetings, the committee members should fill up pauses, and should be able to take the leader's place, if necessary; they should keep a record of all who take part in the regular prayer-meeting. One society makes each of its committee members responsible for one meeting each month.

The committee may prepare programmes and topic cards, may make a list of all who ought to be members of the society, then divide the names among the committee members, and seek to win them for Christ.

Social-Committee Conference,

The seventy-five minutes of the social committees' conference, in charge of Rev. J. Spencer Voorhees, were packed with as many suggestions from half as many persons. It was recognized that the work of the committee is to develop such a spirit among the members as to enable them to win others. It was recommended that the names and addresses of all visitors can be secured in its guest-book.

The social committee can render service to the church by taking an interest in its social features and by furnishing entertainment for the older people. It may furnish social opportunities that will meet the wider needs of the community and enlist the interest and friendship of those outside the church until the unbelieving shall know that we are Christ's disciples by His spirit.

The "Other-Committees"-Conference.

The conference for information, music, calling, and pastor's aid committees had as leader Mr. Walter L. Jaeger of Colorado.

The following were some of the suggestions offered:

Give each member of the information committee some country for special study and report.

The music committee should always be on time so that a song service may be held as soon as it is time for the meeting to begin.

The calling committee should call on the sick, on strangers present at the last meeting, and from house to house; and the entire committee may call regularly weekly on those that may thus be brought into the society.

The pastor's aid committee may offer the pastor its services for any line of work, pay for the pastor's telephone, take care of notices for the Sunday services, and act as the pastor's private secretary.

How to Read the Bible with Expression.

"How to Read the Bible with Expression" was the theme of one of Miss Margaret Koch's conferences, and drew a large and interested audience.

Miss Koch emphasized the point that even those that have not the opportunity for the study of voice-culture may be able to read with expression if while reading they experience the truth of the portion read.

All Endeavorers have the chance of reading the Scriptures in public in the Christian Endeavor society, and possibly in the Sunday-school. Expression makes all the difference between success and failure in reading.

Miss Koch gave some demonstrations, after which the audience read with her 1 Cor. 13, the striking effect of which was equivalent to a sermon on love. The twenty-third Psalm, read in the same way, made a strong impression. This conference will help to call attention to possible beauties in reading the Bible aloud to which many have been blind.

State Presidents' Conference.

The conference of State presidents brought together a company of about fifty, Rev. Edgar T. Farrill of Wisconsin being the leader.

The matter of State papers was considered, and the plan that found most favor was that a kind of bulletin be sent through presidents of local unions to members of every society, the expense to be met not by subscriptions, but by including it in the State budget. The budget system was approved as the best general method for managing the finances.

The opinions favored biennial State conventions with an institute or rally at some attractive resort in the alternate years. Much attention should be given to the discussion of practical methods.

An important subject under consideration was the formation of a federation of State and Provincial union presidents and ex-presidents. Secretary Shaw spoke of the plan, and New Jersey's president, Mr. John T. Sproull, presented the draft of a constitution, which was discussed. The plan was adopted and the following officers were chosen, President, John T. Sproull; vice-president, A. W. Johnson, of California; secretary, T. N. Jayne, of Minnesota; treasurer, C. H. Stewart, ot Manitoba. The new organization is designed to add greatly to the efficiency of the work by promoting co-operation among the states.

State Secretaries' Conference.

Under the presidency of Tennessee's State secretary, Mr. A. S. Wilson, Jr., a goodly number of State secretaries—splendid workers, all of them—met to discuss their especial work. They talked about the best way to reach the individual societies, the best way to promote the efficiency campaign, the best method of keeping records, and other practical problems.

The "Four Hundred Club," whereby Illinois raised $2,000 to support a field secretary, was described. First each secretary in the State received a postal which read enigmatically, "Your Man Is Our Man." Later came a postal bearing only the words, "Watch for Card No. 3." No. 3 was a letter fully describing the plan of raising the money by the gift of five dollars a society.

The District of Columbia union works "flying wedges" of union officers, two or three of them at a time going out and visiting a society. The district sends out blanks calling for many facts from each society, and if these are not filled out the "flying wedge" gathers the statistics on the spot.

Vermont's 220 societies are expected to send in to the State secretary *monthly* reports of work done, and often the necessity of sending these reports stirs them to do something worth reporting. From these reports the State secretary makes out a message which is sent to all the societies and read at the consecration meetings for the month.

Field Secretaries' Conference.

The conference of Christian Endeavor field workers held Tuesday morning was conducted by the president of the International Field Workers' Union, Walter D. Howell. The largest number of field workers met on this occasion that ever were gathered at any time before in any one place. Many helpful ideas for progressive work in the field were voiced and passed along to the comrades in this devoted and splendidly capable band of Christian Endeavor specialists.

Dr. Clark praised highly the work of the secretaries during the two years past, and expressed his conviction that the future advance of the Christian Endeavor movement lies largely in the hands of the trained field workers. He earnestly urged all present to do all in their power to help to get field work done in every State and Province as soon as possible.

Mr. Charles G. Stewart of the Manitoba Christian Endeavor Union, already a generous supporter of the field work there, offered to contribute one-third of the sum necessary to employ a field secretary for any territory not now served by such a worker. This offer was enthusiastically received.

The officers of the Field Workers' Union elected for the new term are:

President, Karl Lehmann, Interstate Field Secretary.

Vice-President, Paul C. Brown, Field Secretary for California.

Secretary-Treasurer, Miss Florence Langham, Field Secretary for Indiana.

Editor Field Workers' Exchange, Walter D. Howell, of THE CHRISTIAN ENDEAVOR WORLD.

State Junior and Intermediate Superintendents' Conference.

This conference, which was led by Miss Lillian E. Hayes, secretary of the Junior and Intermediate National Union, was prefaced by a meeting of this union. One of its first acts was to vote ten dollars to the International Headquarters Building.

A summer school for training Junior workers was discussed, and a motto for the year was adopted: "Better Lives for Better Service."

The question of when and how to use banners was raised. It was suggested that banners and pennants be awarded to societies: first, making an increase of fifty per cent; second, having systematic study of missions; third, giving to missions; fourth, sending reports to the State superintendent; fifth, having a superintendent that uses Christian Endeavor helps.

State Treasurers' and Finance Committees' Conference.

The number of treasurers attending this conference, which was led by Mr. W. M. Ells, treasurer of New York State union, did not measure up to the importance of the subject.

The following are a few suggestions: A card follow-up system is recommended; be moderate in suggesting the amount desired from each society; be prompt in making appeals at the opening of the year; be prudent in the use of funds; adopt a budget at the beginning of the year, apportioning a fixed amount for the work of each department, and stick to your budget.

Urge the necessity for early payment of all pledges—the work must go on; funds may be secured by the use of a circular letter, a monthly paper, or personal appeal. New York has used a chart with 200 squares, each representing five dollars; this chart was hung in the convention hall, and the societies subscribed for one or more shares. Subscriptions may also be secured from others interested in the work. If these subscriptions can be secured annually, a very valuable source of income may be built up.

Conference of Quiet-Hour Workers.

The live leader of this conference was Mr. L. D. Gribben of Pittsburg, Penn. The conference emphasized the great need among young people of increased spirituality, a need which the Quiet Hour seeks to supply.

The prayer-meeting committee should make a list of the members of the society, and endeavor to enroll them as Comrades. Those who hesitate may be urged to observe the Quiet Hour daily for two weeks, as a trial.

Have a special meeting once each month for prayer and Scripture study; carry a pocket Testament all the time, and use it. A nurse told of taking loose-leaf texts to some of her patients. The secret of success is to plan well, and to work the plan well.

Conference of Tenth-Legion Workers.

From all parts of the country delegates came to the Tenth Legion conference, which was led by Mr. W. L. Amerman, of New York, who is the founder of the movement. The discussion dealt with the principles and the methods of giving a tenth part of one's income to the Lord.

"Never forget to use the tithe as a minimum," it was said. "Aim to develop Christian stewards who will spend as little as possible on themselves that they may devote the more to the Lord's work."

But "the tenth is no fit measure for giving by many a prosperous Christian; such persons should, indeed, tithe their incomes, but *living on the tenth*, and giving the nine-tenths to God. "Children, who have no problems of self-support to trouble them, easily reach a higher ratio than the tenth, many of them learning the beauty of giving at least the half.

THE FINE CANADIAN DELEGATION.

"To start a tithing campaign in a society devote a weekly meeting to this topic, with testimonies from those that have practised giving a tithe. Take a ballot as to the adoption of this standard.

"Such a ballot will reveal the practice of your members, and may induce some to decide." [The United society supplies these ballots at fifteen cents a hundred.]

It is well to follow each mission-study course with an extra session on the principles of giving.

The Esperanto Conference.

Among those that attended the Esperanto conference conducted by Rev. R. P. Anderson, associate editor of THE CHRISTIAN ENDEAVOR WORLD, was Rev. George H. Hubbard, of Foochow, China, the man who organized the first Christian Endeavor society in the Celestial Empire. He pointed out the difficulty of teaching Chinese the English language. In eight years they can be taught to speak poor English; in two years they can learn to speak good Esperanto. Educators in China are ready to introduce Esperanto into the schools if they can only be sure that Chinese can use it in their dealings with European nations. Mr. Hubbard is himself an Esperantist, and has issued a leaflet with Esperanto lessons in Chinese.

Mr. Anderson spoke of the growth of the international spirit, and showed the need of an international language to enable men of all nations to comprehend one another. He pointed out the great service an international language can render in travel, in commerce, in science, in literature and other fields. Esperanto was advocated because of the ease with which it may be learned. An outline of its achievements was given.

Mr. Lewis B. Lüders, a Christian Endeavor Esperantist from Philadelphia, gave a sample of Esperanto.

On the motion of the secretary of the New York Esperanto Association it was resolved to urge upon the House of Representatives at Washington the passage of House Resolution 220, which calls upon the national Board of Education to appoint a committee to examine the claims of Esperanto as an international medium of communication and to report to the House

Rev. Mr. Catlin of Blossburg, Penn., gave a sample blackboard lesson on Esperanto.

Consultation Hour.

An excellent and highly appreciated feature of the forenoon sessions was the Christian Endeavor consultation hour, conducted by Mr. John R. Clements, New York State president, Secretary Shaw, and Dr. Clark. Many workers took advantage of this opportunity of getting advice from an expert on their difficulties.

Here is a specimen question and reply: "At what age should Juniors graduate?" Mr. Clements in answering strongly urged the formation of an Intermediate society to receive them. If there are not enough boys and girls to form such a society, then raise the age of Junior graduation. If the Juniors will not stay, graduate them into the Young People's society, but see that older Endeavorers take special care of them, giving them work to do, and making them feel at home.

Dr. Clark himself led the consultation hour in the Temple on Monday morning. The hall was well filled and the audience was eager to ask questions and to tell experiences. It is seldom that a question is entirely new to the founder of Christian Endeavor, for all questions have been asked over and over again in many places during the thirty years of Christian Endeavor history; and Dr. Clark's long experience, and his knowledge of how societies and unions in many parts of the country have sought to solve the various problems, make him an ideal and a wise leader.

In connection with some questions he emphasized the pity that in many churches having many Juniors ready and willing to form a society no one can be found to superintend them.

What shall we do when the young people go home after the Christian Endeavor service, instead of staying to church? One pastor told of successfully running his society on Friday evenings, thus getting past the difficulty. Another society, that meets on Sunday evenings, resolved to keep this part of the pledge loyally, and attend the church services. The older members of this church prefer the back seats, so the society marches in a body into the front seats and fills them up The church-members no longer complain that the Endeavorers do not attend. They are too much in evidence for complaint to be entertained.

Open Meeting for Union Workers.

No one but Secretary Shaw could preside in the best way over this important meeting, which brought together scores of the bright young men and women who are at the head of our Christian Endeavor unions.

In his opening words Mr. Shaw emphasized the necessity, if the Efficiency Campaign is to be a success, that our unions shall take the lead and show the societies just what is to be done. They knew just what to do in an Increase Campaign, but they will not know what to do in an Efficiency Campaign unless they are directed.

In the second place, Mr. Shaw urged that the unions should spend less money on non-essentials, such as printed programmes, and more on advertising the meetings and getting those to attend that ought to have their inspiration. Mr. Shaw told of an influential denominational leader, who has held that Christian Endeavor was "played out." He came to Atlantic City by special invitation, and went away with his idea of Christian Endeavor completely revolutionized.

Secretary Lehmann called for the best plans to reach the individual societies.

Answers: Hold regular congresses, the officers and committee chairmen of the societies meeting to discuss Christian Endeavor problems. An extension committee of eight specialists along different Christian Endeavor lines meets with those interested, and holds group conferences, afterwards uniting in a general conference. Get at the society officers, and you will accomplish more, often, than if you meet the whole society. Send a committee to the society prayer meeting, let the committee analyze the meeting and then meet the prayer-meeting committee and tell it how it can better the meetings it has in charge. Get into the society executive-committee meetings, with the additional advantage that such meetings may thus be held where they are not ordinarily held.

What are the best kinds of union meetings?

Answers: Those that have snap. Meetings that show how. Meetings that are distinctively Christian Endeavor. Meetings that deal with some definite work of the union, such as the work for foreigners done in Scranton, Penn.,— work which in a single meeting led 32 Italians to join the church; or such an endeavor as the Indianapolis evangelistic committee and its personal workers' classes.

Suggestions for country unions: An interchange of leaders among the societies. Pack some society in hay-wagons (most Endeavorers will ride in hay-wagons when they won't ride in Pullmans) and come *en masse* into the prayer meeting of some other country society.

Should a local union do a work in a city, or interest the societies to do the work?

Answer: Get the societies to do the work, except that there are certain large endeavors, such as mission work or country-week work, that need the co-operation of all the societies.

The question of the pastors that do not believe in Christian Endeavor came up, as it always does.

Answers: Take them to live societies and show them the work in operation. Hold meetings in which the Endeavorers tell what Christian Endeavor has done for them. Help the pastors in their work. Don't "call the pastor down," but get him to help in the work. Get the whole society to attend the church prayer meetings and take part in them.

This session, which will mean so much for Christian Endeavor, closed with a very helpful consecration service conducted by our trustee, Bishop U. F. Swengel, D.D. With songs, and many prayers, and testimonies of devoted purpose, these union leaders filled twenty minutes as full of power as twenty minutes can well be filled. It was a deeply moving sight to see the splendid company raise their hands as they sung, "Consecrate me now to Thy service, Lord."

The last word was a prayer in German by Secretary Blecher of the German Union, followed by the singing of "Blest be the tie" and the doxology.

Open Meeting for Society Workers.

A great crowd of society workers met in the Temple on Wednesday morning, under the leadership of Dr. Grose, to exchange ideas on society work. No one came with a prepared speech, but many, as it proved, were ready to answer Dr. Grose's question. "What is your society doing?"

Everything went with a snap — no hesitation, no waiting. The house was packed, and a big crowd stood in the doorway,

One society reported holding two meetings, one in the week. Another did the same thing, but held the meetings one in the church, the other in a schoolhouse, showing the outreaching influence of Christian Endeavor.

The second Presbyterian society of Chicago holds two open-air meetings each week during the summer.

A Waterville, N. Y., society takes charge of the prayer meeting when the pastor is on his vacation.

One society prints on the topic-cards a full directory of its members' names and addresses. Another has a quarterly which prints announcements of socials, tells of work done, and sketches work projected. This is a strong spur to the committees, which are expected to tell each quarter what they have done and what they plan to do.

Dr. Grose is an ideal leader. The question, "How do you pay for it?" brought out the idea that a quarterly may be paid for from the general funds, or a single page of advertising may meet the expenses of a four-page sheet.

A Paterson, N. J., society collects clothing for the poor, and arranges Saturday-afternoon rambles to which non-members are invited.

A great many societies have charge of the Sunday-evening services, a fact which led Dr. Grose to suggest that the pastor in many of these instances may well be freed to go out and preach to those that have no preaching-service.

Another question by Dr. Grose, "How many societies furnish flowers for the pulpit which are later taken to the sick?" brought, on a show of hands, a forest of responses. It was demonstrated, further, that many of the workers try at the same time to get into personal touch with the sick.

We heard of societies that aid in Sunday-schools. A lady from North Carolina told of the Willard Industrial Institution for mountain boys, which has a fine Christian Endeavor society. Some of the boys who used to make whiskey have been transformed into temperance speakers.

Besides holding services in hospitals, many societies visit almshouses, homes for the aged, and institutes for the blind, singing and reading for the inmates, and making life a little less dreary.

A sewing-school, with a kindergarten for children, is conducted by one society, while another reported regular work done at a Boston Rescue Mission.

Christian Endeavor is an educational and citizen-making force. In a town of 6,000 inhabitants, where there are 1,500 foreigners, a society seeks to help these strangers to a better knowledge of English. A show of hands again proved that many societies undertake work of this kind.

A report by one society of union services of Christian Endeavor and the Epworth League brought out the fact that such combinations are fairly common. Dr Grose impressed upon delegates the possibilities of union meetings of societies, especially during the summer months.

Only one society reported holding meetings on the church lawn on Sunday evenings. This was a Baltimore society, showing that the method, which was successful, applies to large cities and not only to small cities or towns.

The advantages of systematic giving were illustrated by the experience of a Pennsylvania society which had been giving twenty-five dollars a year to missions. Adopting the weekly pledge system, the amount jumped the first year to one hundred and twenty-five dollars and the second year touched the two-hundred-dollar mark.

Another show of hands indicated that almost every society represented supports in whole or in part a missionary on the foreign field.

Beautiful work was done by one group of young people, that of sending to shut-ins weekly letters containing some of the best of Sunday's sermon-thoughts.

An institution for the blind in Philadelphia has about 1,500 pupils who during their eight years' course learn much in the Christian Endeavor society.

A different kind of work was done by a New Jersey society which took a religious census of the community. Every member of the society helped, cards being used to collect the information. Dr. Grose pointed out that this is a necessary work on which all the societies of a town or city might combine. It would help to make clear the kind of people that are in the community, and at once reveal how many of them are foreigners.

A Philadelphia down-town society, whose church is in a Roman Catholic district, finds a helpful work in holding Sunday-evening open-air services, which the pastor attends, and which have resulted in the conversion of both Jews and Catholics.

From the Christian church in Nashville, Tenn., a missionary went to the foreign field and died there. The society has established a memorial cot in a hospital in the country where the missionary died.

Finally, a Ridgewood, N. J., society filled a great need by placing a number of Bibles in the hotels of the city.

From the Temple the audience marched to the main auditorium, where Dr. Tomkins led a consecration service.

Those that were privileged to be present will long remember his heart-searching and helpful talk on the three words that he chose for his text, "My Dear Christ." Each of these words constituted a division of his subject. He laid great weight upon the importance of personal relations with Christ. We must be able to say, "The Lord is *my* shepherd."

"How many of you," he asked, "before you go to the Christian Endeavor meeting or the Sunday-school, bend your knees in your room and pray God to give you His blessing, in order that you may pass it on to others?" The personal possession of Christ counts for much in this world.

"It is not enough to know that we are Christ's; we must know that He is ours. 'My Christ.' Can we say it? Is He ours?"

Then came a few tender words about the word "dear," applied to God and the things of God. "I wonder," said Dr. Tomkins, "if we Protestants have the tremendous, whole-souled devotion to Christ that was common enough in the days, for instance, of Thomas à Kempis. We remember the saint that said that his soul could find no rest until it found rest in God. Have we this burning devotion which makes us go to church because we really cannot stay away?"

Then followed some words about "Christ." The speaker told the story of the origin of Charles Wesley's hymn, "Jesus, Lover of my soul"; told of the sparrow that, pursued by a hawk, sought refuge in the poet's bosom, and inspired the words that generations have sung and will continue to sing. "Write these words in your Bibles: 'My Dear Christ,' and try to make them the power of your life — Christ the Son of God dwelling in us, and we resting in Him."

CHAPTER XV.
THE FIELD SECRETARIES.

That magnificent band of field workers direct from the firing line of Christian Endeavor thrilled a large audience in Auditorium Endeavor on Wednesday afternoon. Flushed with victory and faces beaming, each one in turn presented glowing reports of work accomplished in their respective States during the campaign just closed. To make the point of contact with these dynamic forces was just what the vast audience desired, and in appreciation gave them tremendous applause. It was a field workers' session throughout.

Treasurer Lathrop, who presided, introduced Mr. Walter D. Howell, secretary of the Field Workers' Union, and Mr. Howell led a unique opening service made up entirely of field workers. Secretary Rottmann played the piano. Secretary Brown led the singing, and the words of the first song, "Somebody," were by John R. Clements, much of whose time is spent in the field. When "The King's Business" was sung, the field secretaries sturdily sung the chorus by themselves. Miss Koch, one of whose specialties is public Bible-reading, read the Scripture.

Every Saturday night about nine o'clock the field secretaries pray for one another, and they ask that other Endeavorers remember the field workers at this time. Such a prayer for his fellow workers was next offered by Mr. Howell.

California led off, as it should just now, in the splendid series of rapid-fire talks from the field secretaries, and Secretary Paul Brown divided the six minutes with Secretary Hannay of the Intermediates.

Mr. Brown declared that the success of the work in California grows from their insistence upon the surrender of all to Jesus Christ.

Mr. Hannay told how "the driftwood of the whole world" comes out to California, and the lamentably meagre Christian population have a fearful task to evangelize the State. Christian Endeavor has a wonderful home-mission work to do in California.

Secretary Jaeger spoke for Colorado and Arkansas, fields a thousand miles apart. Colorado fell short of its quota in the Increase Campaign because the thorough work of Mr.

Jaeger's predecessor, Karl Lehmann, left only two or three dozen possible churches that were without Christian Endeavor societies. In Arkansas Mr. Jaeger was asked several times whether there were any Christian Endeavor societies outside the State, so that much information had to be given; but nowhere in the country is there a State that is a more fruitful field for Christian Endeavor than Arkansas.

Illinois was discussed by Secretary Gates, whose Gatling-gun sentences met with continual applause. That State sent 200 delegates to Atlantic City. Their goal of 625 new societies in the Increase Campaign meant a gain of about fifty per cent. Five months ago Illinois had 100 of those 625 societies; now they have gained 630 of them!

Secretary Poling of Ohio reported 731 of the 760 societies assigned to his State to gain. He urged that if the Efficiency Campaign is to succeed, we must first set ourselves to the completion of the International Building project, which spells efficiency in Christian Endeavor throughout the world. Then, if these new plans are to succeed, new leaders must be developed; and Ohio has set up as its watchword "Leaders!"

Mrs. Hutchison, Ohio's Junior field secretary, told about the long-continued work for the children of the Buckeye State. Last year, however, she found a pastor who had never heard of a Junior Christian Endeavor society. There is work to be done still.

Treasurer Lathrop introduced Miss Lanham as "a little woman representing a very important State"—Indiana. As so large a part of our Endeavorers are girls, the woman field secretary has a large work to do. She must illustrate the womanly characteristics, and often must help wipe the dishes so that the woman of the house may go to church. Indiana has more than reached the 475 societies which was her goal in the Increase Campaign.

At this point "The King's Business" was sung by the District of Columbia chorus, using words written by Secretary Gates before he went to Illinois.

Feld Secretary Lehmann was hard put to it with only six minutes in which to give an idea of his work in thirty-two States during the past few years. He told of the whirlwind campaign in the District of Columbia, with its 57 services in 21 days; of Alabama, with its gain of 56 new societies in two years; of Nevada, just organized for the first time; of Nebraska, with its State convention of 52 delegates transformed into a convention of more than 600, with its debt of $200 changed into gifts of $1,900 to support a field secretary, and just now with a gift of $1,000 to the Headquarters Building.

Kansas spoke through its vigorous Secretary Jones. He

Mr. W. L. Ammerman,
New York.

Mr. William Phillips Hall.
New York.

Rev. Claude E. Hill,
Valparaiso, Ind.

Rev. H. A. Denton,
Troy, N. Y.

Miss Marion B. Crowell,
New Hampshire.

Rev. Willis L. Gelston,
Philadelphia, Pa.

Mr. Sidney A. Clark,
Dartmouth College.

Miss Tyler Wilkinson,
Texas.

Rev. H. I. Marshall,
Burma.

was once introduced thus: "This thing is an experiment; I refer to our field secretary." But when Secretary Jones took hold, only nine months ago, Kansas had but 53 of the 400 new societies assigned to it. Now it has 491 of them! A good idea carried out in Kansas is a corresponding secretary's five minutes in each society meeting, given up to a report from that important but too often negligent officer.

Miss Koch was introduced by Treasurer Lathrop as from a State peopled by Mainiacs. She spoke of "butter" Christians — those that say, "O, it ought to be done, but — ." She told of four young people actually in Christian work that got their inspiration in Maine's admirable Christian Endeavor summer school. Miss Koch's work reaches out into the regions of the lumber-camps, and is full of stirring events, some of which she described. Her closing words were a plea for the retention of the prohibition law which Maine has enjoyed for fifty years.

Secretary Clark of West Virginia was kept away by sickness, and at this point an earnest prayer for his recovery was made by Dr. James L. Hill.

Secretary Voorhees, when a Massachusetts pastor, had a church most thoroughly organized in Christian Endeavor, with all kinds of societies, from Senior to sub-Junior. He told how he had been encouraged by the good words for Christian Endeavor spoken at Atlantic City by so many distinguished men, from President Taft down. He expressed the thought that Christian Endeavor was brought into the world to save the church, bringing it back to the simplicity and courage of the gospel; and, through the church, to win the world for Christ in this generation.

The Old Granite State, said Miss Crowell, is the smallest State with a field secretary. She told how New Hampshire, small as it is, has organized 57 new societies in the past two years. The young people have the right spirit, but need to be told how to do things. "Why, I thought you were going to be an old lady," said one girl when she saw Miss Crowell on a Christian Endeavor trip; but she found out that wisdom does not always depend upon age. In another place it was necessary for the field secretary to help clean out the church preparatory to one of her own meetings.

After a verse of the field secretary's hymn, "I love to tell the story," New York spoke in the person of Dr. Bernard Clausen. He told how, from December 1, 1909, to July 1, 1911, he has travelled on Christian Endeavor errands 22,507 miles, has visited 130 conferences, 230 rallies, and 179 county conventions, and addressed 61,600 persons. Half of the collections at rallies addressed by the field secretary go to the county and half to pay the field secretary's traveling expenses, which have been paid from this source, and a little to spare.

Miss Wilkinson has an immense task to meet the Christian Endeavor problems of Texas, and she told of some of the Christian work needing to be done in that vast State, with thousands of new settlers pouring into it constantly. Christian Endeavor societies there are sure to represent many States and denominations, and our society affords the only common religious platform on which they can stand. She pleaded with the Endeavorers to train those that are going to Texas so well that they will be leaders of Christian work when they arrive in their new homes. Texas was asked to organize 145 new societies, and did organize 166.

After an appeal from Dr. Darby for aid in carrying on the proposed Christian Endeavor extension work among the colored people of the South, we heard Secretary Rottmann, the field secretary with the "little" field of Wisconsin, Minnesota, the Dakotas, and all of western Canada. He described the varying conditions in this great region. Minnesota and Manitoba have done better for the Headquarters Building than any other part of America.

Mr. S. A. Martin is to be Junior and Intermediate field secretary of Manitoba, thanks to the splendid generosity of Mr. Charles G. Steward, who assumes his support. He proved himself throughout the Convention to be a live wire for Christian Endeavor, and in a few vigorous words he told why he believes in Christian Endeavor for the boys and girls.

Finally, Mr. Shaw was properly introduced as "the greatest field secretary that Christian Endeavor has ever had." He told how he had met on the Board Walk two drunken fellows pushed in a wheel-chair and flaunting three Christian Endeavor flags. Mr. Shaw tried to buy the flags, but failed. Then he tried persuasion. "Would you like to have the organization to which you belong misrepresented here in Atlantic City?" No, they wouldn't. "Well, you are misrepresenting the organization to which I belong." "Whazh that org'zashun?" "It's Christian Endeavor, a religious society; and with those flags, if you don't look out, you are likely to be conducted into a prayer meeting." "Thazh so? I thought C. E. shtood for Civil Engineers!" They got rid of those flags speedily after that; but they were not far wrong, for Christian Endeavor is a society of civil engineers! But it is money that makes the wheels go round, and Mr. Shaw's urging was that the Endeavorers everywhere should give liberally to support the splendid work of the field secretaries and of Christian Endeavor everywhere, represented by the reports of the afternoon.

CHAPTER XVI.

TRAINING FOR MISSIONS.

Auditorium Williston.

The missionary element pervaded the whole Convention, but a unique session in Auditorium Williston was devoted to the topic "Training for Missions." The programme announced no names of speakers; but speakers, and strong ones, were not lacking to tell of their own experience in both the foreign and the home field.

First was Rev. W. H. S. Hascall, who went to Burma when twenty-one, and has also been a pastor in this land. In Bassein, Burma, the members of the Christian Endeavor society seek earnestly to win the Buddhist boys, who are first asked to repeat verses, then consent to become associate members, and finally express a wish to become Christians.

Mr. Ralph R. Stewart, a young man going to teach in the Gordon Mission College in India, spoke of being moved by the conviction that the mission field is the best place for a young man to invest his life.

Miss Johanna Louise Graf, from Mardin, Turkey, told how most of the Christian Endeavor boys, both active and associate, in her field give the tithe, and all the money that is given outright.

In response to Dr. Clark's suggestion, by a loud "Ay" the audience voted to send greetings to their brother and sister Endeavorers in Mardin.

Mr. W. I. Shambaugh, representing China, told of inspiration received at the conference of the International Missionary Union at Clifton Springs, N Y.. They wore badges bearing the initials I. M. U., but dropped the periods, and made them read, "I'm you"; and he wished that all might have the same spirit.

The first missionary to introduce Christian Endeavor into China, Rev. George H. Hubbard, brought a message from Mr. and Mrs. Strother, and displayed a banner sent to the Convention. He pointed out the significance of tiny mirrors along the edge of the banner. Confucius had seventy-two disciples, represented in the temples as reflecting his glory. So the Christian Endeavor followers of the Lord Jesus Christ must reflect His glory.

Dr. Clark had asked Mrs. Hubbard to sing in Chinese, but instead she read "Jesus loves me" in Chinese, and Mr. Hubbard sung it, asking the audience to join in the chorus, the first time a Christian Endeavor audience has sung in Chinese, Dr. Clark suggested.

Born a Catholic, his mother having wished to be a nun, his father having wished to be a priest, Rev. J. V. Kovar, introduced as once interpreting for Dr. Clark in Europe, now engaged as a missionary to Bohemians in Pennsylvania, testified that Christian Endeavor is the best means to win his people to Christ.

There is just one Ruthenian Christian Endeavor society; the people have never before been represented in a Convention. But Rev. Theodore Halenda told how he came to America in 1898 to make money, but was found by a Bohemian missionary, was led to Christ, and was moved to fit himself for work among his people in Pennsylvania.

"What is it you are going to do?" was the way in which Rev. Lapsley A. McAfee opened the service of intercession that followed. "For whom are you going to pray? Why are you going to pray for them? Do you believe you can move things in China right here? How many of you feel a real desire to do this? Now will a number of you stand, and let us have several prayers, one after another?" A succession of brief prayers filled the next few minutes, earnest and definite.

The echoes from mission fields were continued by Rev. George William Wright, formerly a Chicago Endeavorer, now at work in Manila. The old method in the Philippines "is this book closed," said he, holding up the Bible; "the method of our denominations, of course, is this book open."

Miss Ella M. Varian, of Vicksburg, Miss., where she is working among the colored people, said that her first inspiration to missionary work came through Christian Endeavor, and Miss Clotilde Pretlow, laboring in Cuba, characterized the society as their own right hand in their work.

Next came four representatives from Burma, Rev. H. I. Marshall, Rev. and Mrs. C. H. Heptonstall, and Miss N. Ma-Dwe Yaba, who told of the influence of Christian Endeavor on them personally and in their work. Miss Yaba told how she used to be put to shame because she could not take part in meetings and lead them. She was asked to do so, and resigned from the society. She felt that she needed training, and this led her to America. She then taught the audience to sing "Jesus loves me" in her own Karen, as she has taught kindergarten scholars.

"I have loved Christian Endeavor, and shall continue to love it to the end of the days," said Rev. Herbert Anderson, formerly president of the India Union, "because among the most beautiful things it does it gives to every one a world-vision."

A fitting and impressive scene closed the session. Dr. Clark asked who among those present were planning to enter service in the mission field, home or foreign. The company that responded was swelled in response to the next request for those to stand that would say, "Here am I," if they should feel that they were needed in the missionary service. Then a prayer especially for those that had risen was offered by Rev. John Barstow, whose son is at work in Turkey. Then the feelings of all were further voiced in a prayer by Dr. Ashburn for those abroad, those going, and especially for Mr. and Mrs. Strother, secretaries for China.

As many of those that spoke bore witness to the influence of Christian Endeavor in leading them to the mission field, doubtless in future years not a few will have cause to look back to Wednesday afternoon's meeting as having been a powerful factor in bringing them to a like decision.

CHAPTER XVII.

A FEAST OF ADDRESSES.

This chapter embraces the majority of the addresses delivered during the Atlantic City Convention. It is a veritable feast of addresses through all of which run the golden threads of Christian Endeavor. We employed this method of compilation in order to save time for the reader in locating these helpful and inspiring addresses.

"There is an eminent statesman," said Dr. Clark, "who peculiarly endeared himself to Christian Endeavorers by going clear across the continent when he was Vice-President, to address our Seattle Convention. I refer to the Hon. Charles W. Fairbanks, former Vice-President of the United States, whom we all love, and who has come to address us on the subject, 'How Foreign Missions Promote Fellowship.'"

The Endeavorers rose to receive the honored Christian statesman, whose fine address follows.

It is a fact very gratifying to me that I have attended a number of your Conventions. I am not to blame for it; I simply could not help it. I have got into the habit of accepting your invitations; my record is unbroken to-day; and I assure you it will not be safe to extend to me any invitations in the future unless it is intended that I shall accept. Christian Endeavor is not the expression of a moment. It came in response and it lives in response to a need as wide-reaching as the human heart; and for this reason it will continue a vital and energizing force for centuries and centuries to be.

The wide-spread influence of Christian Endeavor is a subject for general congratulation. Christian Endeavor is one of the most efficient agencies of the church working in all the principal countries throughout the world. It is bringing people of different races and different religious denominations into closer and still closer fellowship.

Four years ago I had the honor and pleasure of delivering an address before your great Convention in the city of Seattle. Two years ago while on our journey around the world I received an invitation from Dr. Clark to deliver an address at the World's Convention of Christian Endeavor in the ancient city of Agra, India.

The exigencies of travel rendered it impossible for me to reach Agra until two days after the close of the great gathering in that city. The enormous tents in which the meetings were held were still there, as evidence that a vast Christian assembly had been drawn from all quarters of the globe. Americans were there, British were there, French and Germans were there: in short, each of the leading countries had made its contribution to one of the most significant conventions in recent years. In the course of my travels I met many who had attended it; all were agreed as to the wide-spread results which had flowed from it.

One of the chief effects was to impress upon the minds and hearts of all a realization of the tremendous power of Christianity in bringing all nationalities from the uttermost parts of the earth into co-operation with each other for the advancement of the Kingdom, and for the maintenance of peace among men. All who participated in that Convention returned to their homes with a quickened sense of responsibility to their fellow men and with the emphasized appreciation of Christianity as an energizing force in the lives of men and in the upbuilding of nations.

The bonds of fellowship among peoples whose blood is alien to each other were strengthened. The people of India, where superstition has so long prevailed, who have been bound to their idols through countless centuries, and who are wanting in the power of co-ordination for the common good, saw in the assembled hosts at Agra, under the banner of the cross, the manifestations of a power of ultimate redemption to millions in spiritual darkness.

We hear much in these latter times of the awakening in the Orient. There is also an awakening in the Occident. The Christians of America are coming to realize their responsibility to our own country and to those countries which are yet in darkness.

How Foreign Missions Promote Fellowship.

One of the most significant movements of the day is the wide-spread interest shown among the Christians of all denominations, in all quarters of America, in behalf of our foreign missions. There has been nothing like it since our first missionaries were sent out into heathen lands. There is much hope in it—not only for those who are the primary objects of the solicitude and effort of our own people, not alone because of the benefits which will accrue to millions in other lands, but because of the good which will come to our people as a result of their activity in work of such broad humanity. As we devote ourselves to others, as we tend to lift them up into new dignity and new life, we inevitably exalt ourselves; we strengthen our Christian fibre; we quicken our own sympathies; we give an added impulse to our energies in the cause of well-doing.

The foreign-missionary movement is awakening our churches to an appreciation of their larger duties and limitless opportunities, and they become in a very especial degree its beneficiaries; with an increasing sense of their responsibility and with an added realization of their duty will come deeper and broader consecration and increased purpose to meet them.

Missionaries from American Christian churches are among the foremost in the missionary field. They are to be found everywhere, devoting themselves to the betterment of others, to the advancement of their spiritual, intellectual, and moral welfare, with a zeal which challenges our admiration. They are carrying to the most distant parts of the earth the blessings of the Christian religion and the principles of American liberty in government, which are exerting a profound influence upon those in whose behalf they labor. They sacrifice the comforts of home and fellowship with their own countrymen in order that they may advance the welfare of people who are alien to them, and not infrequently they are the victims of the ignorance and superstition of those for whom they leave country and kindred. Many of our missionaries in years past suffered martyrdom; they placed all they had willingly upon the sacrificial altar of Christian service.

The missionary field is not so remote as it was a few years ago. The instruments of trade and commerce are bringing the peoples of the earth continually into closer contact with each other. There are no longer any unexplored regions; no longer any peoples who are unfamiliar to us; no longer any hermit kingdoms or nations existing in a state of complete isolation. The telegraph and printing-press, the railways and steamships, interchange intelligence and the commodities of the peoples of the earth. What is transpiring in one country is quickly known in every other.

One nation cannot, therefore, be indifferent to the welfare of other peoples—and it should not if it could. In some manner, through an overruling Providence in the affairs of mankind, nations have come to have more or less intimate relations with each other, and to be bound in a certain degree to the fortunes which attend each other. The discoveries of science, developments in the manifold arts, growth in political government, advancement in general in one country, have a very especial bearing upon the progress and welfare of mankind everywhere. There is no achievement in the realm of science and art, and trade and commerce, or in government, which does not concern the entire human family. It is to the interest of each nation that every other nation should be well ordered, devoted to the preservation of human liberty, the dissemination of those things which make most for the welfare of the human race.

It is a part of our Christian belief that we should have a care for those less fortunate than ourselves; that we should, to the best of our ability, light the pathway of those who are still in darkness.

Our missionaries are an honor to themselves and to our country. They carry with them wherever they go the Bible of our fathers and the flag of the republic. They carry to others knowledge of the Christian religion, and fill them with an appreciation of the strength and majesty of a great Christian people. While they do not concern themselves with the political affairs of others, yet as they awaken their minds to Christianity and the dignity of Christian manhood they fill them with a craving for a larger liberty and a natural participation in the government of their temporal affairs. The result wherever the missionaries have gone has been that absolutism has gradually yielded and constitutional government is coming more and more to take its place.

There is a profound and significant awakening in Japan and in what was until recently known as the empire of Korea. The Chinese dragon is languidly opening its eyes to new light. There is an awakening also in the vast empire of India. In short, in all countries where our missionaries have gone a change in immemorial conditions, customs, and superstitions is manifest.

Some may think progress is slow; but when we measure the advance to-day with that of a decade or two ago, we observe that the advance has indeed been rapid; and when we contemplate the comparatively small number of missionaries, and contrast them with the millions and tens of millions in whose behalf they labor, we are filled with amazement that they have accomplished so much, and with pride and gratitude that they should have virtually expatriated themselves and have responded so nobly to the Master's command.

Our missionaries are making friends for America—a consideration of no small moment when we contemplate the manifest destiny of the republic. Foreign missions tend to promote fellowship between our peoples where they are established. The fact is that the foreign-missionary movement promotes peace among the nations; it tends to establish good relations among them, which will greatly diminish the possibilities of war.

We hear much of peace and arbitration, and God grant that it may not be an idle dream! What is accomplished, and what is being accomplished, in the promotion of this world-wide desire is due to the influence of the great nations where Christianity prevails most; in short, the greatest Christian nations are those which are doing the most to usher in the time when reason and justice, and not brute force, shall be all-powerful in the adjustment of international disputes.

It is a happy circumstance that the United States is taking the lead in the matter of international arbitration, and that Christian Endeavor has accomplished so much toward this great end. President Taft has struck

THE VIGOROUS BAND FROM MAINE.
Including the fine representatives from the parent society in Williston Church, with their pastor, Rev. Jesse Hill, in the centre above the banner.

THE NEW HAMPSHIRE DELEGATION

the high note of our national purpose; and if he shall succeed in effecting conventions of arbitration between the United States and the leading powers of the world, as comprehensive as now proposed, he will win the foremost place among the friends of universal peace; it will be the crowning achievement of his public career, and rank him among the benefactors of the human race.

In his advocacy of peace he has but given voice to the teachings of the great Christian churches of America.

The United States may well lead in the movement for international arbitration, for no other nation will question her exalted motive. We do not stand for arbitration because of any question as to our material resources, or doubt as to the superb courage of our men. We are for it because it is fundamentally right, in line with Christian progress. It must be so, or Christian civilization is a failure.

Our missionaries are bringing people in foreign lands together; they are awakening in them a spirit of mutual interest and mutual helpfulness; they are teaching them co-operation in matters which concern the body politic; they are showing them their duty to each other, and how helpful service among themselves in a broad and generous spirit promotes the welfare of the entire community. Our churches, mission schools, Young Men's Christian Associations and Young Women's Christian Associations, hospitals, and other forms of missionary activity, are working a revolution in the habits and customs of many; they are bringing them into co-ordination with each other; and are filling them with an appreciation of their oneness and of the good which is to come to all who work in a common cause.

CHRISTIAN ENDEAVOR TRAINING FOR CHURCH-OFFICERS.
By REV. JESSE HILL, Pastor of Williston Church, Portland, Me.

Friday, Afternoon, July 7.

Christian people have been aptly divided into three classes, shirkers, jerkers, and workers. The marks of a worker are judgment, self-reliance, and initiative. Individuals of strong personality and singular forcefulness are educated for leadership by a natural and involuntary selection. Competent leadership, which can plan, adjust, and inspire the church and make it the rallying-point of those that love the Lord, is the most persistent need of the church.

The theme presupposes two things. First, that churches will furnish to qualified young people the opportunity of leadership. Church boards ought not to be close corporations and self-perpetuating. All society drill needs to be supplemented by laboratory practice. The development of leadership depends as much upon co-operation as upon theoretical instruction.

Second, that there is no panacea which is guaranteed to cure every church crippled for officers in thirty days or money refunded. Organizations do not change the nature of things or convert juniper-trees into kings of the forest. We must recognize the time element in constructive work. All plans fail when they are merely schemes. The best reports come from those that reach down to the foundations.

Training for officers begins in a definition of goodness. Goodness is efficiency. The energy that we once spent in keeping young people out of things we now spend in getting them into the best things. A person is wicked who is not a breeder of moral enthusiasm for doing good.

Christian Endeavor develops officers by magnifying the unrivalled sphere of activity in the church. There is more religion in the world to-day than ever before. This is the day of the social consciousness. Men want to help the world. But the church is often crippled because we have permitted our leaders to carry on the most fruitful religious work outside of religious organizations. The Christian Endeavor Society insists that the church is a vital necessity. It is coining a new phrase, "Back to the church." The church has a ministry which can be rendered to the world only through its channel.

The Endeavor society trains officers by insistence upon the concrete. The very training of the committee directs and equips these leaders with a definite conception of what it means to be a church-officer. The birth of the devotional frame of mind came to many a church-officer of today from his experience on the prayer-meeting committee. The present interest in missions, in systematic giving, and evangelism has received a great impetus from the committee work, which exalts these purposes. The history of Williston Church shows the result of the thirty years of Endeavor, where out of thirty-eight of the present time twenty-five came from the training received in the Young People's Society of Christian Endeavor.

The demand of the hour is for leaders of strength, intelligence, tact, and consecration. The hordes of organized evil and the unorganized forces of indifference are never to be feared if the young people capitalize themselves for their work. Spiritual dynamics are possible only when the divine impulse becomes fundamental in the lives of men. Moral leadership is the result of the new vision and close contact.

CHRISTIAN ENDEAVOR TRAINING MINISTERS.

By Rev. George B. Stewart, President of Auburn Theological Seminary, Auburn, N. Y.

Friday Afternoon, July 7.

Our present concern is not with what Christian Endeavor has thus far done in the work of training ministers so much as with what it may do in this direction under proper inspiration and guidance. Statistics would tell us, if we could get them, what has been accomplished thus far, but in the absence of statistics we may get our inspiration from certain general considerations.

1. There is need for ministers. They are indispensable. An army must have officers. Captains of industry are necessary to the vast industrial enterprises of this day. Religious leaders are needed to marshal and direct the great host of moral and religious workers.

This is an age of great lay activity. There never were so many and varied opportunities for religious service by laymen. This is the laymen's age. Within the last half of the preceding century arose the Young Men's Christian Association, the Young Women's Christian Association, the women's missionary societies, brotherhoods, Christian Endeavor, and numberless other lay agencies. By this same token the demand for competent leadership of this array of lay forces is vastly increased. The ministers are the natural leaders, and they are thus afforded superb opportunity for efficient service.

2. There is need for ministers trained for the present day. The old-style training of ministers was admirably adapted to produce the kind of ministers needed in former generations. But the ministers to-day face a situation distinctly different from that of former days, and they must have different training. Such a gathering as this was unheard of when I began my ministry less than a third of a century ago. This fact, which is but one of a multitude of similar facts, reveals the thoroughgoing character of the change in the church and in Christian service. The minister must know truth and life and how to fit truth to life. He must organize and direct the religious forces of the community. He must understand and utilize the forces that are socializing religion. He must by

disposition and training be qualified to lead the present and coming religious movements.

3. There is need for a spiritual ministry. It might be thought that we need ministers that can "do things." The emphasis is placed here by the trend of church life. But the great need is for men that hear the Lord, that have visions, that are prophets, that look through the seen things and behold the unseen. We must have men that know the value of the things of the Spirit, that crave for themselves and their people the fruit of the Spirit, that prefer to make men and women to receiving members into their church, that put being above doing, and attainment above getting. We need men that will say with Paul, "What things were gain to me, those I counted loss for Christ, yea doubtless, and I count all things but loss for the excellency of the knowledge of Christ Jesus, my Lord."

Christian Endeavor has open to it a fine field of service for the church in supplying this need. Here are three things our organization can do in this direction:

1. We can inspire young men with an ambition to serve.

The society catches them young, and deals with them in their formative years. It can impress upon them that it is their supreme duty to serve their fellow men.

2. We can train them to do things. Ours is a "doing" society. Here young men get a taste of church-work, and that too under the most favoring conditions. Naturally, they ought to want more, and they will, if the society does its duty by them.

3. We emphasize spiritual things. Our organization is pre-eminently a spiritual one. We aim to train young men to listen to the call of duty, to be faithful at any cost, to be ready for self-denial, to seek spiritual things above all others.

Our societies for these three reasons and for others ought to become the recruiting-stations for the ministry. Pastors should use their societies for this purpose. The officers and committees should consciously aim to make their society a training-school for the ministry. They should ask their pastors to present the claim of the ministry upon young men. The young men in the society should prayerfully consider the claim of the ministry upon them. Almost without their being aware, in the faithful performance of the work that the society gives them they will be drawn toward this exalted calling, and will get the first lessons in preparation for it.

ENDEAVOR TRAINING MISSIONARIES

By Rev. H. I. Marshall, Tharawadi, Burma.

Friday, Afternoon, July 7.

I sometimes wonder whether I am more of an Endeavor-trained missionary than an Endeavor-training missionary, but yet I am expected to speak to-day more about the latter phase of the topic, and so I shall try to present to you a few of the problems, as well as to show you something of the progress of Christian Endeavor in Burma.

1. We have the great inertia of the ignorance, the thraldom of the superstition, and the bigotry of the idolatry, of the people to overcome. They have been wrapped in the mantle of the darkness of paganism for generations. For example, they say to us that they know what we say about religion must be false because we also teach that the world is round when every one can really see that it is flat. The bondage to the evil spirits binds them from birth to death, and determines all the events of their lives. The animism of the hill tribes and the Buddhism of the Burmans alike are opposed to everything outside the narrow circle of their customs.

2. The material the missionary has to work with in building up a Christian church is like timber long subjected to being warped out of true, and can be brought to the line only by long-continued pressure. The stability of character that is the growth of generations is not yet theirs. Their sense of proportion does not yet lead them to distinguish between the temporary and the permanent. One pastor once wrote to Dr. Smith, president of our theological seminary, saying that he had searched the Bible through to find whether it mentioned anything about young people's societies, and since he could find no mention of them he felt sure they could not be right. I remember having a long conversation with a newly organized society, trying to convince them that it was not incumbent on them to conduct elaborate disciplining of members, as does a church.

3. The aim of the missionary in training Christian Endeavorers is to develop the converts into a strong self-supporting, self-propagating, indigenous Christian church; to train the young people of to-day to become the leaders of to-morrow.

4. We are thankful to say that results are in evidence. The Christian Endeavor societies bring together the young people of our Christian villages, and give them something to do. They learn to take part in meetings, to manage affairs, to do helpful things for others, and so become active Christians.

Our people are very fond of music. The young people love to get together and sing. Non-Christians come in to help form a choir. These choirs have sung the gospel where we could not preach it. I could tell of many instances where they have rendered the missionary or native evangelists great help.

Then, again, there is growing a responsibility for evangelistic work. Certain members are chosen each week in many of our societies to distribute tracts and to preach to heathen people with whom they come in contact. One pastor said that he found that the Endeavorers were doing more than he was, and so he had to bestir himself to greater activity.

The Tharawadi district union of Christian Endeavor supports five evangelists in heathen villages, and at least one church has been organized as a direct result of their work.

Buddhist kyaungs (monasteries) are bound to give way before the oncoming Christian hosts. I rejoice that the eight thousand Christian Endeavorers of Burma are having no small share in bringing about this transformation from darkness to light.

TRAINING WITNESSES.

By Rev. Alexander Gilray, D.D., Toronto, Canada.

Friday Afternoon, July 7.

For what service do these witnesses stand? "A true witness delivereth souls." If this, then, is their work, how all-important that the training should be thoroughly adequate!

First. We must begin at the very gateway into the kingdom of service. Jesus Christ has left no doubt as to the vital importance of this first step. "Verily, verily, I say unto thee, Except a man be born anew, he cannot see the kingdom of God." Every witness must know how these things can be, before he is ready to train.

Second. When he can say, "I know whom I have believed, and I know that my Redeemer liveth," he is prepared for the college of prayer, by means of which strength, wisdom, and courage are secured to those that would bear testimony before men for the glory of God. We read, "But they that wait upon the Lord shall renew their strength." What significance there is in this word "wait"! In its first setting it means to twist the hemp strands so that the cable rope is laid, with which tons and tons of material can be lifted to great heights. So the soul that bears or waits upon God becomes entwined with the divine, and goes forth in new might to mount aloft, to run swiftly, to do the business of the King, and to walk steadily and perseveringly when the road is rough and dark, and its end far out of sight.

During the great Welsh revival a minister preached with marvellous power. He was asked how he got such power. "My heart was heavy," he said, "for men. One evening I knelt there," pointing to a spot where the carpet was shabby, "and cried for power to preach as I had never preached before. Midnight came and the stars looked down on the sleeping valley and the silent hills; but the answer came not. So I prayed on until at length I saw a faint gray shoot up in the east. Presently it became silver, and I watched until the silver became purple and gold, and on and up on the mountain-crests blazed the altar-fires of a new day; and then the sermon came, and the power came, and I preached, and scores fell down before the fire of God. That is how I got that sermon."

If Dr. Clark had done nothing more than call the Christian Endeavor weekly prayer meeting and the Quiet Hour into existence, he would have conferred inestimable blessings upon millions of young lives and upon the church throughout the world.

Third. There must also be a vision. "Where there is no vision, the people perish." The first time we heard the honored founder of Christian Endeavor preach was when he was in retreat because of overwork. His theme was, "Seeing the invisible." Moses doubtless prayed much in the wilderness of Horeb, but it was only when he turned aside to see the great sight that he received his commission and delivered his people from their cruel bondage. It was after Isaiah saw the Lord "high and lifted up" that he said, "Here am I; send me." And what a mission he accomplished! When the apostle Paul had accomplished twenty-six years of unparalleled service and suffering, he declared that he had accomplished it because he had not been disobedient to the heavenly vision; he saw Jesus in the way.

It is told of Doré when crossing the Italian frontier on one occasion that he had mislaid his passport, and was called upon to prove his identity. This he did by taking a sheet of common paper and a piece of charcoal and drawing the homely, manly features of Victor Emmanuel. The officers at once knew that only Doré could draw like that. Challenged by the world, may we not let men see the nobler features of the face of our King? "By this shall all men know that ye are my disciples." Christian Endeavor teaches how all its members may "practise the presence of God." The first two disciples met with Jesus, and came forth, saying, "We have found the Messias."

Fourth. The next vital step in training witnesses is the daily reading and study of the word of God. No one can estimate the number of young people that have entered into the great circle of Bible-study instituted by Christian Endeavor. More than ten thousand members of Christian Endeavor read the Bible through in one year under the wise leadership of that ardent Bible-student, Professor Amos R. Wells; and vast numbers followed in succeeding years, that they might experience the meaning of that beautiful prayer, "Open Thou mine eyes, that I may behold wondrous things out of thy law."

Fifth. For this training of witnesses there is another part most essential. When our Saviour was training the twelve and the seventy, He not only taught them the laws of His kingdom, and wrought miracles before their eyes, but set them to work to heal and to preach and to cast out evil spirits, and this even whilst they were yet babes. Work, and plenty of it, is vital to the training for soul-winning, as it is to all departments of human life.

It is related that, when men are repeating the creed in one of the churches of the East, it was their custom at a certain point to draw out their swords, indicating that they were ready for action if need be. Thus the members of Christian Endeavor should be ready for service at once.

This year of deeply impressive and tender memories to our honored leader will be marked by memorial services held on September 12 at Aylmer and Ottawa. In these services there will be revealed a life heroic and beautiful. And, whilst prayer and faith distinguish that life, yet, when we read "My Mother's Journal," the outstanding feature is the greatness of the work that that mother organized in her sorrow and carried on to a successful issue. No Christian Endeavorer can read "My Mother's Journal," we venture to think, without a deeper feeling of gratitude to God for the son of such a mother, and a profound desire that all his fellow Endeavorers might have in their possession a copy of this memorial volume.

In this connection we are reminded that the word "witness" is also rendered "martyr." We are apt to confine this latter to those that seal their testimony by their blood, whereas every true witness is a martyr. Trial, persecution, or death does not make martyrs, but rather declares or reveals them as such.

Into this training of witnesses, therefore, there must enter

(1) Confession of Christ,
(2) Waiting continuously upon God,
(3) A vision of Jesus,
(4) Service; and
(5) There must ever be absolute dependence upon the presence and ministry of the Holy Spirit. "Not by might, nor by power, but by my spirit, saith the Lord."

SERVICE OF INTERCESSION.

By Rev. H. F. Shupe, Editor of *The Watchword*.

Our leader has given us as our new watchword, "Efficiency." Efficiency implies potency. Power comes from God; power comes in answer to prayer.

An aviator at the completion of a successful flight was congratulated. "It is a wonderful thing to conquer nature," said the friend. "We cannot conquer nature," replied the aviator; "we learn nature's laws, and conform to them." The divine law of power is prayer.

Our Lord spent the hours of a long night in prayer; the next day he selected the right men to carry on His work in the world. Prayer, prolonged prayer, brought Pentecost. Prayer, inspired by the Holy Spirit and interpreted by Him, will make Christian Endeavor potent.

Following these remarks a number of prayers were offered, and the assembly joined in the prayer, "Lord, send forth workers."

TRAINING FOR TEMPERANCE REFORM.

By Mr. H. H. Spooner, Secretary, Connecticut Temperance Union.

The beginning of training in this line of work must be on ourselves, for he who cannot govern his own spirit will never be able to go very far in leadership of others. Let us group this around three words:

The first is training to be *sweet*. We have had many Isaiahs, too many Jeremiahs, with their denunciations and lamentations; now we need workers, who by a sweet, sunny disposition will win those who cannot be coerced into an interest in these subjects.

With it let us be wholly and entirely sensible, taking to the tasks a willingness to admit that we do not know all that is known, and a very earnest desire to learn, and by the added knowledge to commend ourselves to others as using to the utmost that somewhat rare and always helpful virtue called "horse sense."

And then we must be *strong,* ready for any emergency, with eye and ear and arm trained to push the battle to the farthest possible point and hold every inch of gain against all comers.

With this equipment in our own hearts we shall take up work in lines of reform with a threefold motive running through it all.

We shall be *sincere,* not following a whim, not riding a hobby, but in deadly earnest, realizing that lives are at stake and longing with all our hearts to keep them from the evil.

With our sincerity will run an undertone, deep, strong, resonant, which will make us realize the meaning of our second word *stern,* and which will hold us true to our course, no matter how heavy the pressure of criticism or resistance may become.

We shall have but one ultimate goal in mind, one splendid vision, which will brighten every dark place, clear every obstacle, cheer every lonely hour, the vision of *saving.*

Of course our boys and girls must be brought to total abstinence. Of course the appetites already formed must be overcome, the poor, far-fallen rounder lifted up again, the woman in the lowest depths helped back to decency and hope. Of course "the saloon must go" and its foul presence never pollute another soul, but all of these are but steps toward the ultimate goal. Through all our training must run, if we are to do our best, that last, best, sweetest word, *salvation,* for young and old, clean and unclean; and he who trains to reach that ultimate goal is the one best fitted to lead in temperance reform.

The Christian Endeavor Society has unequalled opportunities for such training.

I speak from my own personal experience through a quarter-century of membership. The blessed old "iron-clad" pledge honestly taken and faithfully kept will open to any seeking soul the opportunities for service. These followed earnestly will furnish an equipment that will send the willing worker out to battle sweetly, sensibly, and strongly for the salvation of his fellow men.

CHRISTIAN ENDEAVOR TRAINING FOR LIVING.

By Rev. H. A. Denton, B.D., River Street Church of the Disciples of Christ, Troy, N. Y.

Living is a higher and further process than existing. Animals exist. Men may live. Not all of them, however, rise to this height of human possibility. This is the dividing line between the animal and the human. It is not the similarity or dissimilarity of bone and muscle and tendon that enables us to draw the line between ourselves and grandfather chimpanzee, but the difference between existing and living.

Living is the Difference Between Saint and Sinner.

Existing is to be borne on by the current of forces. It is to conform. Living is the turning of the current. Its aim is change. Transformation is its great word. Existence submits, drifts, and is passive. Living is active. The one surrenders the fort; the other takes it. Right living is the end of gospel pronouncement. It is the practical difference between saint and sinner. Only a good man lives.

Fast living is a misnomer, since the thing meant is not living, but dying. The so-called fast life is the toboggan-slide of the grave. It is not lived. It is swept on ahead of a flood of passion and appetite and lust. Living is a far different thing. And the difference between a saint and sinner is that the one conquers his world and the other surrenders to it; the one exists; the other lives.

Living is Christian Endeavor.

Living involves action, and action is endeavor, and ideal endeavor is Christian Endeavor. It does things. The Golden Rule of the Orient was a rule of existence, not of life. It forbade the doing of things to others we would not have done to ourselves. Not so with the Golden Rule of our Lord. It teaches us to do the things to others we would have done to ourselves, and, to use the words of the quaint David Harum, "do it first." Normal living is not having things done for one, but doing things for others.

Christian Endeavor trains one to do for others with the help of Christ the things one would have done for himself. There is nothing beyond this. Philosophy can reach no further, and theology has nothing better. But with Christian Endeavor it is neither philosophy nor theology, but the joy of one's heart daily set before him. It is based upon the fact that normal living is Christian Endeavor. What a flood of light this throws upon all nature, as well as that pursuit of one's goal called living! Vicious and immoral conduct obtains only when one falls from the plane of right living, or is deflected from the highway of holiness the Almighty has made for us.

Christian Endeavor training is the end of spiritual laziness. No more servants that will not serve; no more deacons that will not deak; no more ushers that will not ush; and no more corresponding secretaries that will not sec. The hookworm of the soul and the sleeping-sickness of the heart find their germicide in the Christian Endeavor doctrine that normal living is Christian Endeavor.

Christian Living is Just Living.

Christian Endeavor training proceeds upon the presumption that Christian living is simply normal living. It is living; that's all. It is only thought of as a certain kind of living because we have erred as to what living is. Many important features of Christian Endeavor training grow out of this recognition.

1. An early beginning is an important consideration in Christian Endeavor training for living. Most lives are ruined before the training process begins. We dare not wait with the boy or girl until the traditional age of church-membership. Nor do we feel satisfied to let the public schools make the beginning. Christian Endeavor must do that. So we have the Junior society of Christian Endeavor, the Young People's Society of Christian Endeavor, and the Senior Society of Christian Endeavor. We begin in time, and keep it up until the race of life is run, believing that, if Christian living is just living, its period of training reaches from the cradle to the grave. It can not, so far as we know, go further; but it may begin earlier in a Christian Endeavor parentage.

2. By emphasizing the doctrine that Christian living is normal living Christian Endeavor has removed religion from the plane of the artificial and the unreal. Cant has been abolished. Religion is a real thing, and its speech can be spoken by a common man in the terms of the every-day life. It has made it seem not only possible and desirable to be religious, but the perfectly natural thing to do.

3. With the naturalizing of religious training have come the nature signs of life: red blood, vigor, action, perfect fruit. Old-time church

Mrs. Grace Livingston
Hill-Lutz,
Swarthmore, Pa.

Fanny J. Crosby, Famous
Hymn Writer,
Bridgeport, Conn.

Mrs. Charles Hutchison,
Jr., Field Secretary for
Ohio.

Miss Margaret Koch,
Field Secretary for Maine.

Miss MaDwe Yaba,
Burma.

talk was long on sound and short on action. The new life brought by Christian Endeavor training is conventionally oratorical, if not always oratorically conventional; and it can put ideas over the plate. It can both talk and live the life of red blood and high ideals. A little service does not give it palpitation of the heart.

It has been so that a young woman could prepare for a week for a society function, using all her nice hand-painted china pieces and borrowing from her friends, working all day before, and standing far into the night to have people "giggle, gabble, gobble, and git," to use the words of an eminent author, and to dream dreams of great joy over the triumph for weeks to come, ready to go to it again, and upon being asked to lead a devotional meeting, or to do some spiritual service for humanity, she would throw up her hands and gasp for breath. A change has come. We are nearing, let us hope, the end of a situation like this.

Christian Endeavor has trained us for a living that finds its constituency in the young people of the rich and the poor, the learned and the unlearned. And in this convention, perchance, will sit together in the Lord the one that was "born in the terraced house and the one in the street below," quite forgetting the difference that man makes in the unity that Christian Endeavor training has realized. It may be that the young student that has been reduced to the plainest fare, and has even known pangs of hunger, and has been satisfied to have his coat cleaned and trousers creased again to come to this convention, will sing from the same book with the young man that has not known want, and wears his fraternity pin, and is arrayed like King Solomon in dress. It is the spirit of Christian Endeavor. And this uniting of the classes and the stations of life is more wonderful than the lying down of the lion and the lamb together. It is that splendid democracy of heart and brain and brawn for which our Lord wore the thorn-crown.

4. Christian Endeavor training, like approved pedagogy, which makes play of the pupil's work, brings the Christian life into some hope of the universal realization of its aims. It makes Christian living a delight. What true Endeavorer does not feel this way about it? He is not a Christian soldier because he has been drafted, but because he could not restrain himself from enlistment. And the great undertakings of the church challenge the best that is in him.

It has not always been so. Many times the ravens of despair have flapped their black wings over our heroic undertakings, and chanted the refrain of Poe's raven, "Nevermore!" But this is not to continue. We will not allow these black fowls of gloom to sit upon our church spires and chant "Nevermore!" They will not light upon the pastor's dome to find a home. They will not perch upon the pallid busts, napping deacons, and cast a shadow on the floor from out whose gloom our contribution-baskets shall be lifted nevermore.

5. We have had a generation of Christian Endeavor training for living, and we are beginning to get results. Younger men wearing C. E. pins are coming to the front in legislative bodies, calling loudly for square dealing and honest legislation. Prosecuting attorneys wearing our emblem upon their inner hearts, if not upon their lapels, are digging up and exposing graft. Christian Endeavorers that have to do with foods and refreshments are becoming Christian enough to make a wholesome loaf of bread, a genuine cake, an unadulterated dish of cream.

Young business men are spurning the short weight and the scant measure. In Kansas City an Endeavor business man spurned from his presence a scales salesman who had begun to show how much his scales would save the merchant in the course of a year.

Humane methods that regard the lives of the industrial army are being adopted by young stockholders and operators who got their training in the Young People's Society of Christian Endeavor.

The ends of the earth are full of men and women we have trained, and they are giving us a new China, a new Japan, a new Korea, a new India, and, most wonderful of all, are healing the Sick Man of Europe. Light is breaking everywhere, from the haunts of the medicine-man of equatorial Africa to the sacred city of the Grand Lama. It is the result of **man-training**.

It has taken the church all the centuries since the first to learn the **business of man-training**. The training of animals has come down to us from ancient times, but the training of men to live is a new thing. All known animals have been trained to some extent. Even the flea has been slowed down to a walk and trained to draw a miniature chariot. But Topsy "just growed," and but for Christian Endeavor so should we have done. Train, train, train, train men to live!

A beautiful young woman, one of the many that have no special aim in life further than to be pleasant and to enjoy the pleasures of society, was dressing for a ball. As she was fastening a diamond ornament in her hair so that it would be seen as advantageously as possible from the seats of the onlookers as she whirled through the softly gliding company of waltzers, her little sister entered the room.

"O sister, how it shines! I wonder if the stars in my crown will be as pretty as that."

"Why, little dear, what do you mean?"

"Our Junior superintendent said we should have stars in our crowns in heaven if we won souls for Christ. I want stars in my crown," said the little tot, as she skipped back and forth and innocently out of the room.

"'Stars in my crown,' and 'win souls for Christ,'" the young lady said to herself, "what does that mean?"

She went to the dance, but something seemed to have chilled her enthusiasm, and long before it was over she requested her escort to take her home. At the entrance door she said good-night, and mounted to her room, taking off her ornaments, thinking, thinking, thinking, thinking of the remark her little sister had made.

Then she went to her little sister's room. There she lay upon her snow-white cot, her curls falling about her head and smiles playing upon her innocent face. The little flower had closed its petals for the night — white, sweet, innocent — to open them on the morrow more beautiful than ever. She looked for a long time into that sweet face.

"Dear little girl," she said, "you want stars in your crown. You shall have them. And I am going to be the first one. Henceforth my life for Him."

CHRISTIAN ENDEAVOR HOSPITAL WORK.

By Rev. E. L. Reiner, of Chicago.
Member Hospital Board, Chicago Christian Endeavor Union.

In this retreat of suffering there are 1,645 patients, with never less than 1,200. Sixty-five per cent are Roman Catholics, thirty-five per cent comprising Protestants and all shades of other religious convictions. In one year, we believe, almost every nation under heaven will have had a subject there.

Our work began in a very modest way sixteen years ago, when a few Christian Endeavorers visited the hospitals each Sunday afternoon with bouquets of flowers with Scripture texts attached, distributing them among the patients. Later we were permitted to distribute religious literature, Testaments, and so forth. At a subsequent period we began systematic personal work. This work has grown so that a Christian Endeavor chaplain is maintained there, giving all his time to spiritual ministrations to these unfortunates.

The work is further helped by a Light-bearers' Circle, numbering seventy-five, composed of young people of our sister organizations.

At a recent Sunday-afternoon time for reports one of the ordinary, every-day Endeavorers said: "I wish to thank God for answering prayer. Four weeks ago, as I approached a young man as he lay upon his cot, and tried to tell about the Saviour, the only response was a grunt of disapproval. Next week he consented to my intercession to God for him; the next he did the same. To-day that young man is rejoicing in his Saviour."

Some one has said, "Adversity reminds men of religion." The Chicago Christian Endeavor Union hospital board knows the truth of this statement by actual experience among the sick and other unfortunate dependents in our county institutions. We also know that the reason the spiritual work in these places has not been greater is because we have not shown the inmates a genuine religion until recent years.

Our Endeavorers carry forward an organized work in many of the places one day each week, but in the Cook County Hospital we labor seven days a week.

CHRISTIAN ENDEAVOR IN PRISON.

By Judge Edgar M. Warner,

Superintendent of the Prison Department, Connecticut State Christian Endeavor Union.

In France prisons are called "homes of the forgotten." Many times they are such in America, but Christian Endeavorers believe in kind, friendly visitation. They bring hope to the despairing, courage to the despondent, the gospel of salvation to the undeserving, regeneration for degeneration, victory for defeat. This is work Christ delights to honor. It was by no accident that the first redeemed soul to enter paradise after Christ's death on Calvary was a guilty but repentant thief, or that the first person to recognize and greet the risen and glorified Saviour was Mary Magdalene.

Forgiveness of sin and restoration to righteousness is one of the greatest facts in life. Christian Endeavor proclaims this. Letters come from Wisconsin, Texas, Missouri, Iowa, Kansas, Connecticut, and many other States, telling the same splendid story. Christian Endeavor prison societies have been organized about fifteen years. The prison topic-cards are similar to those outside. Some have officers from local societies, others elect inmates to these positions.

The societies have their committees, who do good work. They assist the chaplains, and always work under their direction. Local societies send gifts of books, pincushions, pictures, handkerchiefs, and calendars for Christmas. Some send Christmas letters, not signing their names; these are much appreciated. Some societies furnish music at the meetings, vocal and instrumental, on special occasions. One reports a fine programme every Christmas Day. Others collect literature, good magazines, religious papers, or books. Bibles are always welcome.

One superintendent writes a letter on the Christian Endeavor lesson, and sends a copy to each prison society in his State. The workers hold meetings, distribute tracts, or books, and Bibles, in some cases have personal talks with the men. They try to obtain places and work for discharged prisoners, meeting them at the prison gate, and in general extending a helping hand to every man who feels discouraged. They sometimes act as probation officers without pay. They often urge the enactment of laws, like the probation law, the indeterminate sentence, and others. They work for the observance of Prison Sunday, the fourth Sunday in October. They send circular letters to stir up the clergy to observe Prison Sunday.

Results.

The results of this work are encouraging. As a general rule, prisoners that are in the Christian Endeavor society are very thoughtful, sincere students of the Bible. Many sound conversions result. One man converted in prison is now a Bible-school superintendent at his former home. One worker writes, "During three years of my observation I have not known one active participant in the Christian Endeavor meetings to be returned as a parole-violator."

Field.

The field for Christian Endeavor in prison is broad enough. Every prison or jail in the United States should be often visited by kindly Christian Endeavor committees. This is foreign and home missionary work combined, for there are aliens and native-born in our prisons. Christian Endeavor is both a hospital and a life-saving station. The main object is to show the prisoner that God loves him and that there are people outside who will gladly help him. This work is such that it must be handled by wise and experienced people, and Christian Endeavor societies send their most judicious members to engage in personal work with prisoners.

No nobler work can be found for Christian Endeavor than to wake up the church to the duty of a reform in jails and prisons. Surely God never meant to have in the United States 400,000 human beings in jails and prisons, or awaiting trial. It is no part of His plan.

County Jails.

At most State prisons there is already started a fairly good system of law, but in almost every county in the United States there is a jail managed under a system that ought not to be tolerated anywhere.

One of the results of this vicious police-court and county-jail system is the drunken rounder, the weak, wretched loafer, who makes the journey from saloon to gutter, police court, and jail every few weeks. He often has no home but the jail and no object in life higher than drink. One man I know of has been confined in jail in short terms thirty-two years merely for drunkenness. The best-informed students of jails speak of them as schools of vice and crime. Agitate, agitate, till this miserable system of law, a crime against criminals, is abolished from the face of the earth.

Prison work is imperative in its demands, and should be met; but Christian Endeavor may well devote time and care to preventive measures. Keep the men and boys out of jail. The probation law, which keeps men at their work, and saves the wages for the family, is a great improvement on the old method of sending every petty offender to jail and forcing the family to apply to the town for support. Last year probation officers in Connecticut saved the families $30,000 in wages and the State $6,000 in fines. Similar good results are reported from other States. Look after the boys; see that they have playgrounds and decent sports in the cities and manual training in schools. Let every man in Christian Endeavor be a big brother to some boy.

One earnest worker writes: "Urge Endeavorers to do all in their power to keep men from having to come to prison. Those in prison cells, twenty, thirty, or forty years hence are little children now. It is ours to keep them from falling by the way. The Christian people could bring about conditions that would leave our prisons empty if they would only rise in the power and might the Saviour is willing to give. Why can't the church wake up?"

Things to be done by Christian Endeavor in His name and for the sake of suffering humanity.

1. Organize for your State an efficient prison and jail department if you have none.

2. Observe Prison Sunday each year. Wake up the churches and the public.

3. Urge the passage of good laws, especially one providing for probation officers to take charge of unruly boys and men; the indeterminate sentence of criminals, and State control or abolition of county jails; establish in each State a farm colony for drunkards.

4. Banish the saloon, and kill the drink habit; drive out the deadly cigarette, cheap shows, and gambling; guard the children and youth so that the children of to-day may not be the prisoners of to-morrow.

5. If you are willing, I wish you would use the little Prayer Cycle. Pray earnestly for all prisoners and prison officials, and that all workers may have "grace, grit, and gumption"; grace to handle difficult problems in a civil, courteous manner, treating opponents kindly; grit, to keep at it until success is secured; gumption, to do the right thing, in the right manner, at the right time.

"I was in prison, and ye visited me. Inasmuch as ye did it unto one of the least of these my brethren, ye did it unto me."

FLOATING ENDEAVOR.

By ALFRED S. COX, Chairman of the Floating Committee, Philadelphia Christian Endeavor Union.

Floating Christian Endeavor on board ship presents the greatest opportunity for practical, heart-to-heart evangelistic work among the sailors and seamen generally.

To the men who sacrifice the pleasures of home and country, who face the dangers of the deep, we owe a certain duty while in port; the duty and privilege of presenting the plain, unvarnished gospel of Jesus Christ. These soul-sick men of the sea are only too eager to drink in the message of love and cheer in the moments permitted on board ship.

One of the most practical things Floating Endeavor can do that will be of service to the sailor en route is to provide each one with a comfort-bag containing many useful articles necessary to the sailor. In this bag we also place the Book of Books written in the language of the sailor. If all the messages of cheer, love, encouragement, and hope that were sent out by Floating Endeavor across the sea could be returned to-day by wireless, and relate their story, what a mighty testimony it would be for that branch of Christian Endeavor destined to relieve, help, and work with and for the men of the sea!

CHRISTIAN ENDEAVOR AMONG THE LEPERS.

By JOHN JACKSON, F. R. G. S., Secretary, Mission to Lepers in India.

The above title is strikingly suggestive of two things. First, the fact that there should be any Christian Endeavor among those outcast and destitute people suggests that the work of missions is penetrating to the lowest depths of human need. Next, it is a striking testimony to the development of the Endeavor movement that it should have extended to a people seemingly so unlikely and hopeless; but we may gratefully accept the fact as an indication of the far-reaching effects of Christian missions.

There can be no question of the dire need of these destitute people for all the help and hope that Christian missions can bring to them. Accursed by their own creed, regarded as unclean by their own kindred, driven out to wander or to die, they represent the lowest depth of suffering and misery. No part of the whole work of missions is more practical and Christlike than to shelter, relieve, and evangelize the many thousands of homeless lepers to be found in the great lands of the Orient.

The Mission to Lepers in India and the East in an international and interdenominational society, which exists solely for the relief of lepers and the rescue of their untainted children. The disease, while incurable and contagious, is not hereditary; and therefore the offspring of leprous parents may be saved from the disease, and the mission has twenty homes in which these children are being trained for useful lives. In the eighty stations at which the society is at work, comprising India, China, Japan, and the Philippines, there are no fewer than four thousand leper converts. Among these the work of Christian Endeavor has found a place, and has proved the means of great encouragement and help to the lepers in their Christian life.

One of the first Christian Endeavor societies to be formed among the lepers adopted the title of "The Sign-post Christian Endeavor Society." They explained this as meaning that just as the sign-post could not move, so they, being lepers, could not leave their asylum; but like the sign-post they could point each other to the right way. This society is at Sholapur in the Bombay Presidency, India.

Another society insisted upon contributing from their own scant allowance the funds necessary to send their native pastor as their delegate to the Agra Convention.

At Purulia, in Bengal, where the mission is caring for nearly six hundred lepers and their children, there is a large and flourishing Endeavor society. Once a week the members conduct a special service in the church of the settlement. Their programme is an elaborate one, containing about a dozen items; but they are all very keen and proud of their society. The principles of Christian Endeavor are especially appropriate to such a community. They are encouraged to help one another, and it is not an uncommon sight to see two or three lepers, who have the full use of their hands, binding the wounds or dressing the sores of others much worse than themselves. At Canton in China there is also a well-organized Christian Endeavor society among the lepers in the village outside the city.

The work of ministering to these outcasts is one that should appeal to all Edeavorers. It is at once philanthropic, medical, and missionary, and constitutes an object-lesson of true Christianity which greatly impresses heathen peoples.

CHRISTIAN ENDEAVOR AMONG THE COLORED DENOMINATIONS OF THE SOUTH.

By Rev. W. J. Darby, D.D., Assistant Secretary of the Presbyterian Board of Education.

The Field.

With one-tenth of our entire population belonging to the negro race, and most of it in the South, the measure of this responsibility is evident. Of the religious denominations concerned, the Methodists and Baptists largely preponderate, each having a negro membership of about one and three-quarters millions. Other denominations have probably a half-million, making a total of four millions of people among whom the Christian Endeavor organization has a wide-open door for service. In one branch of Methodists, the African Methodist Episcopal Church, under the leadership of a member of our Board of Trustees, already there are twenty-five hundred Endeavor societies.

The fact that in the two large denominations mentioned there are forty-one schools and colleges, on which the membership spend a million dollars annually, and the further fact that they contribute a quarter of a million dollars for foreign missions, are sufficient to show the aggressive spirit and marked liberality of their people. With the beginning already made, the barriers to the progress of Christian Endeavor are not by any means insurmountable. Among colored Presbyterians and Congregationalists the Society is always welcomed.

The Movement Proposed.

The design is to secure sympathetic co-operation among all the colored denominations, in order that their young people may receive from Christian Endeavor the incalculable blessing it has in store for them. At the same time, the aim is to enlist white Endeavorers in the Southern States in helpful co-operation, so that, while racial distinctions and limitations are duly recognized, in line with the public sentiment of the Southern people, yet the stronger race shall aid the weaker, and by mutual burden-bearing the law of Christ be fulfilled. By action of our Board of Trustees a committee has been appointed to advise and guide in this large and important movement. Under their direction an executive committee representing most of the negro denominations has been organized, and active work has already begun. Within the past few weeks city unions have been formed in Richmond and Baltimore, and others will speedily follow. The first aim will be to establish the Society permanently in as many local congregations as possible, and then with city and district unions proceed in a systematic way to disseminate the principles of Christian Endeavor.

The Good It Will Do.

It will help to develop and train leadership. The race must look chiefly to the Christian schools for its consecrated leaders, but not all the captains and commodores come from West Point and Annapolis. From the ranks that cannot reach college or university there must come a great host of practical workers, or the Kingdom must seriously suffer. Think of it, nine millions of people; and in all the schools, in process of training for the ministry, for teaching, and for the professions, there are scarcely more than three thousand young men and women. Again, in this training process Christian Endeavor adheres rigidly to the essentials, the word of God, prayer, and the practice of Christian fellowship. Herein is the power of the pledge. Thereby prospective leaders are drilled in things that make steadfast Christian character, strong men and women whom the people can trust.

The internal welfare of the denominations will be promoted. The processes of Christian Endeavor point toward unification, a consummation devoutly to be wished where splits and divisions have wrought such fateful havoc. The negro denominations are afflicted with multitudes of small congregations resulting from divisions of various kinds. To unify the people will strengthen the congregations, and they will then be all the more able to sustain good pastors. Through the various unions pastors and members of the weaker churches will be brought happily into contact with the stronger, and inspiration and instruction will result. The end must be the creation of a higher standard for pulpit and pew among this great mass of small communions.

It will be a guaranty of denominational fellowship. The negro has been noted for the intensity of his denominationalism. He makes a rabid sectarian; but turn him about, and his emotional nature quickly absorbs the spirit of good fellowship. Being a good imitator, the negro is learning that the spirit of the age is toward unification, agreement in the essentials, and in non-essentials charity. To this changed order of things he is rapidly adjusting himself. In the true spirit of Christian fellowship the negroes are "getting together." Neither are they slow to learn that by thus coming closer to one another in the religious life they can do all the more for the good of their race. Nothing can promote this spirit more effectively than Christian Endeavor.

And surely Christian people of the white race, regardless of denomination, whether they have Christian Endeavor or some other form of organization for their young people, surely they will be broad enough to encourage such a movement as this among the needy black people of our own land, precisely as they encourage the coming together of Christian people on foreign soil, regardless of denominational divisions. Let the interests of the race be made the paramount issue. The negro will do it if the white people do not interfere.

The Supreme Question.

Shall the Endeavorers of both races in the Southland meet loyally the test imposed by this advance movement of our Society? In the cities of the North they are trying to meet it in behalf of the foreigners that have come to our shores. Why not in the same spirit adapt ourselves to the pressing needs of these millions of a race that came to us, not of their own volition, hundreds of years ago? Shall we measure up to our responsibilities, and enter the open door of opportunity with wise management of the many delicate questions that must arise and with abiding consecration to duty in behalf of a cause that must be pleasing to Him whose gospel is offered to all the peoples?

CHRISTIAN ENDEAVOR AND CIVIC PROBLEMS.

By Rev. J. S. McGaw, National Field Secretary of the National Reform Association, Pittsburg, Penn.

Four years ago Christian Endeavor took a step ahead of the general procession in the consideration of civic problems. You announced the theme "The Kingdom of God and the State." You took your stand on the word of God and loyalty to Christ in all relationships in life.

America is now in the throes of a great moral crisis. The lines were never more clearly drawn. Two democracies are contending for the dominance of the national thought and life. On one side stands the Christian democracy, represented by this Christian assembly and the rank and file of the evangelical church. On the other side is the secular democracy represented in the Secularist Union. The teaching of the Bible in our public schools, the civil Sabbath, the national Thanksgiving Day, the Christian inscription on our coins, the chaplains in our various institutions, are all under fire in every State in the Union.

The second line of battle is the abolition of our national legalized sins. The liquor traffic, the divorce-mills, the legal sanction or toleration of Mormonism, and the social evil with its attendant white-slave traffic, must go; and any law that supports them must be allowed no longer to disgrace our statute-books.

The third line of battle is the assimilation of the foreigner.

The Bible made America, and you cannot make Americans without the Bible. We must push home missions, evangelism, and the Bible in our public schools, or America will be over-run and taken by southern

THE BEAUTIFUL CORRIDOR OF STATE BOOTHS.

This picture was made before the booths on the left were fitted up. Moreover, it can give no idea of the brilliant color effect.

Europe and the Orient, as was Rome by the Huns and the Goths in the fifth century.

America as a nation must be brought to Christ. Not only does the safety of the nation depend upon it, but the honor of the Lord Jesus Christ demands it. Jesus Christ died for the redemption of organized society. In John 3: 17 the word translated "world" means organized society. This is the blessed gospel to the nations.

The Lord will never see the travail of His soul nor be satisfied until we have a redeemed earth wherein dwelleth righteousness. "This gospel of the kingdom shall be preached in the whole world," and it is ours to begin in our own land and proclaim from one end to the other that as a nation we may repent and accept as fundamental to our national welfare our forefathers' political creed, namely, that God is the Creator of nations, Jesus Christ is the King of nations, and the law of God the only true basis of civil law.

"Fling out the banner! heathen lands
 Shall see from far the glorious sight;
And nations, crowding to be born,
 Baptize their spirits in its light."

THE BEST THING I HAVE SEEN IN CHRISTIAN ENDEAVOR.

By Rev. George William Wright, of the Philippines.

The first thing in Christian Endeavor brought to my notice in the Philippines was the society at the Tondo Presbyterian Church in Manila. This church was begun largely under the leadership of Don Felipe Buencamine, the secretary of state to Aguinaldo. He invited a Presbyterian missionary, Dr. James B. Rodgers, to organize a Methodist church and cable the news to Bishop Potter, then the bishop of the Episcopal Church in New York. So, you see, we early had something of an idea of interdenominational fellowship in the Philippines. This Tondo Christian Endeavor Society, meeting upon each Friday night, has been the training-school for many of our preachers.

Christian Endeavor is an idea in the Philippines even before it becomes an organization, and it has not been a society for young people so much as for all. Nevertheless, we believe it will peculiarly adapt itself to the new age that has come upon us and be of great value among students and young people generally.

Please remember that there are upwards of six hundred thousand students in the public schools of the Philippines; and these young people are not only studying altogether in our language, but they are getting with that language our ideas and ideals, and learning much of our methods. They are playing baseball, and it is becoming their national game.

I found a Christian Endeavor meeting one of the most helpful ways of providing an evening service for the students of Ellinwood Seminary. We began by having a song service and address by the missionary, and after three or four Sabbaths the students were invited to take part, and later have entire charge of the meetings; and a full-fledged Christian Endeavor society naturally resulted. As the students go back from their studies in Manila, they are encouraged to organize Christian Endeavor meetings as the most natural way of giving expression to their own religious sentiments and at the same time opening up work in places where it has not as yet been begun. And, speaking of the very best thing I have seen in Christian Endeavor in the Philippines, I would say it is the testimony that I have heard these students give at our Ellinwood Christian Endeavor meetings upon Sunday evenings.

And we have something we should like to add to all the splendid words of this Convention regarding international peace. It is this, that we in the Philippines absolutely disclaim having anything to do with talk of war between Japan and the United States. If war comes, it will be, if present indications mean anything, because of yellow journalism.

THE BEST THING I HAVE SEEN IN CHRISTIAN ENDEAVOR IN JAPAN.

By Rev. George Fukuda.

In the present day the greatest questions in the world find their solution in the fact that God loves man and man loves God. There is a way of communication between man and God; man may have eternal life through Jesus Christ. Whosoever believeth in Him shall not perish, but have everlasting life. While we were yet sinners, Christ died for us. Such is His wonderful love to man.

Now, Japanese Christian Endeavorers have two great ideas, which they are most eager to put into effect: one is to hasten the regin of peace, through Jesus Christ, among all nations of the world; and the other is to unite into one body all Christian denominations within this century.

If you are all standing as one body to work the active works of love for Christ and the church, you must fight a great battle for peace throughout the world, and for all humanity in His name. I believe that is the will of God. Hereafter one who obstructs international peace between one country and another must be recognized as a public enemy.

Christian Endeavor must aim to oppose all unjust war, because war is a great sin against Christ's law of love. I hope to see the Christian Endeavorers stand as a sacred band of peace-makers. We have a duty in this matter. Do not suppose that the Japanese are good fighters because we have had two great wars in the past twenty years. The Japanese do not like to fight unless some danger menaces the country.

Our emperor desires peace eagerly. He is a peace-maker like your President. So we heartily hope to have eternal peace between these two great nations. Our experience in the past two great wars perhaps you know. The great statesman Count Okuma is the president of the Japan Peace Society; he is one of the sympathizers with the Japanese Christian Endeavor Society.

Early last year, when Dr. Clark arrived in Tokyo from India, Count Okuma proffered a cordial welcome to Dr. Clark and his party in his beautiful garden, and he made an address expressing sympathy with the great movement of Christian Endeavor. So Count Okuma is one of the honorary members, and he is a good friend of Dr. Clark and of all of you too.

It is not only Count Okuma: our Emperor also granted an audience to Dr. Clark. He listened to a presentation of the principles of the Christian Endeavor Society throughout the world, and he gave a most gracious response.

Japanese Christian Endeavorers have a great mission in Japan and China and India and elsewhere; also we have a duty as peace-makers between all nations through Jesus Christ and His churches.

Our Christian Endeavorers have not only a mission as peace-makers in the world; we hope to unite into one body the different denominations under the name of Jesus Christ. I believe this is the principle of the Christian Endeavor Society. Surely I believe this is its greatest work for the kingdom of Jesus Christ.

THE BEST THINGS I HAVE SEEN IN CHRISTIAN ENDEAVOR IN BURMA.

By Rev. H. I. Marshall, Tharawadi, Burma.

I like rapid fire in others, but for myself I should like the time it takes for loading and firing an old-fashioned flint-lock to tell about Burma.

Of the many best things, I can only give you two pictures. The first was on the deck of a steamer in the Rangoon River, with a deck reserved for our party of seventy Burmese and Karen Endeavorers on the way to the Agra World's Convention. Another deck of the boat was filled with a herd of natives returning to India from Burma. They looked more like donkeys or apes than real human beings; so dull were their faces, so dirty and unattractive and passion-ridden were they. We turned from them with a sigh.

But, returning to our Endeavorers, what a beautiful sight met our eyes! They were so bright of face as well as of costume, so neat, so attractive in every way. There were preachers, teachers, laymen, and several young women. It was inspiring to hear them gather by the rail and sing our dear Endeavor songs.

A gentleman standing by me remarked, "If one wants an argument for Christian missions, let him go and look down on that other deck, and then come and look down here, and see the difference."

The second picture is at Agra. The great viceregal camp so many times filled with the splendor of an Indian durbar is now filled with the princes of the House of David in Christian Endeavor convention assembled. Near by is the Taj Mahal, that monument to an undying love. It glistens in the tropical sun. By moonlight it is a dream in marble. But my first glimpse of it showed it as a *shadow* against the rising sun. So are the splendors of heathendom but the dark tombs of dead men in contrast to the rising Sun of Righteousness. May He soon be seen in all that dark land.

CHRISTIAN ENDEAVOR IN BRITISH GUIANA.

By Hy. O. Cendrecourt.

The Christian Endeavor movement in British Guiana is doing much to solve one of the greatest problems that confront the Christian church to-day—the recruiting of young men and women to fill the various positions in the churches.

There has always been a great leakage between the Sunday-school and the church, but the societies have done perhaps more than any other agency to conserve the young life of the church.

The movement has captured and is making good use of one of the finest approaches to the young—the social and literary activities, which prove a very effective means of securing and retaining the interest of the young people, thus giving a very much needed interpretation of Christianity, an interpretation such as the Master Himself gave when He said. "I am come that they might have life and that they might have it more abundantly."

Apart from the strategic importance of the work the movement has proved a great evangelizing agency. Most of the results, and perhaps the most lasting and effectual, do not admit of tabulation or statement. Lives have been transformed and made useful in the cause of Jesus Christ because of Christian Endeavor, the full effect of which cannot be estimated on this side.

Perhaps the most inspiring thing about our work is the great opportunity before it. So far we have touched only the fringe of possibility. What is needed, next to the self-sacrificing labors of Christian men and women, is a vital connection between the larger work here and the pioneer efforts there. We have come to associate helping the cause in foreign lands too much with the giving of our money. You can help, I feel, in a much more effectual way; you could keep in touch with the work and inspire the workers. We need encouragement, the benefit of your wider experience. I feel therefore that this Convention is going to mark a new epoch in Christian Endeavor. You will go to your homes with your sympathies enlarged, your interest in the foreign work awakened, we to our various fields of labor, inspired for greater tasks and prepared for greater conquests in the cause of Christian Endeavor, because we met at this Convention.

THE BEST THING I HAVE SEEN IN CHRISTIAN ENDEAVOR.

By Rev. Friedrich Blecher, Germany.

I have seen seven threads twisting themselves together into one, comprising 421 Young People's societies, with 12,170 members, 73 Junior societies, with 750 members, 1 Mothers' and 1 Floating Society, making a total of 496 societies of Christian Endeavor with 13,689 members. This is the history of German Christian Endeavor for sixteen years.

We have sent considerable literature into our neighboring countries, to introduce Christian Endeavor. One of our clerks called these packages "bombs," of course "bombs of peace." They caught fire, and from them have come 15 societies with 280 members among the Germans in Russia, 7 societies in Slavonia and Croatia, and a society in each of the following places: Bohemia, Austria, Transylvania, Brazil, Haifa (Palestine), Kamerun, Ponape (Caroline Islands), and Nauru (Marshall Islands) in the South Seas.

This all means practically a miracle in the lives of these 13,689 members of these societies, as they accepted Jesus as their Lord and Master. We cannot rest until we see these figures doubled, so that others too may understand how not to live for themselves, but "for Christ and the Church," to march in line for the One who gave His life for us.

We have seen how Christian Endeavor assists young people to understand the secret of a life of victory, and to conquer mistakes and dangers, and overcome temptations and the enemies of success.

We have seen how the first words of our pledge, "Trusting in the Lord Jesus Christ for strength," not only lead our young people to a better understanding, but grow into a mental necessity to become one with Christ throughout all one's life (Rom. 6).

We have seen how young people have been brought up to become a legion of victors (Rom. 8: 37), so that they can assist their weaker companions to overcome difficulties and thus enjoy true happiness in the Lord.

As Christian Endeavor leads us to Christ, so does Christ own a true Christian Endeavor (Luke 4: 18). Therefore the important experience, a testimony of one of our leaders, "The Lord is more truthful to Christian Endeavor than we are."

We have seen grow out of our midst 726 laborers for the Lord, 15 missionaries in the Caroline Islands, one mission vessel, 30,000 marks ($7,500) last year for home and foreign missions, about 2 3-4 millions of books and pamphlets against filthy literature, 161 Sunday-schools, with 10,000 children; while many have said that they could hardly do without our Christian Endeavor paper, the *Jugendhilfe*.

Original prejudice has been overcome, enemies have been changed into friends, Christian Endeavor servants are in demand, and recognition was even obtained from our Emperor, at our twenty-fifth anniversary. through the fruits of Christian Endeavor.

THE BEST THINGS I HAVE SEEN IN CHRISTIAN ENDEAVOR IN CHINA.
By Rev. George H. Hubbard, Foochow, China.

The best things we know are superlatively excellent because of their relation to persons. And the best things in China are also the best in all the world; namely, (a) the reaching out of the soul to God; (b) the reaching out to others; (c) the reaching on in continued fellowship with God and man.

1. The best things at the beginning came through two women. One of them stands now before you dressed in Chinese costume. She made the home centre where the first Chinese Christian Endeavorers gathered in 1885, and we taught them, with Miss Newton as interpreter, the Christian Endeavor way of taking a firmer hold on God.

2. The best in continuance has appeared in the work at Shaowu; and this banner designed by Dr. Yao of that place has a message for us all. He was early as a Christian Endeavorer under the tutelage of Dr. and Mrs. Walker, and as such has carried the gospel message into Kiangsi and down the Yangtze.

3. The best in the present opportunity is shown as Mr. and Mrs. Strother, who visit in the old-time evangelistic spirit as fast as possible cities and villages in the twenty-three provinces of China. This string of cash received by them at Wenchow is the gift of a poor Christian Endeavorer for the building of a new headquarters at Boston. Let these speak the world-wide message of peace and good will to men, which Christian Endeavor continues to echo for the angel band in every land.

All these teachings are summed up in this symbol of the cross which I present to you in the name of our Chinese Christian Endeavorers.

THE BEST THING I HAVE SEEN IN CHRISTIAN ENDEAVOR IN JAMAICA.
By Rev. J. W. Ford, President of the Jamaica Christian Endeavor Union.

Let me say first that I do not believe any of us can see the best thing in Christian Endeavor until we have ourselves been filled with the Spirit of God, and this empowering Spirit has reached out through us to those in our societies and churches.

The best thing I have seen, first, in Junior Christian Endeavor work is the planting of twelve pennies by twelve Juniors of Orange Bay. They did this by taking a penny each, buying a cocoanut and sugar, and making it into sweets to sell, or using it in some such way, each as he chose. In three months these twelve pennies were returned as twelve shillings or three dollars; and at the request of the Juniors were sent, one dollar to Cuba, one dollar to India, as some of the children were India's sons, and one dollar to Africa.

Second, the best thing in group work. One committee appointed by the Orange Bay Christian Endeavor is the open-air band. These Endeavorers go to neglected districts where the people lounged in their dirt and rags all day Sunday, and held open-air meetings. At Spring Garden the people asked for an afternoon Sunday-school. The Endeavorers organized and carried on one. Then they said, "We must have a place for our school, especially when the rains come on." The Endeavorers said, "All right"; and the people joined hands, cut the poles, bamboos, and cocoanut boughs necessary, and built a booth, which I dedicated two weeks before I sailed. This work has brought several useful members into the Christian Endeavor society and one into the church.

Third, the best thing in the individual. At another of my stations new officers were elected early this year. Two or three weeks later I saw the new chairman of the lookout committee, and asked how he was getting on.

He said: "Well, minister, me getting on well, sir! Me chairman of the lookout committee, so me been looking out. Me see some of those children not going to Juniors; so me look out for them, and they go now. Me see some older ones growing careless; so me look out for them. Me see some children who don't go to school [education is not compulsory in Jamaica], and me see their parents. You see that brown boy in school; I look out for him, and I'm pleased of that."

"Yes, Samuel, that's fine."

"Yes, minister, and you know old Constable Joseph; he has been very bitter against our church for years because he don't understand us. I been looking out for him. I'm chairman of the lookout committee, you know; so I must be looking out."

And the last day I spent in the mountains I had the joy of receiving old William Joseph and another man whom he had brought to Christ, with a class of more than ten others, into the fellowship of the church in that mountain station.

THE WORLD-WIDE INFLUENCE OF THE BIBLE.

By Rev. Herbert Anderson.

The chairman introduced Rev. Herbert Anderson as a missionary for twenty-five years in India, the secretary of the Baptist Mission of London, who had twice been president of the Christian Endeavor Union of India, Burma, and Ceylon, and who acted in that capacity at the World's Christian Endeavor Conference held in Agra in 1909.

Mr. Anderson brought the salutations of the ancient East to the New World, and on behalf of forty thousand Indian Endeavorers expressed heartfelt gratitude for all the prayer, sympathy, interest, and gifts that have linked the United States to the East in Christian Endeavor bonds forever.

Speaking on the theme of "The World-wide Influence of the Bible," he reminded his audience that the apostle of Bible-translations to the East was the founder of Protestant missions, William Carey of Serampore. As a village pastor in England he had shown special linguistic faculties, and could read his Bible in Hebrew, Greek, Latin, French, Dutch, Italian, and his mother tongue before he started for India on his missionary career. One of the ideals of his life was to give to every man in every nation a copy of God's word in his own tongue. A magnificent tribute to his untiring devotion and extraordinary scholarship was that before he died, with the help of his colleagues, Marshman and Ward, and pundits he had translated, printed, and published complete Bibles in seven languages, New Testaments in twenty-three others, and portions of the Word in ten more. It is to the honor of the Anglo-Saxon race on both sides of the Atlantic that they have followed Dr. Carey in his great work.

Mr. Anderson dealt with the passage of the Book through the world. The Bible Societies of Britain and America have circulated three hundred million Bibles, Testaments, and portions since their foundation in the early years of the nineteenth century. Their annual circulation is now more than ten million copies, and the best proof of the vitality of God's book is that last year they circulated more than half a million copies more than in any preceding year of their history. The hunger for truth in central Europe, Russia, China, India, Egypt, and Korea was then referred to, and gratifying circulation was reported.

The second part of Mr. Anderson's address dealt with the power of the Book in the world. The indirect influence of the Bible was remarkably shown in the attitude of religious leaders in the East, both past and present. Educated Indians of all religious creeds are reading it, and devout men feed their spiritual life upon its truth. The whole religious thought of Asia is being penetrated and permeated with Bible knowledge, so that the sayings of Jesus are becoming household words. Christian civics are the standard of life; the homes of the people are being sweetened; social wrongs are being ameliorated, and national character uplifted.

In conclusion Mr. Anderson referred to the direct influence of the Bible in the conversion of men, giving illustrations concerning a Buddhist gentleman, a Hindu student, and a Mohammedan agriculturist from his own missionary experience. He urged American Endeavorers to love the word of God, and to aid its dissemination by supporting the American Bible Society.

INTERNATIONAL BROTHERHOOD.

BY REV. F. J. HORSEFIELD, President of the Christian Endeavor Union for Great Britain and Ireland.

Monday Evening, July 10.

It would be almost impossible to conceive of any topic of vaster and more vital importance, and at the same time one more dear to the hearts of Endeavorers the wide world over, than the one assigned to me, that of "International Brotherhood." Such a theme appeals to our highest instincts, stirs our patriotism, brings before us a vision of unspeakable magnificence and of eternal import.

Endeavorers, at least, have long dreamed of the dawning of a day when war should be no more and when the brotherhood of men should be clearly realized. And now the dream is coming true. It is being demonstrated that the recognition of the brotherhood of all men is no mere Utopian idea, no idle imagining of some sentimental visionary, but that is rapidly becoming an accomplished fact; and we, the two English-speaking nations of the world, are leading the van in bringing this to pass.

But I would add further that Christian Endeavor is playing no small or insignificant part in hastening on the dawn of this long-looked-for-day. For Christian Endeavor is no mere local or ecclesiastical organization, caring only for those that are within the immediate circle of its influence and work, whether in your land or in mine; but it embraces in the mighty sweep of its purposes and prayers the whole range of humanity. There is no national narrowness any more than there is any ecclesiastical exclusiveness about Christian Endeavor. Nor is it in any sense a political organization, engineered by men of this party or of that, for the advancement of their own particular aims; but it embraces and unites the best men and women of all political creeds in a common effort to elevate humanity; to bring a touch of glory into the dense darkness of heathenism and the spirit of the gospel into the counsels of civilized nations throughout the whole wide world.

What, then, has Christian Endeavor to say on the subject of international brotherhood? What are its ideals? what possibility is there of their full and final accomplishment? and how shall the accomplishment be brought about?

First, the ideals of Christian Endeavor include a *complete recognition of all national and individual rights*. God "hath made of one blood all nations of men for to dwell on all the face of the earth"; and their kinship is proved by the fact that they are stirred by the same emotions; have to a large extent the same longings, hopes, regrets; respond to the same touch of loving sympathy; and feel alike the thrill awakened by the voice of pity. Being brothers, all men, whatever the color of their skin or the place of their habitation, have indisputable rights that ought never to be taken from them by violence or force; and there must be in the future a clearer insistence upon this fundamental truth. We have long ago so far recognized this as to abolish slavery, but there are still some respects in which there is room for improvement in this matter, not only between nation and nation, but also in industrial circles as between masters and men.

But our ideas include, secondly, the *abolition of* war. With all our hearts do we in England thank God for the magnificent lead of the President of the United States in his message to Congress in December last, and for Sir Edward Grey's reply. The Indians reverenced the peace-pipe, which was borne through the wilderness by the messengers of friendship. Whoever travelled with it was sacred. No warrior dared oppose him, and he was welcomed everywhere without fear. Equally honored henceforth by all Christians shall be your President as the man that wrought to bring peace to the world.

We are one in our language, one in our ideas of freedom, one in many of our religious and philanthropic institutions; and war between England and America will henceforth surely be held as an unthinkable crime.

During the war in South Africa two soldiers, a Briton and a Boer, who had got separated from their respective regiments, suddenly came face to face. Both instantly raised their guns to fire; but, as they looked into each other's eyes, their arms dropped powerless. They remembered that they were both men and therefore brothers; and, stepping forward, they gripped hands in a strong grasp of mutual respect.   !

We are beginning to realize the cost of war. It is not monetary cost alone, though that is enormous. The expenditure involved by a single shot from one gun on some of our great war-vessels would support several missionaries for a whole year. The people of Europe are to-day paying two-thirds of their taxes for war, that is, for interest on war debts and for maintaining war armaments. Who can calculate what it costs in tears, and widowhood, and desolated homes, and waste of every kind? The recognition of international brotherhood will mean the abolition of war.

We turn now to ask the question, "Is it possible that these ideals can ever be realized?" And the answer comes thundering back, "Yes, thank God! It is possible, and more than possible." We are not daunted in the least by the remembrance of all the blood-stained centuries of the past, nor yet by all the croakings of the hopeless pessimists of to-day. On the other hand, we are cheered by the fact that the world is surely making steady progress in the direction of universal brotherhood and peace. We are being drawn nearer together every year. Geographical distances fail now to separate us, and the barriers of hills and oceans no longer divide, for tunnels are thrown through the one, and telegraphic cables laid in the other. All scientific developments, the innumerable improvements incessantly introduced in mechanics and in the commercial world, all these are binding the nations of the world together as never before.

It has been said that war can never cease till human nature changes. Human nature *has* changed, *is* changing more and more. Who would

Rev. F. J. Horsefield,
F.Ph., England.

Rev. G. Fukuda,
Japn.

Rev. Friedrich Blecher, Mrs. Friedrich Blecher,
Berlin, Germany.

Mr. Enos Bacon, The
Yorkshire Nightingale,
England.

Mr. John Jackson,
India.

ever think now of challenging to a duel any one with whom he had a quarrel on some point of honor? Yet but a little while ago that was the recognized way of settling disputes. And ere long war will become as obsolete between nations as duelling is now between individuals.

Besides, who can doubt that the recognition of our world-wide brotherhood is part of the divine plan and purpose, part of God's programme for the world? "Peace on earth" was the refrain of the angels' song of long ago, and down to us through the long ages comes the sure prediction of the ancient prophet telling of the time when swords shall be beaten into ploughshares and spears into pruning-hooks. It is true that "Beneath the angel-strain have rolled two thousand years of wrong"; and, as if in mockery of the song, men have down the centuries been devising more and more cunning and devilish plans and instruments for hurling each other into eternity. But perhaps the day is nearer than we think; the day

"When peace shall over all the earth
Its ancient splendors fling,
And the whole world send back the song
Which now the angels sing."

Lastly we ask the question, "How can this be brought to pass?" and the answer is threefold:

1. By the *cultivation of a wider outlook*. There has always been a tendency for patriotism to become exclusive. This must be resisted. We must learn to think more of the fatherhood of God, and so shall we get a clearer conception of the brotherhood of man. Ambassador Takahira of Japan, speaking at the Peace Congress in Chicago, said that peace amongst nations could be expected only as the sense of justice amongst nations developed. All swagger of superiority and contempt of manner must be laid aside; right, not might, must rule; and in this great enterprise we must learn to think less of all distinctions of party or of creed as separating forces.

2. There must be the *abandonment of international jealousies* and suspicions. There is a current motto, "In time of peace prepare for war." We generally get what we prepare for; and, if we are perpetually getting ready for war, it is difficult to ensure peace. Far better to say, "In time of peace prepare for more peace."

How glorious a day it will be when Victor Hugo's prediction shall be fulfilled, that cannon will be exhibited in museums just as instruments of torture are now; when the doors of the temple of Janus shall be closed forever; when the sword shall be sheathed, never more to be drawn from its scabbard; when money and ingenuity shall no longer be expended in the invention of diabolical engines of destruction. "When truth and justice triumph, war shall cease"; and we, the two great Anglo-Saxon nations of the world, are hewing the path to peace, opening a gateway through which in time all the nations of the world shall pass

3. This vision of universal peace will be hastened as we seek to help forward the *evangelization of the world*. For the gospel is a message of peace, and our Saviour is the Prince of peace. "He maketh wars to cease unto the end of the earth." He is the great reconciler of men, and His teachings and influence will put an end to war. Christianity's horizon is as broad as the world. "The very soul of our religion," said Max Müller, "is missionary, progressive, world-embracing." The message of the love manifested on Calvary will bind the nations together as nothing else can. For Christ is everybody's Saviour. He came to redeem the savage, to transform the cannibal, to save the Indian, to deliver the African slave from worse than slavery.

When, centuries ago, the citizens of European lands used to meet together that they might start on some great Crusade, they rallied to the cry, "It is the will of God." Endeavorers, we rally to-day to the same cry; the abandonment of international jealousies; the recognition of the fact that each man, of whatever race or color, *is* a man, and that Christ is the door for him as much as for the most lovable man of my own race —this is the will of God. For this we labor, and for this we pray. This is our ideal, our ambition, our watchword, our expectation; and in due time

"The whole world shall honor our charter
  Of liberty, sweetness, and light;
For tyrannies all shall be broken,
  And wrongs all avenged by the right.
The strength of all kings shall be meekness;
  The might of all nations be peace;
Their triumphs shall ever be bloodless;
  Their war-dogs' dread baying shall cease.

"We'll go to the deep sunless valleys
  Flanked in by the mountains of sin:
With torches from God's holy altar
  We'll carry His glory-light in.
And soon through the heathenish midnight
  The day of the Lord shall steal in;
The power of the savage shall languish,
  The might of the saint shall begin."

O for its speedy fulfilment!

Following is a synopsis of the address delivered by the Hon. Champ Clark, Speaker of the House of Representatives, on the subject, "Good Citizenship."

The most distressing spectacle in America to-day is the rush of the people from the country to the city. The country is the place God intended man to live in, anyhow. But the country folks have been moving to the city in such numbers during the last generation that there is not a great rural district in the United States that has not decreased in population.

There would be no trouble in running the republic if you had only country people to deal with. But in the city the inequalities of great wealth and great poverty have sprung up and corrupted our politics. The business people — the "fine-haired" people, I like to call them — take no part in the elections, and the result is that the hoodlum is running the big cities. There is not a town in America where the hoodlums are in the majority, and yet in nine cases out of ten the hoodlums rule the cities. The hoodlum is a busy man on election-day. He not only votes himself, but he is generous enough to cast a vote also for the "fine-haired" man who stays home.

Our forefathers did not fight and bleed for us to stay away from the polls on election-day. They fought and bled to get us an election-day. That's the whole thing the scrap was about, and the man who refuses to do his duty in taking advantage of this blessed heritage ought to be deprived of it altogether.

The problem of the city will be solved only when every man marks his own ballot and does not leave it to the hoodlums to mark for him. The man who fails to vote at two elections should be disenfranchised at once.

A good many people contend that the world is going to the bad. There is not a syllable of truth in it. I suppose as a lawyer, and especially practising criminal law, I have seen about as much of the seamy side of life as any man of the age; and I have a better opinion of humanity to-day than I had when I began; and instead of getting worse, the world is getting better. I said that in a speech I made at Springfield, Mass., last January, and some of the newspapers said no wonder I thought that, for I was going to be elected Speaker of the House of Representative in a few days. I have been Speaker going on four months, and I say it still, and I will tell you one of the evidences that the world is getting better.

In my judgment the day of controversial religion is past, and the day of practical religion is at hand. I do not know what others think about that, but as far as I am individually concerned, I fervently thank God that it is true. When I was a boy back in the hill country of Kentucky, the Presbyterians would not allow the Methodists to preach in their church in the neighborhood. The Methodists would not let in the Baptists; the Baptists would not let in the Presbyterians, and all of them combined to shut out us poor Campbellites. But we have grown numerous; we have grown rich; we have grown powerful, and therefore we have become respectable. Well now how is it? A man of one church goes to one place to hold a union meeting; all the rest of the preachers dismiss their congregations, and go and help him out, they pray, and help him along, and when they get through, they divide up the converts, each fellow taking his own, and I am glad that it is true. People have just as sharply defined religious beliefs now as they ever had, but they have the salutary belief that other people have the right to their opinions too.

Another thing: this is the age of organization. It does not make any difference whether we want it that way or not, that is the way it is. The physical inventions of the last 125 years have brought that state of affairs about, and at last charitable institutions, and philanthropic institutions, and religious institutions are being consolidated to do the work that is common to them, and I say, "God bless the movement everywhere." As far as Christian Endeavorers are concerned, they are supplying a great place in the world by setting the young folk to work. I think that Dr. Osler, now Sir Osler, lately knighted, gave utterance to a statement that approached the idiotic when he said that a man past forty ought to be chloroformed; but, nevertheless, the driving power of this world is in the people that are under forty years of age, and he might have gone still further, and located the driving power in the people under thirty years of age.

There is one other feature about the Endeavor movement that is to be greatly praised, and that is, that it has set more men to work in moral and religious matters than heretofore. I used to know a lawyer that said he expected to pull into heaven hanging on to his wife's skirts. A great many other men were in the same identical predicament, but this Endeavor movement has been filling men with the idea of desiring to get into heaven by their own good works rather than to get in by hanging on to their wives' skirts. It may please you to know—and I am not dead sure that you would find it through the newspapers, because they still seem to think that Congress is a very immoral set of men—three-quarters of all the members of the House and Senate attend to their religious duties in Washington better than they do when they are at home.

The Christian Endeavor movement has entered into public opinion until men in public life have to behave themselves better in public life than they did before; if they do not, they will go out of public life, and it is a curious state of affairs in the United States—it never was that way before until very recently—that the three best-known men in America, Col. Theodore Roosevelt, William Jennings Bryan, and William H. Taft, are almost invariably invited to address the great religious assemblies in America.

HOLDING THE CITADEL.

By Rev. Earle Wilfley, D.D.

Monday Evening, July 10.

In the book of God, spoken by the wise man, are these significant words: "Keep thy heart with all diligence, for out of it are the issues of life." As every nation has its capital, and every city its seat of government, so the heart is the capital, the cidadel, the fortress, the fountain, the source, the centre of all the best things of life. It is the capital of the greatest empire upon the earth, the empire of man. Greater than carving great canals, or ascending mountains, greater than the achievements of man, is man himself, the most interesting thing in all the world. The heart being the source of life, it behooves us to recognize the place and the importance of the well-poised, the well-balanced life.

In the sense in which the Bible uses it the heart is both the intellect, the sensibility, and the will. It is the life, the whole, of man. It is not used simply in the sense of the seat of the emotions, but it embraces the entire man. In these days of feverish haste to do something for Jesus there is the danger that we shall neglect that most essential thing, to be something for Jesus. Before doing there is being. Before taking the citadels of sin we must hold, or, as the word rather means, guard, with diligence our own lives.

Of all creatures to be pitied in this world, to my notion the one to be most pitied is the one who loves the flesh, who loves less than the purest and the best. To love inferior things, to fix one's heart upon things that are carnal, is selfish, sensual, and earthly.

Once a lighthouse-keeper in the great lighthouse at Calais, France, had a distinguished visitor, who said, "My friend, I see you have your lights all trimmed and in order, but what if some of these should go out, or burn dim? what would happen?"

The keeper looked astonished and almost staggered, and said, "Sir, if one of these burners should burn dim, a month from now from America, or two months from now from South America, or six months from now from Australia, would come back a letter to the keeper of the house of Calais, saying, 'On such a night the light of the house at Calais burned dim; the keeper did not do his duty.' Sometimes, sir, when my lights are burning, and I can see their scintillations on the waves of the English Channel, I can imagine that all the world is looking at my light."

If we can only get it into our minds that we are like the lighthouse at Calais, that all the world is looking at us! Unless our light is burning, our hearts stirred with love for Christ, our wills in submission to His will, our whole life well kept, well trimmed, and burning brightly, some tempest-tossed seaman might write back from the antipodes, and say that a lighthouse-keeper let his light burn dim.

A beautiful story is related of Robert Bruce, how just before one of his great battles he said to his soldiers: "My children, this may be our last battle. If I should fall, my children, I bid you cut my heart out, and carry it with you into the battle's thickest point;" and thus they went to the fight. It proved fierce, fast, and furious; and the Scotchmen were falling on every hand; and at last the towering chieftain, loved almost to distraction by his men, was seen to stagger and reel, and to fall. A few of his soldiers gathered around him, but he looked up into their faces and said, "My children, remember what I said." When he was dead, reluctantly, tearfully, and with unnerved hands they cut his heart out, and, when the battle was fiercest and the Scotchmen were being pushed back slowly by the enemy, the Scotch leader took the heart of the great chieftain, hurled it forward, and cried out, "Heart of Bruce go, and we will follow thee."

Christian Endeavorers in the crisis to-day must learn this lesson. We have been saved to serve; we have been trained to train others. If this generation is to be saved, it must be saved by this generation. So you and I must realize that out yonder is the great heathen world dying without God. The foe is powerful, well armed, well equipped. He will die, or he will conquer. So must we. Before us stands our great Chieftain, and, pointing to the enemy, He says to us, "O my children, here is my heart; take it, and bear it out into the world, and win the victory for me." And you and I take the great loving, bleeding heart of the tender Christ, and we throw it far out into the ranks of the enemy, and we say, "Go on, O heart of Christ; we will follow Thee;" and into the fight we go for Christ and the church, to redeem those for whom He died.

Keep thy heart with diligence, my friend, for out of it are the issues of life. The cargoes of blessing will flow from a guarded heart, or cargoes of cursing from one unkept for Christ. God keep us, God guard us, God lead us for His sake, since we ask it in the name of King Immanuel, whose we are, and whom we serve.

THE NEEDS OF CHRISTIAN ENDEAVOR.

BY REV. RUSSELL H. CONWELL, D.D., LL.D., Philadelphia, Penn.

The temptation is great upon us, especially under circumstances like these, to endeavor to appear larger than we are, to appreciate more than we do appreciate, and to present things that are not altogether feasible or practicable; and I have been praying on my way here that the Lord will permit me to say something to-night that my children of the Endeavorers could take home with them, and would not easily forget.

This convention has been full of great inspiration; it has had its wondrous themes, its delightful music. It has had great plans discussed, and the future presented; but I do not believe any of them have come to present the very practical theme that there is in every Christian Endeavor society throughout the entire world the need of an employment agency. If I could after a painful journey say the right thing, say it in the right way, say it so that it should be done, O, how thankful I should be that the Lord sent me to Atlantic City! If to-night all the Endeavorers in this hall, all the Endeavorers in the other hall, would go home and put into effect this fatherly and homely advice, then would Christian Endeavor take an entirely new lease of life, and take a leap forward such as it has never taken before. I hope there will be added another committee to be the employment agency in every Christian Endeavor society.

Lazy people have no place in the world. They are criminals always. Yet they are to be the subjects of pity: they are to be commiserated. Lazy people — O, what can it be in the heart of a man that leads him to imprison himself within the walls of laziness? Did you ever visit a great prison, and stand by the cell door, and talk with the man on the inside? On this earth, no place so terrible, no life so full of woe as the life where one is compelled to do nothing. This is solitary confinement. And yet men and women, Christian men and women, that claim to be followers of the ever-working Christ, can imprison themselves within these lazy walls, and condemn themselves to a life of doing nothing. This is the weakness of Christian Endeavor to-day, the fact that its members do so little. In such a convention it seems full of power, but, when you go out into the societies that have lasted a quarter of a century, you will find that they have died, or are soon to die.

A lazy's man's life is a dreadful life. The lazy rich in this country are the curse of the time. They have all the power, all the force, yet are doing nothing. I am thankful that I am not responsible for $100,000,000, that in the eternities I need not face that great account of what might be done with $100,000,000. There are men living now in this world with money enough at their command to convert the whole world to Jesus Christ. One man could do it. The idle rich, O what a sin it is! How little they know of actual happiness!

What we need is, that our rich should get busy. The remedy is, to set the rich at work. What is the great need of the Christian Endeavor Society? It is, that members should be applying at its doors, rapping continuously for admission, and that the whole church should be interested by it. When will it be so? When it gets an employment agency, and that agency sets every member of the Christian Endeavor Society at work doing something.

Christ went around doing good. He did not stop in one place and say the same thing. He went around doing something; doing good all the time. If every one of you will go home to your society and get your society to appoint an employment-agency committee, that shall give each member something to do and keep them busy in the Lord's work, your Christian Endeavor will soon be a real thing, and exercise its spiritual power to the ends of the earth. That seems to be the one need of a Christian Endeavor Society, that its members should work; and it is a great need.

It is time now that we get down to practical application of the ideas that we discuss here. Some poor, old widow in black comes into your meetings. The best thing you can do is to give her something to do. Find something to do, not only for the sorrowing heart, not only for the monotonous life, but also for those likely to be tempted. Satan finds a great deal for Christian Endeavorers to do nowadays, because they are idle. I often yearn to have something of the power that Jesus Christ had when a crank arose in his meeting and yelled out, "I know Thee who Thou art." Many people are so crazy in their testimony to Christ that it injures His cause. The thing is, to give the man something to do.

If you ask what to do, ask what Jesus did, and do it right in your own home.

"If you cannot in the harvest
Garner up the richest sheaf,
Many a grain both rich and golden
Will the careless reapers leave."

Go and toil in any vineyard,
Do not fear to do or dare;
If you want a field of labor,
You can find it anywhere."

TRAINING IN INTERNATIONAL AND INTERDENOMINATIONAL RELATIONSHIPS.

By Rev. WILLIAM HENRY ROBERTS, D.D., LL.D.

It is a great privilege to speak to the International Convention of the Young People's Society of Christian Endeavor. The privilege is highly esteemed for several reasons:

First, because it is a young people's convention, and the old proverb, "In to-day walks to-morrow," is applicable in a peculiar sense to the church of Jesus Christ. What that church will be in the next generation depends upon the young people of this generation.

A second reason is to be found in the fact that the Young People's Society of Christian Endeavor is definitely a part of the Christian church universal. While it has no official denominational connection, there are those of us who realize that it has interdenominational relations of a vital and intimate character; that it is of and by the church, and exists for the church.

A third reason is to be found in the representative character in which I appear before you. I am not here as a Presbyterian minister, but as the chairman of the executive committee of the Federal Council of the Churches of Christ in America.

This body represents thirty-two Christian denominations in the United States, with sixteen millions of communicants, and therefore a multitude of young people. I tender the congratulations of the Federal Council to the Convention, proffering best wishes for the increasing prosperity and power of the Young People's Society of Christian Endeavor.

Permit me, in dealing with the subject of the evening, to emphasize certain fundamental principles. International and interdenominational relationships, to be effective and beneficial, are to be based upon the great facts that constitute the unities of the Christian religion. Federation and co-operation, when made in any form, are of value only by their general acknowledgment of these unities.

I. First of these unities is the unique and supreme place in Christianity of Jesus Christ as God and Saviour. Beginning with the confession made by Peter, this supremacy has continued throughout the generations, and is the fundamental doctrine of the Christian religion. The acknowledgment of Jesus Christ as God and Saviour is the one thing that makes a man a Christian. The New Testament and the acknowledged Christian creeds emphasize the deity of Christ as well as His manhood in a notable manner. They make clear that by His humanity He is in sympathy with us men, and they also make clear that it is as God that He saves and governs us men. A divine Saviour is the only all-sufficient Saviour, and Jesus Christ is accepted by all worthy of the name of Christian as the divine Saviour who is able to save unto the uttermost all that come to God by Him.

It is evident that in these opening years of the twentieth century the passionate loyalty to Christ of the apostle Paul still pervades the Christian churches. And it is to be emphasized that the one doctrine that binds the American Christian churches in the Federal Council is that of the deity of Christ. It is the first of Christian doctrines, and is fundamental to international and interdenominational fellowship. Only a universal divine Saviour can be the universal divine Lord.

II. The second great unity is the actuality of the church visible and universal. The New Testament recognizes clearly the existence of the church in this character. The fact is that it does not know the Christian church in any other character. Whatever differences arose in the New Testament church, as, for instance, at Corinth, where some were of Paul, and some of Cephas, and some of Apollos, and some of Christ; nevertheless, these diversities were regarded simply as differences of opinion, not as constituting separate churches. Whether we deal with the Gospels or with the Epistles of Paul, Peter, and James, or with the book of Revelation, there is everywhere recognized the unity and the universality of that church concerning which Jesus said, "Upon this rock," namely, the confession of Himself as God and Saviour, "will I build my church." In this day of denominational division we are to remember the New Testament fact as to the unity and universality of the church.

III. A third fundamental fact is to be found in the New Testament statement of the one condition of salvation. Whether we consider in connection with this matter the words of Christ or the utterances of His apostles, in every case it will be found that the only condition of salvation is a profession of faith in Jesus Christ and of obedience to Him. Upon this profession baptism is to follow as the sign and seal of church-membership. You will note that a distinction is drawn between the condition of salvation and the administration of that ordinance which is the sign and seal of membership. They are not to be confused the one with the other. Persons are to be baptized because of their faith in Jesus Christ. They are not baptized in order that they may have faith. Here, again, we need in this day of denominational divisions to realize how sharply and definitely the singleness of faith as the condition of salvation emphasizes the unity and universality of the church.

IV. A fourth unity is found in the general recognition by all Christians of the Word of God as the only infallible rule of faith and practice. Whatever differences of interpretation as to doctrine or government Christians cherish in connection with the Holy Scriptures, these do not affect in any manner their acknowledgment of the supremacy of the Scriptures over thought and life. As we think upon the interdenominational and international relationships of Christians, there is no fact that should be more emphasized than this one. Whatever differences of creed or speech or government there may be among Christians, they all hold to the Scriptures as the one source of truth, and they stamp with the superscription of the denomination only what they all believe to be the gold of divine truth.

V. It is fundamental, further, that we realize the fact of the unity of the human race. The Bible knows no feature of the Godward relation of mankind that does not involve constantly this unity. It affects in a marked manner the whole plan of salvation. Christ was born to be the Saviour, not of one nation, but of the world; for it was the world that was lost. He died upon His cross on Calvary as "the propitiation for our sins, and not for ours only, but also for the sins of the whole world." There is not one gospel for the European and another for the African, one way of salvation for the American and another for the Chinaman. All are included under the salvation that is from sin, and all are salvable through the faith that is in Jesus Christ. This unity of the race in its lost estate and in the possibilities of redemption is fundamental to Christian thinking and planning. The church of Christ, to use an old figure of speech, is "separate as the billows and one as the sea."

Having the great facts in mind, of one Christ, one church, one condition, one Bible, and one humanity, the duty of co-operation on the part of all who bear the Christian name becomes apparent. I rejoice, in this connection, in the results that have been already wrought by the Society of Christian Endeavor, both in this country and throughout the world. Speaking for many Christians, I am glad of the work accomplished by the venerated president of the society, and tender to him the gratitude all Christians should feel for the services which he has under God rendered to mankind.

CHRISTIAN ENDEAVOR'S BEST — THE FIELD SECRETARIES.

THE BEAUTIFUL FLORIDA BOOTH

INTERDENOMINATIONAL AND INTERNATIONAL FELLOWSHIP NECESSARY TO WORLD-WIDE EVANGELIZATION

By Rev. L. B. Wolf, D.D.

Two things are ever found in close connection—a great cause, followed by a hearty response on the part of consecrated men and women. So it has always been in the world. Great souls in civil, national, and religious movements have always arisen and met the demands of the hour. In religion a Huss, a Jerome, a Luther, a Calvin, have realized for the world the highest conception of spiritual liberty. In national and civil affairs, a William the Silent, a Cromwell, a Washington, have led in great world-movements.

No cause of humanity is like that, in scope, breadth or vastness, which Jesus started. But the world has slowly interpreted it. Men have limited His work by their vision. But now the issues are being joined, and the conflict is drawing to a head all the combined powers of good and evil. Movements that demand a world's consideration are only parts of the stately march of the purposes of God. A world-wide purpose of evangelization calls for world-wide planning, and a kingdom of universal sway will result. Every Christian Endeavorer is called to do his share in this world-wide task. As a member of the church of Jesus Christ his task is a definite part of the task Christ committed to His church.

We may state the vast task in terms which God has put in our mouths or in the matchless words of Christ, "My name shall be great among the Gentiles, saith the Lord." Every knee shall bow and every tongue shall confess that Jesus Christ is Lord. "And they shall come from the east and from the west and from the north and from the south." Such is the divine scope of the task as stated in heavenly terms by God and His Son.

Set forth in terms of to-day, we should say that every prayer-wheel of Buddhism shall cease to whirl, every temple to Vishnu or Siva shall resound to hymns of praise to Christ; that cries to Rama, Hari, Vijiam, Maha, Siva, shall no longer be heard; but instead, "Thou only, O Christ, art worthy to receive honor and praise and power and dominion, for Thou hast conquered"; that every mosque shall add to its cry, "Great is Allah, only Allah is God"; "Great is Christ; only He is Saviour"; that every light of Asia shall be lost in that Light which, coming into the world, lighteth every man; and that the fetichism of darkest Africa shall be forgotten in the splendor of Christ.

The hour in world-evangelization demands readjustment of forces, and the home base is the place where this readjustment and combination of the forces must take place. These are not the days when we should send four or five "brands" of Methodism; or about the same number of Presbyterianism, English and American; several species of Baptists; pure, purer, and purest forms of Lutheranism; varying types, High and Low and Broad, of Episcopalianism, into the foreign field. The nations are drawing closer together, and the church must do the same. The church must call a halt and stop emphasizing denominations, valuable though they may be, and nations, great though they may be.

World-wide evangelization calls for world-wide terms, and these terms are found only in the school of Christ and in the great ecumenical creeds of the world. The unity of our faith is more important than the union in matters of government. The combination must come by learning to love, serve, yield, and give, as Christ did. We may cease trying to discuss a common denominator for the denominations, and may spend our energies in discovering a common Lord, who came to carry a common message of a common need, who called His church to a common task, and who promised to give universal victory.

It may not be out of place to say that the trouble of combining our forces and of fellowship does not lie in the foreign field among the foreign missionaries. I would not magnify what union might accomplish. I would not say we can double our forces and double our output by combining; but I would say, and say it with all my heart, that combination will make us stronger in the foreign field, especially in the great centres of population and the great cities, where overlapping and waste are more apparent. Now is the time for great central Christian colleges in India and China and Japan. The various Christian missions ought to meet on the platform of Christian education, and work together. There are vast possibilities, too, of combination and co-operation in medical work, in the preparation of Christian missionaries, as well as united evangelistic work in the great centres of population.

The hour demands a readjustment of our missionary forces on the foreign territory, and that readjustment depends upon the view taken by the church on the home base. We must save our faces as denominations here at home before the representatives of the various nations that are coming to our land as never before from every land; and we can best do this by combining, federating, uniting, in the great work of world-evangelization.

The world-wide evangelism may become the lever not only to lift the church into true spiritual power, but to develop in it, above all, true unity of life and power. What the form of government may be in the great Eastern nations is a matter that no one can settle now, but the task of evangelizing at present is so big and so commanding that it must appeal to all. The highest endeavor and the deepest consecration are demanded, and above all the call to every one is to have supreme faith in God's plan and His Son's atonement for the world. Most majestically the following lines voice the faith of God's people:

"God is working His purpose out as year succeeds to year;
God is working His purpose out, and the time is drawing near;
Nearer and nearer draws the time, the time that shall surely be,
When the earth shall be filled with the glory of God as the waters cover
  the sea.

"From utmost east and utmost west, wherever man's foot hath trod,
By the mouth of many messengers goes forth the voice of God.
Give ear to Me, ye continents; ye isles give ear to Me,
Till the earth may be filled with the glory of God as the waters cover
  the sea."

THE OPEN DOOR OF OPPORTUNITY.

By Rev. J. C. Caldwell, D.D.

World-building is not so interesting as man-building. Some men hold that tasks are interesting in proportion as they are difficult to perform; if this be good logic, then swinging worlds into space must take consideration secondary to building a man in time. We have no intimation that God had any trouble stringing planets along the path of His power; yet the centuries unite in the verdict that God has had much trouble in producing the divine style of manhood. Therefore it is safe to conclude that God never undertook a vaster plan than to build a man. Worlds play out His purposes in the harmony of gravitation. They spell out His plans in the law of obedience; but man oftentimes thwarts those purposes and destroys those plans by setting his own will over against the will of God. Thus he wanders, a kind of lost human Pleiad, through the space called time, always and ever coming to himself, but never wholly arriving. Yet man is God's world,—greater than any star world twinkling in space, because he feels, he loves, he thinks, he wills.

This is an age of thought. Thought rules the world; the thinking mind is the growing mind; the growing mind is the active mind; the active mind moves the man; and the man that moves helps to move the world.

I see the alphabet, twenty-six letters, fine in form, but forceless and useless until man by the power of thought takes these letters and joins them together, and writes up all of our literature, science, philosophy, and theology.

This is also an age of work. Never before were there so splendid opportunities for work as now. The fields are white to the harvest. Beckoning hands from the Macedonian kingdom are calling us to come over and help them. The young growing up hungry of mind and heart are appealing to us, and because we do not heed their appeals they feed on the husks of the world, and are dissatisfied. The great question for us to consider is the salvation of the present generation. By work the mind is redeemed from the thraldom of ignorance; the body from the curse of laziness; the earth from thorns and briers; and the spirit from the habit and power of sin. What has been accomplished without work? Absolutely nothing. The Micawbers of the race, those who are always waiting for something to turn up, have been the world's biggest nuisances. Christ said, "I must work." The servant must be as his Lord. There are no favorites, no exceptions. "To every man his work." Hence John, writing to the church at Philadelphia, said, "Behold, I have set before thee an open door, the open door of opportunity."

This is also an age of getting ready to work. It takes trained men and trained women to do things to-day. Willingness, main force, and awkwardness will not do. The prepared man will always get the best place and receive the best pay. The church as never before is calling for and demanding trained workers.

The Christian Endeavor movement, which was started thirty years ago by Dr. Clark, under the guidance of the Holy Spirit, is an open door to train young men and women to do in a systematic way what they used to do in a spasmodic way. It trains them how to be every-day practical Christians. It is indeed a most beautiful sight to see young men and women living a life hid with Christ in God in the home, on the streets, in the busy marts of trade, everywhere.

This young people's movement has opened a door for the reading and studying of God's word, which "is a lamp unto my feet and a light unto my path." I thank God more young people are studying the Book to-day than ever before.

It has given them an opportunity to pray, not to say prayers, but to pray; for there can be no prayer unless backed up by faith. If we ask God for something and do not believe we are going to get it, He will not disappoint us; we shall not get it. We also must remember God is not going to do for us what we can do for ourselves. Prayer is the silence of a soul absorbed in God. The keeping of the Quiet Hour every morning alone with God will change the whole complexion of the day, and life will mean more to you than it does now.

Then there is the open door of service. I like the great motto of the Salvation Army; it must have been born for those workers in the warm heart of the mother of the Army, Catherine Booth. Their motto is, "Saved to serve." Some seem to put the period after the first word.

That is bad punctuation and worse Christianity. We are saved to be savers. There is needed the divine Saviour and the human saver. Only he that has been saved can help somebody else. The tingle of experience in the blood attracts men.

A minister noted for his striking way of putting things was preaching upon the words that were spoken of Paul and his companions, "These that have turned the world upside down are come hither also." He said there were three points to his sermon: first, the world was wrong side up; second, it had to be gotten right side up; third, we are the fellows to do it. Friends, that is our duty, and God cast upon us the task of the times:

"He has sounded forth the trumpet that shall never call retreat;
He is sifting out the hearts of men before His judgment seat;
O, be swift, my soul, to answer Him; be jubilant my feet;
Our God is marching on."

This God-given movement has opened a door of larger fellowship, helping to answer the prayer, "That they all may be one," breaking down denominational lines, breaking down racial lines, realizing as never before that "one is your Master, even Christ, and all ye are brethren"; that God "hath made of one blood all nations of men for to dwell on all the face of the earth, and hath determined the times before appointed, and the bounds of their habitation."

And so to-day we can meet upon this common platform as representatives of the world, and join in exclaiming, "Glory to God in the highest, on earth peace, good will toward men." This is emblematic; may it also be prophetic of the times when

"The war-drum throbs no longer, and the battle-flags are furled
In the parliament of man, the federation of the world."

I do not know what you may think is the solvent for all the racial differences in this world to-day; but for me I firmly believe as I stand here to-night that the only panacea, the only cure, for all the racial misunderstandings is the religion of Jesus Christ, and the Christian Endeavor movement has done more to bring about harmony among the races than anything else extant.

A MESSAGE FROM GERMANY.

By Mrs. Friedrich Blecher.

I am very glad to greet you as sisters in Christ from across the Atlantic Ocean, and I wish to thank you for the many stimulations that we have received from the Society of Christian Endeavor. At first, we believed that Christian Endeavor was not adaptable to our German conditions. But after a trial was made, about sixteen years ago, it grew more and more, and we then saw that Christian Endeavor was a very good means to win the young people, through the young people, for Christ.

The Young People's Society has become dear to us for its definite principles. As we did not know a better translation for Christian Endeavor, we called it the Young People's Society for Decided Christianity. The Young People's Society requires from its members the same as the Bible requires of every true believer—full surrender of heart and life to the Lord.

The Christian Endeavor Society has become so dear to us because it takes a clear view of this purpose, and because it does not permit any indecision such as is found so often in other societies.

Did not our Master say, "Feed my lambs," and not, "Play with them"? One of our German pastors has said he has discovered that the most earnest Christian Endeavor societies are the most prosperous ones.

The Christian Endeavor Society has become also dear to us because of its good and wise organization, as it puts every member to active work, and there is no place for the drones and the know-betters.

We have found, after all, that it was God that put the idea of Christian Endeavor into the heart of our dear, honored Dr. Clark. Many a pastor has called the Christian Endeavor Society the heart of Christian life in his congregation, where the members of Christian Endeavor have tried in humility to serve their pastor and their church.

We often talk of beautiful meetings, but let me ask, When are our meetings beautiful? When the beauty of our Lord will be opened to the souls more than ever before, especially when the young people find their joy in the Lord, and are not lost in the things of the world.

Let me give you a few statistics of our Endeavor work in Germany:

The German Union supports at this time a general secretary, three field secretaries and six clerks in our central office. It comprises 420 societies, with about 11,000 members, out of which have gone 720 special workers of the Lord. We have twelve state unions. For home and foreign missions our German Union raised last year 30,000 marks. It also mainly supports fifteen missionaries in the Caroline Islands, the German possessions. It has bought the first mission ship, called Peace. In the year 1910 more than three million Christian tracts were distributed, against the influence of the bad and cheap literature. It also established libraries in different societies, with instructive and edifying literature. It also looks after the welfare of the factory girls. We have a Christian Endeavor Garten, a Christian school for housework, in Saxony. In the Garten the girls can have gymnastic exercises, and in the school the girls learn general housework.

The Christian Endeavor Society seeks to strike at the roots of social evils by placing the young people upon the rock of God's word, where alone they can resist the flood of the spirit of modern times, the immorality, luxury, and unbelief.

The German Union has seventy-five Junior societies, with about 1,500 members. It publishes three papers, with a circulation of 17,000 copies.

May the Lord make the Christian Endeavor Society in all lands a life-saving station for many lost souls and a training-school for all its members for good service and to be found worthy at the coming of our Lord.

TRAINING THE BODY TO EXPRESS THE SOUL.

By Margaret Koch, *Field Secretary for Maine.*

I want to say to you, first of all, that you Junior superintendents, as well as everybody else, have just two ways by means of which you can make yourselves known to your children—your body and your voice. When you send for a carpenter to build a house for you, you send for a man that has sense enough to come with sharpened tools. Sometimes you meet Juniors that have not sharpened their tools very well; and so by the invitation of Dr. Clark and Mr. Shaw, I am here this morning to talk to you about this tremendously important subject.

When I talk to the Juniors I ask them to guess a little bit of a word that has not many letters in it, and which begins with H. Only four letters; what is it? That's right, "Help." Now add "r" to it—"Helper." By the way you carry your chest I know that you have the capital H. What is the other word, the antithesis of "help"? Yes, "hindrance"; and that begins with a little "h." Sometimes when you sit in a church with your chest in—the way you listen when your pastor preaches—you say that your pastor is "not a good preacher." The fault isn't always with the preacher.

What will help you to be a physical helper? How should you like to have others sit if you were the preacher? The best way to sit helpfully is with the feet squarely on the floor, sitting up straight, not leaning back against the seat. That's it. Of course it is hard. Everything that is worth while is hard. Let me show you how you can help yourselves to be thus helpful. I will give you an exercise that will be sure to do it, if you will be faithful and take the medicine. Put your fingers on your chest in the region of the third rib. Now let your chest drop way down, and let your head drop way back, and then begin to lift. Imagine a little hook just above your head, right up there. It comes down and fastens into a little bunch of hair right on the crown of the head. Now let that little hook draw you straight up,—your chest down, and arms on a level with the shoulders, remember, then gradually drawing you up. Do it slowly. That lifts your whole body.

I want to tell you something. Nine-tenths of the people that you meet carry their vital organs from one to six inches too low. You know the kind of substance these organs are made of—a soft, spongy substance. The lungs press on the heart, and the lungs and heart together press on the stomach and other organs, and these organs press down on your knees and upon your heels; and so you go around weighing about two thousand pounds all the time. Everything in life that you do pulls you down. You know that you are not so tall at night as you are in the morning.

We have got to do all we can to help the Master do His work through our bodies. What is the little word of four letters? That's it, "life." Now I believe that God wants us to have a thoroughly live body. So many people go around half dead. I feel like taking them by the nape of the neck and shaking a little ginger into them. God cannot use that kind of creature. For His dear sake we ought to be willing to put a little time and energy into ourselves. Your boys and girls are going to look at your faces and woe be to you if the corners of your mouth turn down. This can be helped, however. Rub your faces up; and, when you wash your faces, rub them up. Did you ever notice how cats wash their faces? They are wiser than human beings. Just this little bit of a thing is going to help you to be helpful for the Master. Let Him use that face of yours, and let it radiate with all the power and strength that is in you. Rub it up!

Another thing. How many of you know how to stand correctly and powerfully? Let me say this to you: there is a certain right way of standing, when you can get hold of your audience; get a grip on them. You can push yourself out so that the person on the rear seat cannot but listen. You can seem to project your personality way across the room to the very back seat. Now stand, please. Just lift yourselves on the balls of the feet, in this way. Go up just as high as you can, and come down as slowly as possible. Do all your exercises slowly. Then touch your heels lightly. You will be tempted to go back on them unless you watch yourself, but stay forward. The reason why you want to go back on your heels so much is because the muscles back of the knees pull you back. Put your fingers here on the hip-joints, and just bend forward, making a right angle of your body. Now try it again. Everybody up on the balls of the feet, way up. Let your spirits rise; let your faces shine out. Stay forward on the balls of the feet. What have you in the ball of your foot that you haven't in the heel? A little spring. In your ankle there is a bunch of nerve-centres, and, when you step on the heel, you jar that nerve-centre. When you jar a nerve-centre, what happens to the rest of the nerves? They all get jarred. The body is the only thing, the only tool, we have got to work with; and so we will do everything we can to keep it strong for the Master.

Now a little suggestion with reference to your voice. How many of you have ever thought it made any difference what kind of a voice you use? I want you girls to listen a minute. How many of you have ever heard a voice like this—characterless, no force, or energy? Now put your hands at the diaphragm, the thumbs at the side, and hands spread out in back and front, like this. Now inhale—exhale. Now place your hand here at the front, and push out. Make a fist of your diaphragm. Push out again, and hold for a moment. Now put your tongue up in the roof of your mouth, and tell me what you find there. Yes, a cavity. An oval-shaped cavity. That is your second most beautiful resonance cavity in the whole body. The most beautiful one is between the eyes. When you force your voice back into the throat you get absolutely no use of your resonance cavity in the roof of your mouth. You want to get your voice so you will speak right here, with the lips, not in the throat. Now let us try it. Bring the corners of your mouth together. Now try this exercise, pulling the upper lip, then letting go. Put your teeth lightly over the lips, first the under and then the upper. Do it lightly, so as not to injure them. There are more lazy muscles in that upper lip than in any other part of the body. They tell about "keeping a stiff upper lip," but it isn't a good thing for the voice. Now say the word "Poise," softly, lightly, "Poise." I believe that God wants us to do these very things, that radiant life, a life of helpfulness, that comes from your voice, and from your entire being, may be ours. This is the kind of life that will win.

So many people get the impression that the church is a solemn sort of thing, not a radiant, helpful thing; and so they do not care anything about it.

Now one more exercise. Push out here at the diaphragm, and then speak with the lips the one word, "Halt!" Say it strongly, but only with the lips. Learn to do these things and get strong, splendid voices, so that the thing you want to express will carry itself to your hearers. Learn to speak with your lips, and cultivate the strength of your muscles, especially of the diaphragm, and you will find that you will have a voice that people will want to listen to.

For His dear sake, friends, we will do these things, that we may be more effective for Christ. If these few simple suggestions are carried out, I know what they will do for you, and all that will be done for the Master, when we have learned to make the very most of ourselves for His dear sake.

THE CALL FOR FELLOWSHIP IN SERVICE.

By President Ira Landrith, D.D., LL.D.

It is not shouting our shibboleths that postpones the millennium. It is rather our hateful disposition to swat in the mouth the other shouters. And this is true of all kinds of shouters and of all kinds of shibboleths.

Did you read last month that melancholy story about poor John

Starnes, who died in a Southern State after forty years and more as a hermit in despair? Starnes went into voluntary exile because he believed he had slain his own beloved commander, Stonewall Jackson.

It was in the shadowy part of a May day in 1863 that the most intrepid, brainy, devout military chieftain of a dozen generations, with a small company of picked men, stole out from his own lines to do a bit of spying on the enemy, for the purpose of to-morrow's attack. Satisfied, they stealthily returned through the twilight. Suddenly there was a rattle of musketry, a groan and a fall, and Stonewall Jackson lay a-dying, the victim of a pitiful mistake—shot to death by one of his own men. Friend and foe alike deplored the manner of his taking off. And it must have been a cruel disappointment to the hero himself thus to die. It dethroned the reason of John Starnes.

But the history of the Christian church and the story of the warfare of right against wrong runs red with the blood of other Stonewall Jacksons as brave as the Virginia hero and as prayerful as he—shot to death, not by accident, but by deliberate design, and not by avowed enemies but by the professed friends of the cause of Christianity, men and women who had no better reason for their fratricidal mania than that their victims did not belong to their particular ecclesiastical, political, social, national, or racial coterie.

O, the shame of it, that immortal souls and blessed causes should be lost on acount of our narrowness and our meanness! For even yet, while

> "There's a wideness in God's mercy
>   Like the wideness of the sea,"
> There's a narrowness in man's meanness
>   Just as narrow as it can be.

If Paul the princely could be all things to all men that he might save some, surely we ought to be willing at least to be all things to some men, and some things to all men, in order that we may at least save a few. If Jesus could deign to dine with Zacchæus, we might for Jesus' sake occasionally sup with sinners, or breakfast with brethren who have committed no greater folly than joining some other church than ours.

But my theme is "The Call for Fellowship in Service"—not fellowship in the social circle, nor necessarily in the home circle, but in the wider work of world-winning in the name of Him who died for the salvation and religious nurture of all men everywhere. It is a call to the abandonment of any prejudices, or antipathies, or complacencies that have crippled the church of Jesus Christ in its march to the conquest of the world.

At the threshold of the discussion let us, if we can, get rid of a difficulty or two. The Good Samaritan seems to have met all of the conditions of brotherly love when he sent to a wayside inn and at his own cost committed to the care of others the stricken victim he had by chance discovered. And Jesus Himself assumed to select the three disciples whom He preferred as intimates, the sharers of His holiest joys and the companions of His deepest griefs.

Yet there are among us some theorists whose interpretation of fellowship for other people demands the best guest-chamber for every object of Christian benevolence, and an impossible social impartiality toward all classes and conditions of men. More than one religious and civic problem in our own national life would have been solved had we frankly faced the fact that, while no Christian has the right to offend or wound his fellow-workers, every man must be allowed to choose his own close friends, and must respect the rules that govern human society.

Rare prejudices, for example, that are mere prejudices, have no claim to any dignity which Christian people need regard. But race differences that ought to persist cannot be treated with contempt nor adjusted at long range. To be more definite, it is a poor specimen of the genus Caucasian Christian who will not cheerfully and fraternally work with the sincere and earnest African lover of our Lord for the upbuilding of the kingdom of Christ. But he is an equally unwise Caucasian who, in doing so, ruthlessly violates the racial traditions of all the centuries.

Thank God, Christian Endeavor is finding a providentially appointed way to help the brother black man effectively to help himself, his country, and every cause that God loves, without at the same time wrecking itself in the breakers of a social shore that has been the scene of a thouasnd such useless disasters. We shall lose no opportunity to encourage and to co-operate with the sane and earnest leadership of the negro race in creating such a Christlike race-pride and consciousness, and such an intelligent and zealous evangelistic and religious educational spirit as shall tend to make our negro neighbors as consistent Christians and as loyal and dependable citizens as are the members of any other race. When this is done, we shall hear no more fanatical clamor on the one side for a mutually intolerable inter-racial intimacy, nor on the other for the educational, economic, and political oppression of black men by white ones.

The most thoughtful Christians of both races are standing together on this plaform to-day, and if let alone by cheap demagogues, both political and ecclesiastical, the rank and file of both races will agree just here. Racial fellowship, therefore, is necessary to the advancement of the Kingdom.

No less necessary is sectional fellowship. Not only is the war over, but we have heard lately that all Anglo-Saxon wars are over, and henceforth the degree of a man's worth and not the place of his birth shall determine his claim on our confidence. All prejudice is the pitiful, misshapen child of ignorance, and on the site where we come to know each other better we shall people—particularly we Christian Endeavorers shall people—the graveyards of our prejudices. In very truth are we to agree in this Convention that

> "In Christ there is no East or West,
> In Him no South or North,
> But one great fellowship of love
> Throughout the whole wide earth.

> "In Christ now meet both East and West,
> In Him no South or North,
> All Christly souls are one in Him,
> Throughout the whole wide earth."

I have always believed that if the Pennsylvania Railroad had run down South in 1850 there would never have been a Civil War; and if at that time there had been a Christian Endeavor Society holding conventions alternately North and South, the two sections would never have pointed a gun at each other. An old college professor used to say, "Never call a man ignorant; say that he lacks information." What the North and the South need is to know each other.

After Atlantic City, 1911, surely there will be no spirituality-paralyzing international prejudice. If there are ever any more wars among Christian nations—which God forbid!—Christian Endeavorers, though they may respond to the call of patriotism to participate in them, will never have been even remotely the cause of them.

Due very largely to Christian Endeavor, interdenominational fellowship has now become much more substantial a thing than an optimist's iridescent dream. If we had saved all of the ammunition which through the centuries we church people have shot at each other in a worse than worthless war of words over tweedledees of subtle doctrinal differences or tweedledums of church polity, and had turned our guns upon the devil and his army, we should have had the enemy on the run long ago.

Into the field of battling brothers Christian Endeavor rushed thirty years ago with the white flag of the Prince of peace, and only here and there nowadays can be heard a whisper of what erstwhile was a mighty and monstrous arrogance—proclaiming unashamed, "The only way to salvation is through my own little narrow ecclesiastical wicket-gate." There are still

"Many men with many minds,"
And many churches of many kinds.

Long for it as we may, pray for it as we must, the day of the organic union of all the churches seems scarcely to show gray in the east. But it will be the shame of our religion if the churches that are doctrinally and governmentally close of kin cannot be set together in families before the end of another decade. Pity us, O thou trust-forming, combination-creating secular world, if we American Presbyterians, for example, must for even nine more years retain nine different names. But if we cannot have the union of even a few of the denominations, let us have the cordial communion of all of them.

We shall not forget, however, that all true fellowship is founded on loyalty. He, and he only, has the right to love who supremely loves his own.

To thine own church be true,
And it must follow as the night the day,
Thou canst not then be false to any church.

And now let us listen to the many-voiced call for fellowship. Hear the first one in the open heavens yonder, in answer to the Master's intercessory prayer that we all might be one. Every utterance of God, every teaching of Christ, every page of the Bible, is a call to co-operation and brotherhood, and to the bearing of one another's burdens. A few fraternal fishermen, because they hung together, reached in a generation the uttermost parts of the world. What might not present-day Christianity accomplish in a single blessed year if we would but put aside our differences, magnify the vital things in which we agree, and march in solid battle line in obedience to the Great Commission! Brethren, that march ought to begin this very year.

Then there is the call of the times to which we cannot afford to be deaf. Every other cause combines; every other enterprise unites. Evil is organized into a perfectly fitted body—hands and feet and eyes and head and vicious heart and all. It is only the best thing in all the world, the church of God, that has been willing to split itself up into weak and sometimes warring factionism.

Finally, let us heed the definite call of the tremendous need. The work to be done is a peremptory demand for harmony in doing it. The Western farmer who is said to have enjoined his neighbor from erecting a windmill because there would not be wind enough for two was a Solomonic philosopher in comparison with the churchman who seeks for his own denomination a monopoly of the religious activities of the community.

The call of the twentieth century for Christian fellowship in service is a call to the most magnificent task of which the towering ambition of vaulting enterprise ever dreamed. The battles of the church at home and the campaigns of the church abroad are, in comparison with all the wars of all the centuries, as Gettysburg to the brawl of negro urchins in a back alley. We must have interdenominational, inter-racial, interpartisan, and international fellowship if the church is to save its own life in the unequal struggle of a divided Christendom against united iniquity.

The saloon must go, but it will not go until it is bidden to be gone by an unafraid chorus of Christian voices. In response to such a chorus it would long ago have hied itself to its native hell. It is going there from the Southland; and if your people up North do not bestir yourselves we Southerners must insist on a new Missouri Compromise, for "this country cannot exist forever half slave and half free."

Labor and capital must be friends, but that peace-pact will not be signed until the Sermon on the Mount shall be consistently preached in every pulpit and exemplified in every pew.

Poverty and wretchedness and hunger, and the wan pallor of vicarious suffering for others' sins, must all cease. But these blessings of release will loiter until we hush our bickerings, and bludgeon our selfishness, and throttle our sectarianism, and march in lock-step against every foe of humanity.

The unsaved throngs at home and the untaught heathen abroad must be led to the foot of the cross. But this can never be until the hand that leads them is the good right hand of a spiritually united Christendom that as consistently practises the brotherhood of man as it preaches the fatherhood of God.

CHAPTER XVIII

THE CLOSING SESSION.

Another tumultuous sea of sound and of color in Auditorium Endeavor dashed and swelled for an hour before the closing session.

The places for the various State delegations were marked by standards of all the hues under heaven.

It seemed as if most of the Endeavorers were waving something—a gorgeous banner, a C. E. flag, the Stars and Stripes, or only a programme or a handkerchief.

Eager young fellows were standing on chairs frantically waving their arms and leading the yells of their delegations.

Now one yell would surmount the others and ride triumphantly on the hubbub; as this, to the tune of "John Brown's Body":

> "Pennsyl — Pennsyl — Pennsylvania,
> Pennsyl — Pennsyl — Pennsylvania,
> Pennsyl — Pennsyl — Pennsylvania,
>   And the Y. P. S. C. E.
> We are going to California,
> We are going to California,
> We are going to California,
>   In Nineteen, One, and Three."

Now New Jersey's mighty cohort breaks in with the "Glory Song," and carries all before it.

Now the Washington singers on the platform peal out their special Convention song, with its infectious chorus, " 'Rah for the City by the Sea."

Out of the jumble rise half a dozen toy balloons, bobbing up and down and sometimes floating to the brilliant ceiling.

In front the banners of New York and Illinois are conspicuous, Rhode Island's Hope banner, and the purple and yellow of New Jersey.

It seemed quite impossible to check the din, let alone stop it, but Mr. Foster's magic touch quieted it almost instantly, and the last praise service opened as the first had begun, all rising and singing, "All hail, the power of Jesus' name."

Mr. Lincoln led the Philadelphia chorus in the rendering of Kipling's "Recessional," and then, on the request of Mrs. Horsefield, the combined choruses sung "The Song of Victory."

Rev. Robert E. Pretlow, trustee from the Friends, conducted the opening devotional exercises. An impressive feature was the repeating by the great audience after Mr. Pretlow of three sentences: "The Lord keep our ideals high"; "The Lord keep our outlook broad"; "The Lord help us to be patient in the little things."

Dr. Clark announced an important step taken during the Convention, the formation of a Federation of Christian Endeavor State Presidents. The president is Mr. John T. Sproull of New Jersey; the vice-president, Mr. A. W. Johnson of California; the secretary, Mr. T. N. Jayne of Minnesota; the treasurer, President Stewart of Manitoba; the chairman of the executive committee, Mr. John R. Clements of New York. This new organization will do much to keep former presidents in active touch with Christian Endeavor.

After a well-appreciated solo by Miss Preston, the purpose meeting began—the roll-call of the States.

First, New Hampshire, as its delegates were obliged to leave early. The work in this State is much broken up by the mountain ranges, but the Endeavorers expressed their purpose to put Christian Endeavor in the forefront, believing that no other organization under the skies is better adapted to the upbuilding of Christian character. Then a verse of the beautiful State song.

The next two hours were filled with testimonies like these, crowded, varied, vigorous, with great work back of them and looking forward to great work ahead of them.

Representatives from each delegation—no more than four —came to the platform in brisk succession. Usually the State president was the spokesman, sometimes the secretary or the field secretary.

They brought their bright banners with them, sometimes each of the four bearing one. Many of these were the unique banners made in Japan, China, India, and Africa for former increase campaigns. These were displayed as they spoke.

At the close of each testimony from the platform, the delegation of that State, already on their feet, sang a stanza of some song, usually the State Christian Endeavor song, or repeated in concert some verse of Scripture.

Of course we have room for only snatches from these more than fifty worth-reporting utterances. Never are space limitations so perplexing as in reporting the final meeting of one of our great Conventions.

Alabama reported the organization of 61 new societies during the past two years, the State's apportionment being 60. It added $100 to its gift for the Headquarters Building. It is planning new work for the colored youth.

Arkansas promised to fall into line for the Efficiency Campaign.

California intends to emphasize the Efficiency Campaign all along the line, from president down. It will try for one thousand young men and women who will study the Bible systematically for soul-winning. It will work to make Los Angeles, 1913, the greatest International Convention ever held.

Colorado, proud of its gift of Karl Lehmann to national Christian Endeavor, will do its best for the Efficiency Campaign.

Connecticut, the first State to organize a State and a local Christian Endeavor union, seeks also to be first in its loyalty to Christ, and its devotion to those principles which have made Christian Endeavor strong in the past. It has got the campaign habit, and will enter with zest the new campaign for greater efficiency.

Delaware, since last October, has added nineteen new societies and a thousand members. It proposes to do the same—and more—during the next two years. It promises $100 more for the Building "if it is needed"; and it is!

The District of Columbia came forward with a beautiful national flag, which the Endeavorers received by rising and singing "America." "Education, Organization, Agitation" will be the District's motto. It expects the formation of 60 new societies in colored churches. The Washington choir sung a stanza of a song written by Secretary Gates, "The Nation's Capital for Christ."

Florida means to stand firm on the platform which Dr. Clark has established. It will work for better relations between the white and colored young people of the State.

Hawaii had a fine delegate in the person of Mr. S. K. Kamiopili, but he was obliged to leave before the purpose meeting.

Idaho was proud that it was among the first States to secure its apportioned number of societies in the Increase Campaign. It takes for its new motto, "Personal Responsibility." Its purpose is to win Idaho for Christ, believing that "if Christian Endeavor is good for you and me, it is good for somebody else."

Illinois has made good in the Increase Campaign. It rehearsed its success in the campaign for the closing of the postoffice on Sunday, and it asked for prayers that it might succeed in reversing the decision of the Illinois supreme court barring the Bible from the public schools.

Indiana's purpose is to raise $500 for the Building, to keep up its splendid Junior and Intermediate work, and to gain greater numbers and efficiency.

Iowa's representative told the story of the angel who sought to take to heaven the fairest thing of earth. First he selected a flower, then the bloom of youth on a lovely girl's face, then the love of mother watching over the girl. But when he reached heaven he found that the flower was faded, and the bloom of youth also had passed away, and mother-love alone was left—love, the only thing on earth that is fit for heaven.

Kansas, pointing to the Latin motto on its banner, "To the stars through difficulties," seeks a thorough organization of the State work, and more Quiet-Hour and Tenth-Legion members. Kansas can pledge both political parties to the Christian Endeavor goal of "a saloonless nation by 1920."

Kentucky's hope was to stand foremost among the States when we meet in Los Angeles in 1913. The beautiful State song, to the tune of "My Old Kentucky Home," was, as always, greatly enjoyed.

Maine, in loyalty to Dr. Clark, pledged itself to the Efficiency Campaign. Its State song, to the tune of "Tramp, tramp, tramp, the boys are marching," had a hearty ring. A striking feature of Maine's response was the presentation to the audience of the seven delegates from the parent society in Williston Church, led by their splendid pastor, Rev. Jesse Hill. Young Garland, a manly lad in the delegation, was introduced by Dr. Clark as the son of one of the charter members of the first society. His father was only twelve years old when the society was formed, but led one of the first prayer meetings and was one of the early presidents.

Maryland expressed allegiance to the Efficiency Campaign, and—as it never fails to do—won applause by its lovely song to the tune of "Maryland, my Maryland."

Massachusetts's president expressed the purpose of the Old Bay State for better prayer meetings, more efficient committee work, and more loyal service. "Jesus is all the world to me" was sung with much earnestness by the 252 Massachusetts delegates.

Michigan gave one of Dr. Hubbell's grape-canister fusillades: 290 new societies in two years—purpose to furnish every church with a Christian Endeavor society and every Christian Endeavor society with a Junior society—will push rural Endeavor—have two field secretaries and a Junior organizer in the field—$300 more for the Building!

Minnesota has had a prosperous two years following the International Convention at St. Paul; has added 177 new societies; has given about $4,700 to the Building; plans for a second field worker.

Here we had a solo by Miss Ethel Foster, "Teach Me to Pray," with a violin accompaniment by Mr. Sydney A. Clark. Then the roll of States was broken for words from some representatives of other lands.

Canada spoke to the celebration of Dr. Clark's sixtieth birthday, on September 12, at his birthplace at Aylmer, Quebec, and in Ottawa. Glad mention was made of the coming union of the Canadian Methodist, Congregational, and Baptist churches. Canada will soon have three field secretaries. Manitoba leads the world in gifts to the Headquarters Building. The goodly Canadian delegation, each bearing the British flag, sang with spirit "The Maple Leaf Forever."

Great Britain spoke in the persons of President Horsefield and Mrs. Horsefield. They had learned in this American visit that "C. E." means "Continual Enjoyment." "Great Britain is one with you in the splendid enterprise you have before you in the next two years, one with you in the great fight against the drink traffic, one with you in the purpose to lead men to a closer fellowship with Jesus Christ, one with you in the aim to purify national and civic life." The Canadian delegation began to sing "God save the King," and instantly the entire assembly was on its feet singing the British national hymn, and waving anything wavable as Mr. Horsefield waved the American and Mr. Foster the British flag. Then a stanza of "Blest be the tie."

Germany, another Fatherland, received vigorous cheers as Mr. and Mrs. Blecher stepped forward. Secretary Rottmann interpreted for Mr. Blecher as he said in German: "Thirteen thousand six hundred Endeavorers in Germany send you their heartiest congratulations. They give me the commission to thank you for the idea of Christian Endeavor. When ten years ago we realized what were our responsibilities to Christian Endeavor, we sent to foreign countries for Christian Endeavor literature, and translated it. Some of these German translations went to Russia, Austria, and other lands, and started many societies there. We in Germany have written upon our banner the same word, 'Efficiency,' that you have fixed upon for the next two years. We have been counselled to make the principles of Christian Endeavor easier, but we will not give up anything. We stand for Christ, and not for ourselves. He consecrated Himself that we might be consecrated in the truth; and if somebody tells us to lower our banner, we lift it the higher, that all of us may be lifted up with the principles of Christian Endeavor."

After a few earnest words in English by Mrs. Blecher, all in the house of German birth were asked to rise, and fully 250 rose. Then this fine company sang the great German hymn, Luther's "Ein feste Burg ist unser Gott."

India's host of Endeavorers was represented by President and Mrs. Anderson. "The purpose of the Indian Endeavorers is summed up in the motto of one of the greatest of American

Rev. C. H. Tyndall, D.D.
Mt. Vernon, N. Y.

Fred B. Smith,
New York.

Rev. Ira Landrith, D.D.,
LL.D., Nashville, Tenn.

Booker T. Washington,
LL.D., Tuskegee, Ala.

Rev. Howard B. Grose,
D.D., Boston, Mass.

Rev. Sylvanus Stall, D.D.
Philadelphia, Pa.

Rev. Alexander Gilray,
D.D., Toronto, Canada.

Hon. Samuel B. Capen,
LL.D., Boston, Mass.

Rev. Jesse Hill,
Portland, Me.

missionaries, Adoniram Judson: 'Devoted for life.'" They then sung a Bengali hymn that is often sung by the Bengali Endeavorers when they plead with their countrymen to come to Jesus.

Burma had five delegates, and so was better represented in this Convention than any other land across the sea. "The nine thousand Endeavorers of Burma send greetings. We all realize that we have the business of the King in hand. We desire to do more during the next two years than ever before. In 1913, when you will be on the other side of the continent, we shall be celebrating the one-hundredth anniversary of the commencement of missions in Burma. We hope that by that time there will be 100,000 Christians in our own Baptist denomination, and many, many more in the other denominations; and we hope that the number of Burmese Christian Endeavorers will be more than doubled." Then the five sung "The King's Business" in Burmese so admirably as to win great applause.

China's 781 societies spoke through the founders of Christian Endeavor in that great empire, Mr. and Mrs. Hubbard. China is the "banner country" of Christian Endeavor in the literal sense, and beautiful Chinese symbolic flags were shown, one presented to the Convention and one to Dr. Clark.

Japan's two delegates gave a brief but magnificent greeting. They merely rose, stretched up their arms, and shouted with all their might, "Christian Endeavor *banzai!* Dr. Clark *banzai!*" "Banzai" is the Japanese "hurrah!" and means, "May you live ten thousand years!"

The Philippines had for their messenger that cheery Christian Endeavor missionary, Rev. George William Wright. At Dr. Clark's request, Mr. Wright spoke in Filipino, bringing down the house by saying at the close, "And now Dr. Clark will translate what I have said." After the laughter had subsided, however, Mr. Wright added that if Dr. Clark's dictionary agreed with his own, he would interpret his remarks as expressing the desire of Philippine Endeavorers for better organization, many new societies, and much power in all the societies.

Secretary Shaw read this telegram from the president of the Mexican Christian Endeavor Union:

"May heaven's richest blessing rest upon you as you set up the international banner of Christian Endeavor at Atlantic City. Mexican Endeavorers with new liberties rejoice more than ever in this world-wide fellowship. New conditions here open wonderful opportunities. Pray that Endeavorers may play well their parts.   S. G. INMAN."

Also this from Agram, Croatia:

"The first Christian Endeavor conference in any city of Croatia was recently held in Agram, and was very much blessed,

The Lord sent us that dear man of God, Brother Stolpmann of Germany, who was permitted to be a worthy transmitter of the will of God. I hope that in the course of the summer three new societies will be added to our ranks. We will prayerfully stand by you on the occasion of your coming great Convention, and send hearty greetings to all.   SAMUEL SCHUMACHER."

And this cablegram from the president of the European Christian Endeavor Union, from Belfast:

"European greetings.   JOHN POLLOCK."

The Fisk Jubilee Singers then sang two very remarkable songs, "I got a cross" and "My soul is a witness for my Lord." The tremendous applause could be quieted only by Dr. Clark's promise that they should be heard again later in the evening.

Announcement was made of the suggestion of the United Presbyterian rally that an invitation should be sent to the national convention next month of the United Presbyterian denominational society, urging them to join the Christian Endeavor fellowship; and the following was moved:

"*Resolved*, That in response to the resolution from the United Presbyterian rally, we send a cordial invitation to the Young People's Christian Union of the United Presbyterian Church to join our world-wide fellowship by affiliating with us as Young People's Unions of Christian Endeavor, and so make possible an all-inclusive young people's federation, with common methods of service and a common name throughout the world."

This motion was carried heartily and unanimously. Let us all pray that this great step in the direction of Christian unity may be taken.

Secretary Shaw here gave a new summary of the glorious results of the Increase Campaign for the purpose of incorporating information received during the Convention, as that Maryland has reached its quota, and Ohio has added largely to its numbers reported. In honor of the splendid achievements of the Allen League a colored Methodist delegate from Florida was given the floor. Though a young woman, she made herself heard far better than the average man, and brought down the house when she expressed her determination to attend the Los Angeles Convention if she had to start a year ahead and walk there. She asserted the intention of the colored Endeavorers to form State and local unions all their own.

Here the roll-call of States was resumed.

Missouri took for its motto, "Whatsoever"; and for its purpose, to do "whatever Christ would like to have it do."

Nebraska's goal was 240 new societies; it has formed 315. Its purposes include personal work, and the holding of Christian Endeavor insitutes in all districts for the training of "Christian Endeavor experts." It gave $1,000 more to the Building.

New Jersey's mighty host was greeted with cordial cheers as they rose, and as President Sproull spoke for them. They gave $1,000 more for the Building. They will seek to train "Christian Endeavor experts." They sung as their purpose song, "I'll go where you want me to go, dear Lord."

New York, the birthplace of the Tenth Legion, expressed through President Clements its purpose to gain new devotion, new efficiency and new enlargement. Its great company of Endeavorers sung the first stanza of Mr. Clement's popular hymn, "Somebody."

North Carolina has three purposes: to have a field secretary in connection with South Carolina and Virginia; to form a special committee for work looking toward the organization of colored unions; to establish a State Christian Endeavor paper.

North Dakota, a "dry" State, proposes to remain "dry." It will go ahead with Junior and Intermediate work.

Ohio's goodly delegation desired still better county organization, Christian Endeavor education to develop leaders, the vital occupation of the field it has already seized by organizing 730 new societies in the past two years.

Oklahoma, which sent a larger delegation than ever before, will gain more workers by establishing a chain of district conventions. It won great applause by its song, "Fair Oklahoma, the Queen of the West."

Oregon has already started in its Efficiency Campaign, and is moving for a $2,000 field secretary for two years.

Pennsylvania, the great near-by State, sent a monster delegation to the Convention. "If this magnificent arch of Christian Endeavor, resting on the ends of the earth, is to maintain its beauty and increase its efficiency, the Keystone must not only be held in place, but it must be strengthened. And we can do all things through Christ who strengthened us."

Rhode Island, from the days of Roger Williams, has believed in religious liberty. It has always had many Quakers, and so has believed in universal peace. It believes in the federation of the forces of our Lord and the ultimate union of His body, and purposing thus it lifts up its banners and marches on to greater Christian Endeavor efficiency.

South Carolina has no State union, but with the help of God will have one at a very early day. It hopes to get the banner in 1913 for the greatest increase.

South Dakota did not come up to the standard of the Increase Campaign, but hopes to do so in 1913.

Tennessee's 55 delegates made the largest showing from that State since Nashville, '98. They expressed through Dr. Landrith their aim to co-operate with the colored people, and with the Men and Religion movement, and their purpose to help the saloon States to labor for a saloonless nation by 1920.

Texas, through Miss Wilkinson, spoke of the gigantic responsibility of winning for Christ the youth of that vast State. On the twenty-third of July it was to vote on a prohibition amendment to the constitution, and it asked our prayers for victory. At once Dr. Tomkins offered such a prayer. The flag displayed by the large Texas delegation was the old one used when Texas was an independent republic.

Vermont's aim is to form in every society a little group of personal workers, who will go out among the hills and valleys of the Green Mountain State and try to win souls for Christ.

Virginia's young people are largely in the B. Y. P. U. and the Epworth League, but the representative of that State, a Baptist Christian Endeavor pastor, expressed his desire to bring all the young people into federation with the United Society of Christian Endeavor; and there was ardent applause.

Utah had no delegate, but Secretary Paul Brown, who had recently been there, spoke of sad conditions in that State. "If we believe in prayer, let us invest some of it in Utah."

Washington, "the Evergreen State," named for the fruitfulness of its soil, would be known also for the fruitfulness of its Christianity. It aims to develop Christian Endeavor through the services of a field secretary, and through better county and district organization.

West Virginia seeks more societies and better work in the societies. It includes soul-winning work as a part of its efficiency campaign.

Wisconsin has heard God's command, "Move forward," and is bringing forward a splendid body of Christian young people, developed by efficient service.

Turkey's representative spoke last, and gave us the beautiful Arabic greeting, "Peace be to you."

Atlantic City then gave its testimony, through the lips of Dr. Caldwell: "Your Convention has made an impression which we trust we shall never forget. When you are through with your visit to the West and the South, we sincerely hope that you will come back again to Atlantic City. God bless you."

Next came a financial interlude, Secretary Shaw giving out 500 of the Building banks, which were speedily taken by the delegates to be filled. It was a lively time as they were handed out by the ushers. The ever-ready Foster had us sing "Bringing in the Sheaves," and the Fisk Singers charmed us again with "Swing Low, Sweet Chariot." A last call for Building subscriptions brought $250 more from California, $300 more from Michigan and $100 from Georgia.

"The closing word," said Secretary Shaw, belongs to him

who has lived himself into the lives of millions of young people through the past thirty years"; and Dr. Clark spoke as follows:

"*In the name of God set up your banners.*

"This is the banner· Convention of Christian Endeavor. I have never before seen so many banners displayed at one of our International gatherings. You have come here with life and color, with spirit and zeal.

"In the far West, on the shore of the Pacific, *set up your banners.*

"In the North, and in the great land of Canada from which so many of you have come, *set up your banners.*

"In the South, where they are coming forward in this new movement of which we have heard so much during the Convention, *set up your banners.*

"In the great interior States in the vast empires of the middle West, and in the Eastern States where so much of the strength of Christian Endeavor lies, *set up your banners.*

"Banners of peace. Banners of good fellowship. Banners of loyalty to our own churches. Banners of devotion to Jesus Christ our Lord. Banners of new efficiency in His service. Banners of constant waiting upon Him at the mercy seat.

Notice this Chinese banner, brought from the land of Sinim. The cross of Jesus Christ occupies the centre, and upon it are our initials, 'C. E.'

"O friends, on all these banners, by whatever name we call them, let us place the cross of Jesus Christ!

"Christian Endeavor is worthless, and worse .than worthless, unless it is the Society of the Cross of Jesus Christ.

"Let this be our thought, then, for the coming two years; and in the words of the word of God let us say it together once more, all rising and repeating it: *In the name of our God we will set up our banners.*"

For the last time then we joined in the beautiful closing exercise of the programme, we sung softly "God be with you till we meet again," and Dr. Clark pronounced a benediction upon the Twenty-fifth International Christian Endeavor Convention.

CHAPTER XIX.

RESOLUTIONS.

A series of important resolutions were introduced and adopted affecting the vital interests of the Christian Endeavor movement. The first, which was presented by Rev. Howard B. Grose, D.D., at the Trustees' meeting, is as follows:

Whereas It has been increasingly evident that the President of the United Society of Christian Endeavor must have relief from the detail burdens of his office, in order that he may be able to carry out cherished plans for the world-wide success of Christian Endeavor, and be able to do certain literary work which only he can do, and which it is of the utmost importance to our cause and the kingdom of God at large to have done, and at the same time conserve his health;

And Whereas So strong has been his conviction of duty in this regard that he has seriously proposed to resign his office as President, at the coming Convention at Atlantic City in order to gain the relief necessary;

And Whereas We believe that such a step is unnecessary, that it would give the Christian Endeavor cause a staggering blow, be misconstrued and misunderstood, aside from the fact that while Dr. Clark lives it will be practically impossible for him to abdicate or rid himself of concern for the movement in which his life has been wrapped up, and with which the Christian Endeavor world associates him;

THEREFORE

Be It Resolved, That the executive committee of the Board of Trustees of the United Society hereby adopts the following as the basis of the service and relations of the President of the United Society:

1. The President shall be relieved, after January first, of all office work and detail.

2. He shall be released from all obligation to represent the United Society of Christian Endeavor at Christian Endeavor conventions or other public meetings.

3. He shall be released also from the duty of representing Christian Endeavor at other conventions or meetings. That it is the wish of the executive committee that he shall not accept such invitations, on account of other work, and that this shall be made plain to Christian Endeavor State and other officers.

4. It is the intent of the executive committee in this action to leave the President absolutely free in his plans and movements. But, while doing this, the committee wishes to put it clearly on record that Dr. Clark is still President, with no diminution of authority; that he remains the head of Christian Endeavor as in the past; that as President he is responsible for the large direction and general policies of the movement, and that he will be looked to for counsel and guidance, as heretofore. and the committee also records, in connection with this action, its assurance that, whatever Dr. Clark may do, he will be spending his life always for Christian Endeavor.

Resolved, That as members of the executive committee of the Board of Trustees we record our profound gratitude to God for the rare and unique service which Dr. Clark has rendered to a cause that has spiritually developed and enriched a multitude of lives and multiplied many-fold the service power of the Christian church; that we rejoice in the warm Christian fellowship and friendship we have enjoyed with our brother beloved; and that we wish for him long years of service, the best years and best service of his life.

Trustees at Large.

Whereas The Board of Trustees of the United Society of Christian Endeavor was made up originally of the representatives of the denominations, to which were added later the union presidents representing the States, and later still the class of honorary trustees consisting of former members of the Board, whose long connection with the movement is thus perpetual, and

Whereas It seems desirable to enroll among the official sponsors of the Society certain men who, while honored by the entire nation, and deeply interested in Christian Endeavor, cannot be added to the Board as State or denominational representatives; now therefore be it

Resolved, That the United Society of Christian Endeavor hereby amend Section II., Article 3, and establish the office of trustees at large, to be men of national reputation, sympathetic with Christian Endeavor, who are willing to promote the interests of the Society as they may have opportunity. The number of trustees at large shall be limited to twenty-five, and the term of office shall be two years.

The following letter and the accompanying resolution speak for themselves.

To the Board of Trustees of the United Society of Christian Endeavor:

The Christian Endeavorers of the United Presbyterian Church assembled in denominational rally at Atlantic City, July 10, 1911, taking into consideration the loss in Christian fellowship and in training for service that is sustained by many of the young people of our denomination by reason of the fact that they organized in a denominational society and not in Christian Endeavor, earnestly petition your honorable body to extend to the young people of our church an invitation to join the wider fellowship of Christian Endeavor.

The Young People's Christian Union, which is the name of our denominational society, will meet in annual convention in Baltimore, August 3-8, 1911, which fact gives opportunity for the immediate presentation of an invitation.

This petition is sent with the very earnest prayer that it may lead to the rich blessings in all of the societies of our church that some of us have enjoyed.

Very respectfully,
HUBER FERGUSON,
(Acting Chairman).

Resolved, That in response to the resolution from the United Presbyterian rally, we extend a cordial invitation to the Young People's Christian Union of the United Presbyterian Church to join our world-wide fellowship by affiliating with us as Young People's Unions of Christian Endeavor, and so make possible an all-inclusive young people's federation, with common methods of service, and a common name throughout the world.

Rev. Howard B. Grose, D.D., chairman of the committee on resolutions, presented to the Convention the following, which were unanimously adopted:

Thanksgiving.

In view of the fact that Christian Endeavor has during this year passed its thirtieth milestone it is fitting that we should unite in special thanksgiving to God for the providential ordering of this young people's movement from the day of small beginnings to this day of world-wide influence.

We thank Him for the preservation of the life and health of the founder, who has discharged with rare fidelity the great trust of leadership committed to him; for the wonderful extension of the society until the World's Union of Christian Endeavor encircles the globe; for the exceptional work done by Endeavor in foreign-mission fields, where the missionaries regard it as an invaluable training-school for service; for its strong body of efficient workers, from whose ranks have come ministers, missionaries, church officers, Sunday-school superintendents and teachers, and leaders in every line of Christian activity; and for the society rank and file, who constitute a vast working force in the churches and a prepared constituency for other organizations and movements.

We give thanks also for the unwavering loyalty of Christian Endeavor to Christ and the church and to the teachings of the Bible; for its proof that firmly held denominational conviction is not incompatible with interdenominational fellowship, and for its furthering thus of the cause of Christian unity and the close co-operation of all Christian forces in world-evangelization. As solid regiments of a well-compacted army Christian Endeavor moves forward in the unity of the spirit and the bond of peace with Jesus Christ the supreme head and "all one body we."

Christian Endeavor's Aim.

We indorse and adopt the suggestions of President Clark for our aims and efforts during the coming two years:
1. As an international organization the promotion of world-wide peace.
2. As an interdenominational organization a still wider fellowship of all young Christians.
3. As a local organization a campaign of education and efficiency.

We reaffirm the Christian Endeavor principles as restated by him: Outspoken Acknowledgment of Christ, Constant Service for Christ, Loyalty to Christ's Church, Fellowship with Christ's People.

International Peace.

To carry out the first suggestion — to promote world-wide peace — we pledge ourselves to do all that lies within our united power.

We rejoice in the record of Christian Endeavor in this matter, which vitally affects the economic, moral, and spiritual welfare of humanity. We have consistently stood for all efforts to establish peaceful settlement of disputes through arbitration.

We pay unqualified tribute to President Taft for his superb leadership in proposing, for the first time in history, a peace pact that would recognize no cause whatever as justifiable cause for war between two great civilized nations. By this act he has made his country illustrious and his name immortal. The instant response that came from England's noble statesman, Sir Edward Grey, and the mighty rallying of both powerful peoples around the new standard, together with the quick assent of France and other nations, have stirred the pulses of the world and brought the vision of universal peace to the borders of reality.

In this great day Christian Endeavor rejoices with exceeding joy, and will set its whole strength to the support of every measure that will tend to bind all people into brotherhood, remove the oppression of needless armaments, and under the ægis of universal peace secure for every man, woman, and child in all the earth a fair and full chance for life, liberty and the pursuit of happiness.

Three Statesmen.

We are grateful for the presence and participation in this Convention not only of the President of the United States, but, also for the first time, of the Speaker of the House of Representatives, and, for the second time, of the former Vice-President of the United States. Never before in the history of this country, so far as we know, have three statesmen so distinguished and influential thus recognized a religious convention, and we rejoice in this proof of a changing attitude of the political world towards the religious forces of the nation.

William the Peacemaker.

We would express to President Taft particularly our deep appreciation of the cordial words and first-hand news of important treaties, his fine tribute to Dr. and Mrs. Clark, his generous recognition of Christian Endeavor, with its international fellowship, as a factor in peace-promotion, and his expression of confidence in the loyal support of Christian Endeavorers for this cause. We assure the President that he can rely upon the Christian young people of America for solid backing in every forward movement for peace and righteousness. We record our conviction that President Taft, by his fearless utterances, his repeated tributes to the high character and services of our missionaries in foreign lands, and his readiness to throw the weight of his official influence upon the side of our great religious movements, is rendering an inestimable service to the higher interests of his country, entitling him to the great name bestowed upon him by Dr. Clark — William the Peacemaker.

Peace Celebration.

We favor the proposed celebration of the one hundredth anniversary of peace among English-speaking peoples in 1914-15, in commemoration of the Treaty of Ghent, and authorize the executive committee to appoint a Christian Endeavor Co-operative Committee, representing every State and Territory of the United States and the Provinces of Canada, as requested by the national celebration committee. As the celebration is to be made international, the international character of Christian Endeavor makes such a co-operation committee especially fitting.

The Bible in Schools.

We have had before us overtures for an utterance in behalf of Bible-reading and religious instruction in the public schools. We believe that a prime interest of a nation is the moral and religious training of its children and youth, and that the public schools therefore ought to teach at least the fatherhood of God, the brotherhood of man, and the moral order of the universe, or elementary ethics. To that end a way ought to be found to require the reverent reading in all our public schools every day of those selected portions of the Holy Scriptures which proclaim these three truths so vital to good citizenship and to high character.

Surely Protestants, Catholics, and Jews can agree to this; and any who cannot consent, in a God-honoring republic like ours, ought to claim no right of protest which the government is bound to respect.

Sabbath Desecration.

Sunday-desecration creates one of the serious problems of our time. Realizing that the steady encroachments of business and pleasure upon Sunday are not only deadening the conscience and injuring the morality of the people, but are also imperilling the rights of all to a rest-day, we urge Christian Endeavorers to set the example of Sunday-observance and to exert all possible influence in their communities to preserve Sunday as a day of rest and worship.

We must heartily commend and indorse the action of the postal authorities in closing in large measure the post-offices on Sunday, and pledge the Postmaster-General and his assistants the united support of the four millions of Endeavorers of the United States in this action, which is in the interest, not only of the postal employes, but of a Christian civilization.

We urge also upon civic authorities the enforcement of Sunday laws. It is the duty of Christian Endeavor to help create the public sentiment that shall insist on every man's right to his rest-day, and we will aid every right movement that seeks to secure reverent observance of the Lord's Day.

Law-Enforcement.

We commit ourselves anew to obedience to and enforcement of law, and to the support of those officials, and those only, that stand for law-enforcement. If the law is good, failure to enforce it is criminal; if pernicious, enforcement will reveal its evils. Officers of the law who assume to elect what laws they will enforce are no better than other perjurers, and should be impeached and disgraced as perjurers, and that regardless of their office or influence.

But disregard of law is as dangerous in the private person as in the official. We do not recognize either in the private morals of inividuals or in the public prosecution of law-breakers the slightest apology for the existence of a double standard. Just as both men and women must be pure, so must both capital and labor, public officials and private citizens, be law-abiding.

Men and Religion.

With men and boys forming at least forty per cent of its membership, and having stood from the first for a robust and virile type of masculine Christianity, Christian Endeavor hails with joy and indorses with enthusiasm the Men and Religion Forward Movement. As a training-agency for Christian service our organization has been blessed with the privilege of furnishing to this, as to many other great causes, not a few of its leaders; and we urge that in all of the local campaigns of this new movement for the salvation and training of men and boys Christian Endeavorers do their full share, with labor and gifts and prayerful sympathy, to the end that men and boys everywhere may be brought to Christ and into the activities of the churches of Christ.

Mission-Study.

The growth of missionary interest in our societies promises much for the new campaign of efficiency, which demands something to do. We recommend that definite work be undertaken by the societies. Mission-study classes in local societies may become the source of instruction and inspiration for the whole membership. A missionary society will tend to create a missionary church, and a live missionary church will be full of the spirit of evangelism, which is the need of the day.

The Immigration Problem.

In view of the vast inflow of immigration and the obligations which this imposes upon us to safeguard the newcomers with kindly and Christian influences, our societies should find in this migration of races an open door of specific service.

Personal work is the only solution of the immigration problem. Every society is in the midst of a home foreign field, and may engage in direct missionary effort, through elementary teaching of English, through seeking out foreign young men and women, and by friendliness drawing them to society, Sunday-school, and church. Ways are easy if eyes are open.

Our societies will rise to newness of spiritual power if they respond to this divine challenge to evangelize the stranger within our gates. We recommend this as a new and immediate objective for Christian Endeavor, which can here employ its young men especially in noble and needed service for men.

Good-Citizenship Day.

Christian Endeavor is a training-school in Christian citizenship, and we approve, therefore, the suggestion made by the Nebraska Union that the Sunday immediately preceding the Fourth of July be generally observed as Good-Citizenship Day, and utilized by pulpit, young people's societies, and other agencies to promote patriotism and give instruction in civic duties, rights, and responsibilities.

We approve also the suggestion that Christian Endeavor may find room for leadership in the movement for a sane and safe celebration of our national holiday. Societies can originate and help carry out plans and programmes for patriotic services, especially in the rural districts and villages, and thus keep the church in the van of civic progress. Christian Endeavor should have part in all movements that tend to elevate the moral tone of the community and better the conditions of life.

Rural Endeavor.

In view of the increasing attention given to the rural problem by statesmen and educators, it is timely that Christian Endeavor should give larger consideration to the possibilities of our work in the village and country societies. In many localities the rural situation is most serious. We believe that Christian Endeavor, with its peculiar genius and flexible methods, is especially fitted to render a valuable service in improving this situation.

The country and village societies afford a strategic point of attack for the campaign of enlargement and efficiency inaugurated at this Convention. We commend the appointment of a committee on Rural Christian Endeavor by the Board of Trustees, with purpose to conserve and increase the forces of Christian Endeavor in our rural communities.

Christian Endeavor in Negro Churches.

We rejoice in the very encouraging growth of Christian Endeavor among the negro churches of the country, particularly in the South, and in the annoucement from the Board of Trustees that a special committee has been appointed to promote this work, also that this committee is planning to hold in Nashville in July of 1912 a great national federation convention of all the societies of young people in the colored churches of the United States. In all practical ways we urge our white Endeavorers and their unions to co-operate in the organization and development of Endeavor societies and unions among their colored neighbors.

Temperance.

Now as always Christian Endeavor is the uncompromising, implacable foe of saloon endeavor, and is the friend of every sincere and sane agency, society, union, league, or individual laboring for the abolition of the liquor traffic, local, State, national, or international.

We rejoice in the recent temperance triumphs, and in the fact that Christian Endeavorers everywhere have generously aided, often led, in achieving these notable victories.

We congratulate the Endeavorers of Maine for their solid stand against the present powerful attempt to repeal the prohibitory law of that State, and assure them of our sympathy and our hope that they may win in their struggle.

We oppose the manufacture, exportation, importation, sale, and use of intoxicating liquors, and we favor such constitutional provisions and the enactment of such laws, by Congress and by State, Territorial, Provincial, and municipal legislative bodies, as will forever destroy this unjustifiable and intolerable evil.

Specifically we indorse the pending Curtis bill for prompt passage by the United States Congress, for we are unwilling as self-respecting American citizens longer to endure the national shame of a federal forcing of an iniquitous business on local communities and States that have been decent enough to close their own saloons. No revenue law and no interpretation of the Interstate Commerce Law should be allowed to flood with liquor the dry territory of this country, and our representatives in both houses of Congress should be made to understand plainly that the Christian citizenship of America has had enough of their dallying with such measures as the former Miller-Curtis, now the Curtis bill. Let either the law or its Congressional foes be passed, and that right early.

A Saloonless Nation.

We have had before us resolutions adopted by the Oregon State Christian Endeavor convention, and indorsed by the State conventions of California, Kansas, Alabama, Maine, Vermont, Washington, Oklahoma, and Minnesota, proposing a country-wide campaign for national prohibition at the end of ten years following the early passage of a federal law to that effect. In full sympathy with the spirit of these resolutions, and heartily indorsing their aim to free America from its greatest curse and still safeguard the property rights of those engaged in the liquor traffic, we believe that an earlier date should now be fixed for the enforcement of such a law, or preferably constitutional amendment, and we recommend to all Christian Endeavorers and other young people's societies, prohibition movements, and temperance and anti-saloon organizations, a united campaign — a bloodless because legal and moral revolution — for a new Declaration of Independence, "a saloonless nation by the Fourth of July, 1920 — the three hundredth year from the landing of the Pilgrims at Plymouth."

Parting Thanks.

We extend to the Committee of Arrangements of 1911, headed by State President Sproull of New Jersey, our hearty appreciation of the long and arduous service they have given and the fine provision made for the Convention. It will be part of their reward that Atlantic City will go down, not only in the list of memorable Conventions, but in some respects as the most memorable of all. We extend thanks also to the musical leaders and conference leaders, singers, and choirs for their essential aid, and to the speakers, many of whom have come long distances, and all of whom have freely given their services to our cause and made the Convention of great value to the delegates.

To the hotel and boarding-house hosts of Atlantic City, to the churches which have opened their buildings for our use, to the people at large, we acknowledge our gratitude for constant courtesies and favors.

In a stress of weather unexampled in our country we have found in this resort by the sea a large measure of physical relief and comfort. We gladly acknowledge our obligations to the daily newspaper press, which has given us unusually full and excellent reports, this being conspicuous in the case of the press of Philadelphia and of Atlantic City. For all that has tended to make this Convention of 1911 a spiritual and moral blessing we are profoundly grateful.

CHAPTER XX.

Corporation and Trustees' Meeting.

The Temple.

Thursday afternoon of the first day of the Convention, July 6, an unusually large and representative body of men and women assembled for the annual

Meeting of the United Society.

First came annual reports, from Treasurer Lathrop, Editorial Secretary Wells, Publication-Manager Shartle, and Building-Superintendent Anderson. These all showed most encouraging progress made during the two years since the last Convention.

Dr. Clark's report made a brief survey of the thirty years of Christian Endeavor, a report full of cordial words for his many co-workers in the headquarters office and in the field.

He had intended, as Christian Endeavor has reached its thirtieth birthday and he has nearly reached his sixtieth birthday, to resign at this time the presidency of the United Society. The trustees, however, would not hear of such a thing, rightly believing that for years to come Dr. Clark in the presidency of the United Society can do a unique and invaluable work for Christian Endeavor.

Several serious physical breakdowns of recent years, however, have shown Dr. Clark that he must adopt a less strenuous life; and besides, he has much important writing to do for Christian Endeavor. Both reasons lead to a somewhat new relation which he will hold with reference to the United Society, a relation voted with great heartiness by the meeting, as it had previously been voted by the executive committee of the Board of Trustees.

Hereafter, by direction of the Board of Trustees, Dr. Clark is to be freed from the obligation to attend conventions, and is to give his time to the larger planning for Christian Endeavor, and to the writing that he alone can do.

In honor of the great work that Dr. Clark has accomplished during these thirty years for the young people of the world, the trustees passed a hearty resolution of appreciation; and then, rising, sung "Praise God from whom all blessings flow."

Death, removal, and transfer of denominational relations have caused a number of changes in the Board of Trustees, which were voted as follows:

Hon. John Wanamaker, to be Presbyterian trustee in place of Dr. William Patterson (removed to Ireland).

Rev. A. D. Thaeler, to be Moravian trustee in place of Rev. W. H. Vogler (resigned).

Rev. Elmore Harris, to be Canadian Baptist trustee in place of Dr. A. A. Shaw (removed to the United States).

Rev. Frank J. Day, to be Canadian Congregational trustee in place of Rev. E. H. Tippett (removed to the United States).

Rev. Albert W. Jefferson, to be Free Baptist trustee in place of Rev. John M. Lowden (now pastor of a Congregational church).

Mr. George W. Coleman, M.A., to be Baptist trustee in place of Dr. Wayland Hoyt (deceased).

Dr. Earl Wilfley, to be trustee from the Disciples of Christ in place of Dr. F. D. Power (deceased).

Dr. Clark spoke most feelingly concerning Dr. Hoyt and Dr. Power, and the long, devoted, and able service that they gave to Christian Endeavor. He was asked by the United Society to incorporate his remarks in letters to the families of these departed leaders, and Dr. Floyd W. Tompkins offered a beautiful commemorative prayer.

Dr. Clark also spoke very tenderly about the honorary trustee, Dr. J. Z. Tyler, so long held in the grasp of an incurable disease, and Secretary Shaw was instructed to telegraph him a brotherly greeting from the United Society.

The United Society at this meeting established a new division of trustees. We had at first only trustees representing the denominations. Later there were added the union presidents representing the States. Still later honorary trustees (or trustees emeritus) were added, those that, after long service on the board, can no longer serve actively as trustees. Now it has been decided to elect trustees at large, limited in number to twenty-five, who shall be men of national reputation, sympathetic with Christian Endeavor, and willing to promote its interests. As most of the present trustees are eminent clergymen, the new trustees at large will be chiefly laymen.

The new officers of the United Society of Christian Endeavor are as follows:

President, Rev. Francis E. Clark; vice-president, Rev. Howard B. Grose; general secretary, William Shaw; treasurer, Hiram N. Lathrop; clerk of corporation, A. J. Shartle; auditor, Robert H. Bean; editorial secretary, Professor Amos R. Wells; superintendent of Builders' Union, Rev. R. P. Anderson; publication-manager, A. J. Shartle.

At
The Trustees' Meeting,

which followed the United Society meeting, the new class of trustees at large was heartily adopted.

At this meeting also, in memory of his nearly thirty years of loving work for Christian Endeavor, Rev. John M. Lowden was elected honorary trustee for life.

Probably the Board of Trustees has never before held a meeting so largely attended. The gathering was one of splendid ability, widely representing the churches and the States. These Christian leaders were full of enthusiasm for Christian Endeavor. They took a number of notable forward steps for our society, appointing committees of large scope and purpose, whose work will become apparent during the coming months and years.

Probably the largest work done by the Board of Trustees at its Monday morning meeting, from the standpoint of far-reaching influence, was the accepting of the report and recommendations of the committee on work among the colored people of the South, of which Dr. Darby is chairman.

President Clark named, as the beginning of a committee on Endeavor work in schools and colleges, Professor Amos R. Wells, Rev. Willis L. Gelston, Dr. French (of Ann Arbor, Mich.), Rev. Lapsley A. McAfee (of Berkeley, Cal.), Rev. D. A. Poling and Secretary William Shaw; the committee to be permitted to add to its number later.

The trustees accepted the invitation of the United Society officers to hold a retreat at Sagamore Beach, Mass., in July, 1912.

A pleasing feature of the meeting was the introduction of Rev. Herbert Anderson, president of the India Union, to whom so much credit is due for the success of the Agra World's Convention. In a happy little speech Mr. Anderson said: "India owes to you a debt of gratitude that can never be paid. Our Endeavor movement in India, Burma, and Ceylon has a magnificent future before it. We have forty thousand Endeavorers, speaking thirty languages. Our aim is twenty native secretaries to prosecute the work aggressively."

The advisability of a committee on rural Christian Endeavor work was advocated by Rev. C. H. Hubbell, D.D., and on motion such a committee was authorized, which President Clark will appoint later.

SOME OF THE NORTH EAST BRANCH HUSTLERS,
Philadelphia C. E. Union.

A WHEEL-CHAIR PROCESSION AT ATLANTIC CITY.

CHAPTER XXI.

WHAT THEY SAY.

The Christian Endeavor Convention, which closes to-day at Atlantic City, will be notable among these great gatherings for the formal recognition by President Taft of the value of this international organization with four million members, scattered through all nations, in preaching peace and urging arbitration through all the world.

The influence of all this will grow year by year. It brings the summons to international duty uttered by President Taft and to keener municipal responsibility by Speaker Clark. This new development is quickening in colleges and in churches a more vivid consciousness of the demand for social service and for good citizenship. The effect of this is already apparent in the increase of moral movements and a stronger social responsibility for social reforms. The transformation of society is more fully recognized than ever before as being no less the duty of the Christian church in all its branches than the conversion of individual men. — *Philadelphia Press.*

The growth of the Christian Endeavor movement from its small, unpretentious beginning, thirty years ago, to its present membership of nearly four million members is phenomenal, and has proved itself, under God, one of the most mighty religious forces in the world. Inspired afresh by this great convention at Atlantic City, the thousands in attendance will disperse to their respective homes and churches to take up Christian Endeavor work with renewed zeal, and thereby transmit something of their newly kindled enthusiasm to their fellow workers who were deprived of the privilege of attending the convention. — *Christian Intelligencer.*

Christian Endeavor has come back; or, if that offends any enthusiast who is unwilling to acknowledge that it ever declined, let us say that Christian Endeavor is very much all here to-day. The late Convention at Atlantic City, though it indexed a good many particulars in which Christian Endeavor in 1911 is different from the tumultuous boom of twenty-five years ago, certainly demonstrated that there is plenty of vitality still left in this great fellowship of young people for substantial growth and the outthrust of a service that tells.

Whether one admits that there was a sag in Endeavor or not, there is nobody who can deny a wonderful up-climb in the last two years. The trustees, and some even nearer to Dr. Clark than they, admitted confidentially that though the Christian Endeavor founder was building castles far away in Spain when, to the last International Convention, held in St. Paul, he proposed an "increase campaign" that should add ten thousand societies and a million new members to the rolls of the organization before July, 1911. For a movement then apparently at a standstill this sounded like a next to impossible advance. Christian Endeavor had already cultivated its field well, and it seemed that there could not be room anywhere for so big an extension. Besides, there was the very prevalent notion that the young people themselves had lost heart for Christian Endeavor, and would not work for it to-day as its members worked twenty years ago. But the man who for thirty years has been the world's most conspicuous leader of young people knew them better than the many men who doubted them; and the thing which the multitude called impossible came to pass, just as the man who called it possible had planned. — *The Continent.*

The hosts of Christian Endeavor, young and older people, came together at Atlantic City last week from all parts of the country under the inspiration of a record made during the last two years that compares favorably with any similar period in the thirty years' history of the movement. No less than 10,400 new societies have been formed since the Convention of 1909, and a million new members have been added, and during this time plans for a new building in Boston to serve as headquarters have been well advanced. The Endeavor idea may not suit itself to every locality or church; the plant may here and there droop for lack of proper nutrition; but take it the world over, no better method has been devised of interesting young people in the things for which the church stands and in training them for service. It has been a powerful force for unity, and the only opposition to it on this score to-day arises from those who are disposed to exalt denominationalism above our common Christianity. — *The Congregationalist.*

The last time we were in this cavernous structure the G. A. R. was in session. More tumultuous and noisy that throng, not less eager and enthusiastic this, but there is a quieter, deeper tone. These are soldiers in the army of the Lord. — *Rev. J. W. Weddell, D.D., in The Journal and Messenger.*

Feeling of gratitude found expression at night, when Secretary Lehmann, acting for the whole membership of Christian Endeavor, presented to the founder of the Society a simple and beautiful gold watch-chain. It added a touch of human interest that will make this meeting of the Christian Endeavor delegates one of the most profitable the society has ever held. — *The Methodist Protestant.*

In a general way the Convention has been equal to any held within recent years. Not only has the attendance been great, but the interest has been unusual, and the enthusiasm tremendous. — *Reformed Church Messenger.*

The recent Convention of the Christian Endeavor Society at Atlantic City revealed an unimpaired vitality in this great organization. A constantly broader outlook, increased activity, a deeper consecration to the work in hand, has marked the progress of the society since its organization, till it has grown from a small local affair to be, in extent and influence, a "world-power" in as true a sense as England or the United States, and in a far more important sense even than they. For while they are exerting power for material ends, and dealing with material forces, this widely extended society is working for spiritual ends and combating those unseen but powerful influences that are potent for the destruction of humanity.

There has been a fear at times — and sometimes, we are sorry to say, almost a hope — that the Christian Endeavor Society had reached its culmination and was on the wane. We are glad to know that this is not the case, but that steadily, and with increasing momentum, it is growing in numbers and in efficiency. It has found a work to do, and is doing it, and that not only without detriment to any other form of Christian activity, but to the decided benefit of every other. Slight local disturbances there may have been now and then, resulting from lack of tact in leadership; but the net result, and that on a grand scale, has been for the advantage of the church, the young people, and the community. — *The Examiner.*

INDEX

THEMES OF ADDRESSES

A Fatal Mistake 61
Best Things in Christian Endeavor:
  By George William Wright 161
  By George Fukuda 162
  By H. I. Marshall 163
  By Hy. A. Cendrecourt 163
  By Friedrich Blecher 164
  By George H. Hubbard 165
  By J. W. Ford 165
Christian Endeavor and Civic Problems 160
Christian Endeavor and Prison Reform 75
Christian Endeavor among the Colored Denominations of the South 158
Christian Endeavor among the Lepers 157
Christian Endeavor in Prison 155
Christian Endeavor Hospital Work 154
Christian Endeavor Training for Church Officers 145
Christian Endeavor Training for Living 151
Christian Endeavor Training Ministers 146
Christian Endeavor Training Missionaries 147
Christian Endeavor Training for Temperance Reform 150
Christian Endeavor Training Witnesses 148
Christ Our Hope in Time of Storm 32
Efficiency 18
Facts and Factors 22
Feed My Sheep 33
Floating Endeavor 157
Four Messages from the Bible 67
Good Citizenship 97, 170
Holding the Citadel 172
How Foreign Missions Promote Fellowship 142
Interdenominational and International Fellowship Necessary to World-wide Evangelization 177
International Brotherhood . 97, 167
International Peace 37
Message from Germany 180
Needs of Christian Endeavor 173
Service of Intercession 150
Shepherd Psalm 31
The Beauty of Holiness 65
The Call for Fellowship in Service 183
The Evangelistic Message of the Bible 71
The Open Door of Opportunity 178
The Queen's Part in the Kingdom's Work 67
The Uplift of a Race 48
Training in International and Interdenominational Relationships 175
Training the Body to Express the Soul 181
Two Years of Growth 24
Welcome 16
Windows of the Soul 52
World-wide Influence of the Bible 166

FEATURES AND POINTS

Am Meeresstrand 92
Bond of Unity 20
California Pictures 60
Campaign of Education 20
Camp-fire 56
Choral Service 56
Christian Endeavor Experts .. 20
Citizenship 19, 97, 170
Convention Hymn 28
Efficiency Rating 20
Fanny Crosby 58, 59
Fellowship of Churches 19
Field Secretaries 19
Fisk Jubilee Singers 194
Fresh-air Camps 26

INDEX

German Peace Resolution .. 93, 96
Harrisburg Choir 56, 74, 95
Headquarters Building 26, 103, 104
Healing of Naaman 52
Hospitals and Missions 27
Hymn by John R. Clements .. 111
Immigrants 27
Immigration Exhibit 60
Increase Campaign 13, 24
Junior Rally 51
Meeting of the United Society 206
Moving-picture Fight 26
Moving Pictures 95
Notable Features 12
Notables Present 13
Philadelphia Choir 56, 59, 64
Presentation of Chinese Banner 66, 139
Presentation of Gavel 16
Presentation of Watch-Chain 17
Quiet Hours 30
Resolutions 198
Salt Breezes 11
Suggestions 21
Sunday Labor 26
Tenth Legion 28
Trustees' Meeting 208
Washington Chorus 24, 136
World Peace 18, 93, 96, 201

GREETINGS.

Croatia 193
Disciples of Christ 96
Europe 24, 194
Japan 23
Los Angeles 95
Mexico 193
Wilson, Governor Woodrow .. 16

CONFERENCES AND RALLIES.

Conferences:
Boy Problem 121
Christian Endeavor Methods 114
Christian Endeavor Union Methods 117
Clean and Strong 121
Consultation Hour 129, 130
Corresponding Secretaries .. 123
Esperanto Conference 129
Evangelistic Endeavor . 117, 118
Field Secretaries 126
Floating Christian Endeavor 120
How to Read the Bible with Expression 125
Intermediate Christian Endeavor Methods 116

Junior Christian Endeavor Methods 115, 116
Lookout Committee 123
Missionary Endeavor .. 118, 119
Open Meeting for Society Workers 132
Open Meeting for Union Workers 130
"Other Committees" 125
Prayer-Meeting Committee . 124
Presidents' Conference 122
Prison Christian Endeavor Work 122
Quiet Hour 128
Social Committee 124
State Junior and Intermediate Superintendents 127
State Presidents 125
State Secretaries 126
State Treasurers and Finance Committees 127
Sunday-School Endeavor .. 119
Temperance 121
Tenth Legion 128
Treasurers 123
Denominational Rallies:
African Methodist Episcopal and African Methodist Episcopal Zion 77
Baptist 77
Brethren 80
Christian Convention 80
Congregational 80
Cumberland Presbyterian .. 81
Disciples 82
Friends 83
Lutheran 84
Mennonite 84
Methodist 85
Moravian 87
Presbyterian 87
Church of England and Protestant Episcopal 89
Reformed Church in the United States 89
Reformed Church in America 90
Reformed Episcopal 94
Reformed Presbyterian 90
Seventh-Day Baptist 91
United Brethren 91
United Presbyterian 91
German 92
Welsh 93
United Evangelical 93

PERSONNEL.

Albrecht, C. H. 92
Allebach, Rev. Annie G. 85
Amerman, W. L. 128

INDEX

Anderson, Herbert, ...
...... 74, 78, 104, 140, 166, 192, 208
Anderson, R. P. ... 51, 82, 129, 207
Ashburn, Dr. 141
Ashburn, T. 81
Baba, Y. 104
Bacon, Enos ....
.... 14, 22, 55, 57, 60, 86, 102
Baker, G. Evert 82, 105
Bannen, R. G. 84
Barstow, John 141
Bean, Robert H. 207
Bidwell, F. C. 100
Blanchard, F. Q. 81
Blecher, Frederick ....
.... 84, 92, 104, 132, 164, 192
Blecher, Mrs. Frederick ... 66, 180
Blue, Miss Ruth 80
Brack, George M. 102
Breed, R. L. 81
Brooks, Dr. 79
Brown, Paul C. ....
.... 81, 118, 127, 135, 196
Brownlee, Mrs. Alexander 55
Buch, Theodore 84
Burnett, Augustus .... 1.. 94
Burns, G. J. 86
Cale, Mrs. Edna 95
Caldwell, Julian C. 77, 111, 178
Capen, Samuel B. 22, 67, 80, 81
Catlin, L. E. 129
Cendrecourt, Hy. O. 163
Chain, Dr. 32
Chalmers, Dr. 79
Chapman, J. Wilbur 30
Chapman, Mrs. Woodallen 65
Chenoweth, Irving S. 82
Clark, Hon. Champ 97, 170
Clark, Francis E. ....
  15, 16, 17, 18, 37, 51, 55, 56, 57,
  78, 92, 95, 97, 100, 112, 127,
  129, 139, 141 142,, 189, 197,
  ....206, 207
Clark, Mrs. Francis E. 65
Clark, John 137
Clark, Sydney 52, 118, 191
Clausen, Bernard 104, 122, 137
Clements, John R. ....
...... 57, 103, 111, 114, 130, 195
Coleman, George W. 207
Collins, Herbert D. 103
Condon, Mrs. E. L. 83
Conwell, Russell H. 173
Cox, Alfred S. 35, 157
Crandall, Lloyd R. 91
Crowell, Marion B. 123, 137
Crosby, Miss Fanny 56, 57
Darby, W. J. 35, 88, 138, 158
Davis, Miss Nannie 81
Dawson, Edward 90

Day, Frank J. 207
Deckard, W. W. 105
Demarest, W. T. 90
Denton, H. A. 82, 151
Dyer, C. W. 101
Ells, W. M. 127
Evans, Rev. Mr. 93
Fairbanks, Hon. Charles W. ..
.... 86, 107, 112, 142
Fallows, Bishop Samuel ......
................22, 62, 75, 94, 107
Farquhar, Miss Ruth 83
Farrill, Edgar T. 81, 106, 125
Ferguson, Huber 32, 92, 105
Field, Elliot 87
Fismer, A. 92
Fleming, H. 94
Ford, Jefferson W. 83, 104, 165
Foster, Miss Ethel 65, 191
Foster, Percy S. ....
.. 14, 15, 30, 36, 51, 56, 57, 77, 188
Fredenhagen, Edward A. ... 75 122
Fukuda, G. 102, 162
Gates, E. P. 118, 136
Gelston, Willis L. 31, 87, 208
Gerhard, Paul 90
Gifford, Miss Alice 83
Gilray, Alexander 87, 106, 148
Graf, Miss Johanna Louise .. 139
Gribben, L. D. 128
Grose, Howard B. ....
........17, 18, 132, 198, 200, 207
Grubb, N. B. 84
Grunert, James E. 87
Hahn, Albert F. 92
Halenda, Theodore 140
Hall, William Phillips 62, 71
Hall, William Ralph 88
Halsey, A. W. 34
Hanney, Tom 116, 135
Hardcastle, William 101
Harpster, W. S. 93
Harris, Elmore 207
Hascall, W. H. S. 59, 74, 139
Hayes, Miss Lillian E. 83, 127
Heilman, C. A. 100
Heilman, P. H. 84
Henderson, Cree J. 103
Heptonstall, C. H. 78
Heptonstall, Mrs. C. H. 140
Hill, Claude E. 82
Hill, James L... 34
Hill, Jesse 81, 103, 145, 191
Hirschy, N. C. 84
Hogan, Jasper S.: 90
Horsefield, F. J. ....
.... 61, 89, 96, 102, 167, 192
Horsefield, Mrs. F J. 66
Howell, Walter D. .. 114, 127, 135

INDEX

Hubbard, George H. 105, 129, 139, 165, 193
Hubbard, Mrs. George 67, 102, 140
Hubbell, C. H. ... 101, 119, 191, 208
Humphries, Elijah 71
Hunt, L. C. 93
Hutchison, Mrs. Charles .. 115, 136
Jackson, John 35, 60, 157
Jaeger, Walter 100, 125, 135
Jefferson, Albert W. 207
Johnson, A. W. 100
Johnson, W. T. 107
Jones, William A. 105
Jones, William I. 81, 136
Joy, Miss Grace 67
Kamiopili, S. K. 190
Keiffer, Dr. 89
Kelly, Gilby C. 32, 80
Kinports, H. A. 90
Kliefken, William 92
Koch, Miss Margaret 67, 116, 125, 135, 137, 181
Kovar, J. V. 140
Krehbiel, H. J. 84
Landrith, Ira 71, 112, 183, 195
Lanham, Florence E. 101, 123, 127, 136
Lathrop, Hiram N. 22, 135, 206, 207
Lehmann, Karl 17, 100, 104, 121, 127, 131, 136
Lewis, T. H. 109
Lincoln. H. C. ... 14, 59, 64, 95, 188
Lindsey, Ben B. 40, 121
Litsinger, J. E. 100
Loder, Mr. 102
Lüders, Lewis B. 129
Hill-Lutz, Mrs. Grace Livingston 52
McAfee, Cleland 22, 47
McAfee, Lapsley A. 140, 208
Martin, S. A. 138
McGaw, James S. 35, 90, 160
MacNaugher, Samuel 90
Marshall, H. I. ... 78, 102, 140, 147
Mason, A. DeW. 90
Meyer, F. W. 84
Miller, Rufus W. 90
Moon. L. Oscar 83
Morgan, William 93
Morris, Mrs. R. H. 90
Munday, Mr. 93
Neals, Frederick H. 94
Newby, Richard R. 83
Newman, Herman 83
Nichols, Emma O. 65, 119
Nicholson, S. Edgar 83
Nitzschke, F. R. 87
Oberholtzer, H. M. 80
Osborne, Miss May 90
Page, Frederick H. 80
Paisley, H. E. 89
Palmer, C. J. 89
Petrie, Miss M. Josephine 88
Pockman, P. T. 90
Pohlman, A. 84
Poling, D. A. 93, 104, 117, 136
Preston, Agnes Green 24, 189
Pretlow, Robert E. 83, 189
Ramige, Rev Mr. 93
Reiner, E. L. 34, 154
Rice, William 81
Richards, Charles H. 81
Richards, John T. 93
Richardson, Archdeacon J. B. 61, 89, 111
Roads, Charles 85
Roberts, F. T. 93
Roberts, William H. 88, 93, 108, 175
Rondabush, Miss Flora 65
Ross, David 79, 104
Rottmann, H. H. 111, 114, 135, 138
Rundall, Dr. 90
Schaeffer, C. E. 90
Shambaugh, W. I. 93, 139
Shartle, A. J. 89, 117, 207
Shaw, John Balcom 22, 37
Shaw, William 15, 59, 60, 74, 80, 81, 103, 114, 126, 130, 138, 193, 194, 196, 207, 208
Shupe, H. F. 91, 150
Skaggs, J. L. 91
Slagel, Rev. Mr. 93
Smith, Fred B. 61, 69
Smith, O. L. 82, 101
Spooner, H. H. 76, 121, 150
Sproull, John T. ...16, 103, 126, 195
Stall, Sylvanus 84, 103, 121
Stanley, Miss Sada F. 83
Stauffer, Miss Blanche 91
Steele, R. E. 34, 120
Stengel, F. W. 87
Stevenson, T. P. 90
Stewart, Charles G. 127
Stewart, George B. 146
Stewart, Ralph R. 139
Stiles, J. S. 81
Stillman, M. G. 91
Stocker, H. E. 87
Stoddard, Elijah W. 57
Swengel, U. F. 93
Taft, President William Howard 12, 36, 37
Tead, Edward S. 80
Thaeler, A. D. 207
Tomkins, Floyd W. 15, 89, 134, 196, 207
Tracy, William 94
Tyndall, C. H. 52
Van Ormer, A. B. 84

Varian, Miss Ella M. 140
Vogler, William H. 87
Voorhees, J. Spencer 124, 137
Walkey, A. R. 86, 106, 123
Walker, D. N. 102
Walters, Bishop Alexander 34, 77
Wanamaker, Hon. John 207
Wantzel, F. W. 87
Washington, Booker T. 48
Warner, Judge Edgar M. 34, 75, 155
Watkins, E. A. 80
Webb, George T. 78
Weeden, W. C. 14, 57, 71, 73
Wells, Amos R. 28, 57, 207, 208
Wells, L. N. D. 82

Wilfley, Earl 82, 172, 207
Wilkinson, Miss Tyler, 105, 124, 138, 196
Wilson, Jr., A. S. 81, 126
Wilson, W. F. 22, 67, 85
Winey, C. W. 91
Witter, E. A. 91
Wolf, L. B. 84, 108, 177
Wolle, Edward S. 87
Woodrow, Samuel H. 80, 81
Worthington, Ray A. 105
Wright, George W. ...102, 140, 161, 193
Yaba, Miss N. MaDwe ..65, 79, 140

www.ingramcontent.com/pod-product-compliance
Lightning Source LLC
Chambersburg PA
CBHW022354040426
42450CB00005B/182